Recapitulations

by

Vincent Crapanzano

Other Press
New York

Production Editor: Yvonne E. Cárdenas
Text Designer: Julie Fry
This book was set in Dante by Alpha Design &
Composition of Pittsfield, NH

10 9 8 7 6 5 4 3 2 1

Library of Congress Cataloging-in-Publication Data

Crapanzano, Vincent, 1939–
  Recapitulations / by Vincent Crapanzano.
    pages cm
  ISBN 978-1-59051-593-8 — ISBN 978-1-59051-594-5 (ebook)
  1. Crapanzano, Vincent, 1939–   2. College teachers—
United States—Biography.   3. Anthropologists—
United States—Biography.   4. Authors, American—
20th century—Biography.   I. Title.
  LA2317.C23A3 2015
  378.1'2092—dc23
  [B]
                                        2014027388

Disclaimer: The names and identifying characteristics
of certain individuals in this work have been changed to
protect their privacy.

for J A N E

In memory I meet myself.
—SAINT AUGUSTINE

But do I? Do I ever?

CONTENTS

I.

ORIGIN

STORIES

MY PARENTS taught me that it was rude to ask someone what he or she did for a living. Even today, when I am doing fieldwork—I'm an anthropologist—and have to ask people I work with what they do, I feel a slight constriction in my throat. I imagine that my question comes out at a noticeably higher pitch than normal.

When I am asked what I do, I have several answers. "I teach." "I'm a professor." "I write." "I'm an anthropologist." "I'm an anthropologist, but I also teach comparative literature." Each of these answers elicits a particular response. "What do you teach?" "Where do you teach?" "What do you write?" "I took a course in anthropology in college." "I thought about becoming an anthropologist." "That must be exciting." "Anthropology and comparative literature, how interesting." "I don't see the relationship." "I do see the relationship." "Did you know Margaret Mead?"

You are rarely asked how you decided to become a doctor, a lawyer, an investment banker, a consultant (whatever that means), an architect, an actor, an artist, a diplomat, or a taxi driver. But when you say that you are an anthropologist, you are (at least I am) always asked how you decided to become one. What a nuisance! How do you ever know how or why you became anything? All we can do is tell ourselves, tell others, a story that—if we have not conned ourselves—we know is a bit of a fiction. It's a way not only to answer the question or define yourself, but also to stop questions that ultimately lead nowhere or somewhere you don't want to be even if you are there. It's an origin story, a kind of myth, which, like all myths, is an artifice that denies its own artifice. Myths can have no irony.

I have several origin stories that I deploy according to the circumstances in which I find myself. None are true. None are false. Some are pertinent. Some are impertinent. Sometimes I say that I went to an international school in which the students came from eighty-five different countries. I have, in fact, no idea how many different countries they came from—a lot, I know—but I always say eighty-five. Eighty-five does not have, as far as I know, any special meaning for me. I say it was at that school that I became aware of cultural difference. I usually reserve this story for people I find uninteresting. Sometimes I say that I spent the first thirteen years of my life living on the grounds of a mental hospital (before explaining that my father was a psychiatrist attached to the hospital), and that it was there I became intrigued by the range of human behavior. Usually I tell this to people whom I want to shock. Sometimes I talk about a little book of pictures of American Indians from different tribes that fascinated me as a child. What I don't say is that I could never remember all the tribal names.

Often I add—if I like the person who has asked me—that one of my father's patients was an archeologist who walked me through the woods behind our house, looking for arrowheads. We always found some. I remember one in particular. It was a mustard brown, what the French call *jaune*, beautifully carved, softer and less sharp than the flint arrowheads we usually dug up. I wonder where it is now. It was uncanny how the archeologist always knew where to find arrowheads. One day—I think it was the day we found the brown one—my mother and father laughed when I showed it to them, and said that the archeologist had

probably buried it. I wouldn't believe them. They said it was okay.
I was still learning about the Indians and had a fine collection of
arrowheads. Perhaps I would become an archeologist. But the
next time I went out with the archeologist—I can't remember his
name—we came to a meadow where I often played cowboys and
Indians with my school friends Freddy and Bob, and sometimes
Jimmy. The ground was uneven, and the archeologist said that the
hillocks were mounds under which the Indians had buried their
dead. I wanted to start digging right away, but he said we had to
have permission. It was the first time I looked directly at his face.
He had pale blue eyes, very thin lips that were twitching slightly,
and, I think, a gray mustache. His eyes were empty—well, perhaps not empty but ever so slightly, blankly, fearful. I had the feeling that I had pushed him too far, that he didn't know how to
get out of the trap he had got himself in. I never saw him again.

I didn't really want to see him again, but I asked my mother
why I was not allowed to. She said he was having one of his episodes and couldn't leave the ward. "Having one of his episodes"
was my mother's way of saying that he was in a psychotic crisis, what Clara, my nanny (though we never called her a nanny),
called a spell. Clara was also a patient. She, too, had spells. She
would see faces in the hoarfrost on the kitchen windows, and she
never ate bananas because the seeds in their centers were crosses.
Of course, I usually don't go into this much detail. When you
are writing to readers whom you don't know, you are freer to
elaborate—to flutter around fiction. Fiction can sometimes be
truer than nonfiction: a cliché, I know, but one that calls attention to a dimension of the quest for truth that my literalist colleagues and the Christian Fundamentalists I once worked with
have to deny. There is no ethnography—I might as well say it
now—that is free of the fictional.

There is one story I have to tell in detail here. Unlike the others, my decision to tell it seems to have less to do with whoever asked me about becoming an anthropologist than with a compelling need to recount it and an inability to stop doing so or even to shorten it. Having told it, I become embarrassed. It seems inappropriate: an endless monologue that destroys the seductive intimacy of storytelling. I obliterate my audience. I obliterate myself. Why? Seneca, in one of his letters to Lucullus, says that one should make friends with oneself.

Though the story I recount was certainly not responsible for my becoming an anthropologist, it had a profound effect on me—a reorienting one, like a mini-conversion—that may have influenced my decision. It has become dream-like. When I graduated from college, my grandmother gave me a present: five hundred dollars with which to travel. This was a lot of money in 1960. I decided to go to Mexico. I had read a lot about the Aztecs, their sacrifices; the Mayans, their writing; the revolution, the banditti, the corruption, the violence, the whores—they figured in my imagination—and gringo spots that seemed to have nothing to do with Mexicans.

I was going to have an adventure, an exotic one, spectral in my imagination. This sounds childish, and no doubt it is. But to set off on an adventure, as opposed to having an inadvertent one, produces childlike excitement, memories and memory traces that evoke the freedom, the naiveté, and the irresponsibility of play. Behind those memories and memory traces lies the thrill of danger: of a shipwreck, of an attack by Indians armed with bows and arrows, of being held captive in a den of thieves—or of their adult counterparts: a forced landing in enemy territory, an attack by militiamen armed with machine guns who do not understand a word you say, or a kidnapping by Somali pirates. That thrill announces a metaphysical danger: an imaginative collapse, a devastating loss of freedom, an entrapment in reality—a fall.

In fact, I had never had much interest in anthropology or in becoming an academic. I never took an anthropology course in college, though the section man for one of my courses, Karl Riesman, who was studying anthropology, had a far greater influence on me than I realized at the time. He was one of the best teachers I ever had. He had us read Emile Durkheim's *Elementary Forms of the Religious Life* instead of something by Max Weber that the professor had assigned. Karl—he was one of the few section men at Harvard at the time who insisted that we call him by his first name—described the ritual frenzy that produces a sense of social cohesion that intensifies the collective representations by which a society understands itself. None of us really understood what he was talking about, but we were excited by whatever it was that we thought he meant. We were freshmen and had no idea how to distinguish between the significant and insignificant in Durkheim's treatise. I remember poring over it, looking for an explanation of how ritual frenzy could possibly be responsible for the categories of understanding and never really finding one. Not, at least, as Karl described it.

I'm in Chichen Itza, in a Yucatán not yet overrun with tourists. The hotel where I was staying had converted some huts that archeologists once used on digs there into bungalows for some who would not or could not pay for rooms in the main building. The morning of my arrival, a guide offered to show me around. He was about my age, a Mayan, I assumed, friendly and timid. I refused, explaining that I was just a student and would use a guidebook. He seemed disappointed, hoping for once, I thought, to meet someone his own age. After dinner that evening, I sat alone on a darkened veranda to think about what I had seen. Just as I was about to return to my cabin, the guide appeared, sat down, and began asking me the usual questions guides ask. Where are you from? What do you do? Is this your first trip to the Yucatán? To Mexico? In turn, I asked him similar questions. I was tired and bored and wanted to go to bed. At one point in the conversation, he asked me where I was born. I told him, and asked him where he was born. He named a village. Just as I was about to ask him where the village was, he asked me, "Where are you going to die?" I was taken aback. I told him I didn't know. He seemed as shocked by my answer as I had been by his question. I asked him if he knew where he was going to die. He said yes and then told me: down the road, near an enormous tree in a pasture where I had seen a horse grazing that morning. I don't remember any of the conversation that followed.

As I was walking back to my cabin, I kept asking myself what the world would be like if you knew where you were going to die. Our sense of time, space, history, and even that inner experience of the flow of time, *la durée*, which Henri Bergson described, would have to be radically different. Had the guide and I really understood each other at all? Even those banalities we exchanged? I was irritated with myself because I hadn't asked him if he knew when he was going to die. I didn't even know what he had meant by dying. Would the place he referred to be the actual site of his demise or where his soul and perhaps his body, in some altered state, would settle? I promised myself to ask him, but the occasion never arose. When I greeted him the next morning, he seemed embarrassed and said that he had some clients waiting. What, if anything, had he thought of our conversation?

THIS IS the skeletal version of the story. I usually do not elaborate, since most people seem satisfied with it. Some do ask me for more details about the Mayans. I say that I don't know much about them, and this is true. I have never tried to learn anything about Mayan theories of time, birth, and death. This may seem strange and irresponsible for an anthropologist, and no doubt it is. I prefer to leave my story unblemished. I prefer to live with the play of imagination. I suspect that we all have had such formative experiences. They are sacred, idiosyncratically so, couched in danger. We want to leave them free from the destructive force of impersonal facts.

The morning after my arrival in Mexico City, I sat in the bus terminal waiting for a bus to Vera Cruz. I had decided to travel around Mexico before spending any time in the capital. The courtyard behind me was covered with scaffolding, on which workers were replastering. In front of me, just to the left, a worker crouched—I remember his being very small—removing yellow tiles from a column. He tapped them with a hammer and chisel rhythmically, rarely missing a beat, never looking up. His tapping punctuated the conversations I overheard and barely understood. (I had never studied Spanish but understood a good deal because I knew Italian.) They punctuated my own thoughts. One minute they calmed my anxiety; the next they increased it. The bus, needless to say, was late. The longer the delay was, the greater the bustle. Suddenly we heard a dull thump come from the courtyard. No one said a word. No one could say a word. We were all caught in a silencing silence—drawn into a single consciousness. We knew. The thump could mean only one thing. It echoed in my mind, and as I write now, all these years later, I can still hear it, resonating the infinitely prolonged finite moment between life and death. We were locked in silence, anticipation, certainty, and dread. Two stretcher-bearers arrived in minutes, as though they had been waiting in a back hall for the fall. As they carried the corpse out, the silence was finally broken by an army officer in the crowd, a major, I think, who asked in a voice that in the silence was louder than he had expected, *¿Está muerto? Sí, está muerto.* The little man did not look up. He had never stopped tapping. Silence is never so total as to be emptied of all sound. The tapping was part of it.

On the morning after my conversation with the guide, on my way to the hotel for breakfast, I met a couple who were staying in the cabin next to mine. They were amateur archeologists from somewhere in the Middle West, who spent their vacations visiting Mayan ruins. They even had a Chevrolet with an extra-high wheelbase so they could negotiate the dirt roads that led to some of the more isolated ruins. They had heard about a cave, recently discovered, in which there was a temple and asked if I wanted to see it with them. Of course, I agreed. It was closed to the public, they said, but they were sure they'd find a way in. It turned out that Jeff—I think that was his name—knew the guard who led us through one tiny, dank antechamber after another until we finally entered an enormous room with a sculpture, so far as I could tell in the semidarkness, of a female figure in the middle of a lake. It covered most of the room's floor. Jeff and the guard had both brought powerful searchlights, but they were not powerful enough to light the cavernous temple, if it was in fact a temple. There was an airhole in the roof, as I remember, through which a beam of light fell on the sculpture. I had never been in so chthonian—so sacred—a place, and my presence, our presence, seemed to me to violate that sanctity.

Jeff wanted to wade out to look at the sculpture more carefully, but the guard got very nervous and said that was impossible. The way he said this was so definitive, so fearful, so evocative of danger that I was sure he saw it as a violation, too. Jeff would have insisted, had his wife not stopped him. She must have felt as I did. On our way back to Chichen Itza, Jeff told me something he hadn't mentioned before—the temple had been a place of worship until a team of archeologists discovered it a few months earlier. He went on to say something about a purification ceremony that was planned to eradicate the danger caused by the archeologists' intrusion. *Like ours*, I thought. The guard, still visibly upset, had refused to accept the tip Jeff offered him. Jeff wondered whether the guard had been one of the worshippers.

Late the next morning, in the midday heat, I took a bus to Uxmal. It was stifling. I dozed, overwhelmed by a phantasmagoria of colossal, thick-lipped Olmec heads like the ones I had seen a couple of days earlier in Villahermosa—of hands, my hands, amputated hands, covered with blood from slapping vainly at mosquitoes that infested the jungle site; of the heads moaning; of the giant iguanas I had seen sunning in the ruins, totally indifferent to the visitors, yawning, exposing saurian teeth, yellowed like the teeth of a *capitán* who tried to pick me up in a bar in Vera Cruz; of the Mayan guide, innocently inquisitive; of Jeff and of his wife looking emptily at her husband, beckoning me salaciously as she scolded me; of the terrified guard and the little man who never stopped tapping, now a dwarf, now a monkey, now laughing and splashing about in the underground lake, bursting into tears, whining, mourning, caressing the statue, a grimacing Mayan Madonna with brick-like features…I must have fallen into a deep sleep, for on awakening, I looked out of the bus window at the thick, reed-and-liana-strangulated jungle through which we were passing and saw plants killing one another violently, desperately, incessantly to make room for more plants. *Life changeth, yielding place to death, death to life*, I mumbled to myself, pretentiously, in Tennyson fashion. In itself, pretention notwithstanding, it was a banal observation, but it had for me the power—the transformative power—of a vision.

II.

FIRST
MEMORIES

"WE ALWAYS begin before we begin." This was one of the paradoxes that my seventh-grade teacher, Mr. Hilton, put to us. He liked paradoxes—"brainteasers," he called them—but he rarely offered us a solution. He just listened to us try to figure them out, and whenever we thought that we'd arrived at a solution, he would pull the rug out from under us by pointing out a flaw in our logic or by slyly recasting the paradox so our original solutions made no sense. If he offered us any solutions, they were for the most concrete, the most trivial of the paradoxes—for the "stupid ones," Freddy, Bob, and I called them. "They're for girls," we'd say with that disdain that only boys our age could muster. Although Mr. Hilton couldn't resist punctuating his classes with brainteasers, he always reserved the last half hour on Fridays just for them. Sometimes he would ask us to invent paradoxes, and for those, he usually had solutions. He had a slippery intelligence. He was portly and, unlike the other male teachers, who wore sports jackets, he always wore a dark suit with a white shirt and a fanciful tie. He loved to laugh, lowering his chin as he did, producing thereby an exaggeratedly constrained sound that suggested he knew more than he could or would reveal. He was, in fact, the most demanding teacher I had had until then.

"We always begin before we begin."

We struggled with that one. "In the beginning God created the world," someone suggested. (In those days, you said the Lord's Prayer each morning in public schools.) "But who created

God?" I asked. Someone else—I think it was Freddy, because he was Catholic—said, "In the beginning was the word." "And who wrote that? How did he know? Had he been there, he would have been before the beginning of creation." There were other suggestions: precursors of the Big Bang Theory. "But there must have been something there to collide."

Must we begin at the beginning? Can we? Is there ever a beginning? I was born sometime between four and four-thirty in the morning on April 15, 1939. Was that my beginning? (I am not referring to uterine life or the moment of conception, but I could be.) I came, I come, with an inescapable heritage and a fated future—an advent, a coming-to, as an arrival, and an awakening, as though from a coma or a dream.

I am caught in a turbulent swirl, a gyre, a vortex, a whirlpool at once centripetal and centrifugal, casting me there, pulling me here, with no possible footing. As a child, I was fascinated (and scared) by bathwater swirling down the drain, sucking me in, drowning me in some netherworld. Is it a cosmic analog of birth that precedes memory?

My first memories, like all memories, presuppose a past that I do not know, not really, not directly, but only by hearsay. It is hearsay—the possibility of hearsay, the voice of the other, the call that turns memory into defensive memorialization. Freud spoke of screen memories, those exceptionally vivid memories, the truth of which you cannot doubt, which conceal other, repressed memories that, so terrifying, cannot be brought to consciousness.

But aren't all memories screen memories insofar as they protect us from that past, our past, which we do not know but whose existence we cannot doubt—the past of hearsay, of the voice of the other, hollow, abyssal, insistent, insinuating itself around that which we have experienced in such a way as to lead us to doubt—and to arrogant claims of veracity?

A few years ago, two days before I was leaving for Italy, I received a call from a lawyer whom I didn't know. After establishing my identity, he told me he was representing a client who had been in an automobile accident six years earlier and that I was listed as a witness. I told him he must be mistaken, that I had never witnessed an accident, that in all likelihood I was not even in the United States at the time. In a very calm, soothing voice, he asked me if I was absolutely sure: "It is most important for my client. The statute of limitations is about to expire." I answered that I was sure, though I felt my certainty wobble.

"What would you have been doing on a Sunday morning at nine-fifteen?"

"I'd probably be walking my dog."

"Where?" he asked, in an expectant tone that I found burdensome.

I told him.

"Yes, that would be possible."

And then, unexpectedly, he asked me what color the car was, as if I had already admitted to seeing the accident.

"Gray," I said without thinking, and suddenly I remembered the accident. It was not serious, though it could have been. A taxicab, driven by a Haitian man who spoke no English, had rammed into a gray car. I saw it clearly: the frightened eyes of the cabdriver, who was clearly guilty, since, in overtaking another car, he had been driving on the wrong side of the road. The driver of the gray car, an African-American woman, was surprisingly calm, efficient, dressed in a gray business suit. I remember thinking, at the time, that it was the same color as the car.

"Was anyone injured?"

"Not to my knowledge."

"Are you sure?" the lawyer asked. He sounded disappointed.

"To the best of my knowledge," I answered legalistically. His soothing tone was beginning to irritate me.

"The car was rented," I blurted out.

"Yes, that is right. It was a rental car. How do you know?"

"I don't remember."

"What else do you remember?" the lawyer asked, emphasizing the "do" as to cast doubt on my memory.

"Not much. Ah, yes, I do remember translating for the police."

"You speak French?"

I answered that I did.

"Do you remember giving your name to the police?"

"No, but I suppose I did."

"You suppose," he said harshly, as though I were a hostile witness.

I was surprised by his change of tone.

The lawyer went on to ask me routine questions. Did I know either of the drivers? Did I remember any other witnesses? Did I have any financial interest in Avis? The car had been rented from Avis. Finally, he asked me if I would be willing to be deposed. I told him that I had no objection, but that, as I was leaving the next day for Europe for three months, the deposition would have to be scheduled for that afternoon or early the next morning.

"I'll get back to you," he said irritably, "if I can arrange something by then."

"You can always fly me back."

He didn't laugh and never did get back to me. I knew he wouldn't.

The play of memory is not the same as the play with memory.

The lawyer was playing with my memory, as lawyers do. And my memory—I sometimes think of it as an imp—was it playing with me too?

Memories of memories.

I do not remember the first time I remembered my first memory, nor the second nor the third. But I do recall my first two memories in their immediacy—without regard to their later recollections.

The first: My father is taking me to the hospital to see my mother, who has just given birth to my sister. I am not yet three. I see myself dimly, as from the outside. I'm scared, since I know that children are not allowed in the hospital, but my father tells me not to worry. He's a doctor. *But I'm not*, I think. I see my mother. She looks pale and smells funny. My father lifts me up to look through a window in a door to the nursery. We cannot go in. He tells me where my sister is, but I can't be sure I see her, since I can't tell right from left. "Did you see her?" I say yes, but all I know is that I saw a lot of babies. She must have been one of them.

The second: I am playing with a steamroller in the lower garden, near the sandbox, below the fishpond, where the goldfish had frozen to death that year. My parents gave me the steamroller just before my mother went into the hospital. "As compensation," I learn years later, but I can't remember when. (Why a steamroller? Is the burden of having a sister so heavy? In those days toys were still made of metal.)

I hear the car that is bringing my mother and sister home. I hear Clara call me, but I don't answer. She finds me. "Don't you want to see your little sister?" she asks. I don't say anything, but I see myself looking at myself sitting on the steamroller. It is gray. My knees stick up above the seat on which I am sitting. It is too low.

There is no doubt that these dreams concern the birth of my sister, a lack of confidence in my father perhaps. But what interests me is the way my memories are interlarded with explanations that could only come later: knowing the difference between right and left, that children aren't allowed in hospitals, that the goldfish were frozen to death earlier that year...That memories, like dreams, are continually revised, despite a sense of their fixity, is obvious. What is less obvious (at least for me) is that each act of remembering falls between time past and time future: an unknown or excluded past and an unacknowledged future that loops back onto the "memory," configuring it with the moment of remembrance. But the memory, however transformed, is not without effect, for it casts, it tones, the present—the rememberer, his or her circumstances, his or her real or fantasized interlocutors—in a way that may be desired or may negate that desire. Memories gyre like a top. When we think too much about them, they produce epistemological vertigo. I was surprised by how anxious a friend of mine became when I asked her if she remembered the times she remembered a particular memory. "Why do you bother yourself with such questions?" she asked, and I couldn't answer. "Brainteasers," I could have said but didn't.

In both memories I see myself from the outside: dimly, in the first, from no specific vantage point; more clearly, in the second, from Clara's perspective, perhaps, even before she came down to fetch me. Is my seeing myself from the outside, especially from Clara's perspective, a first objectification of myself: a bodiless *I* that has become an embodied *me*? Doesn't Saint Augustine say, "In memory I meet myself" (*The Confessions*, book 10, p. 214)?

The French psychoanalyst Jacques Lacan would relate my experience to babies' fascination with their mirror image: their discovery of their selves, a shattering of what unity they may have felt, a sense of insufficiency, because their image, or so Lacan postulates in his allegory of first self-alienation, would be more coordinate than their disjointed experience of themselves. I felt myself an object pinioned by my gaze and helpless, entrapped by that gaze, by myself. Does it cull all those moments of embryonic self-consciousness that preceded my memory? Or does it hail the self-consciousness that will follow that which I, as I remember, already experienced?

Memories in free fall.

What pleasure do I take in conceptual vertigo?

I took Garrick, my grandson, to the playground a few days ago. He is just six. He wanted me to spin him around on one of those tires that hang from chains, which children seem to love. He wouldn't let me stop. "Faster, Baba, faster," and later, *"Plus vite, plus, plus vite."* He laughed until he could laugh no more. He wobbled around for a few minutes, clearly dizzy, and then suddenly vomited. He told me that he had already vomited three times after having swung on a tire. "Would you do it again?" I asked. "Yes," he said, "but I won't throw up."

Of course, our memories do not normally swirl. We are caught within them as we remain outside them. The space of memory, our entry into that space, however terrifying the memory may be, is not without comfort. Proust bathed himself in the space of his memories. I do this sometimes, when I am driving alone, taking a walk, or on the verge of sleep. I find myself wallowing in them, their associations, which, of course, lead me astray and to the point, or at least to a point. Why do my associations end where they end? Is it mental exhaustion? That certainly is a factor. Or do they bring to the surface—the near-surface—repressed memories? Or do they simply end because the hidden story they tell has come to an end? I have often felt that I am being swept away by a story I cannot know—but know to be uncannily familiar.

Are these stories, are the repressed memories, creations of present-day desires that I prefer not to acknowledge or those that I long to have but don't have? "How can you long to have a desire you can't have when you are in fact desiring that desire?" I hear Mr. Hilton asking. A desire for desire is not the same as that desire. This bovarism—desiring another's desire and trying to live according to that desire—is bound to fail, unless you can fully delude yourself. But who is this "yourself"? Isn't it a precipitate of the other's desire? Are desires ever so distinct? Don't they flow into one another, if only by osmosis? If you live according to the desire of another—Emma Bovary's aristocratic lady, Don Quixote's knight errant—are you not acting? Yes, I would say, but not like a stage actor, who knows that he is acting. There are, of course, actors who so identify with their role that they cannot separate themselves from the character they are playing. It was rumored that Patrick Magee, who played the perverse marquis in Peter Weiss's play *Marat/Sade*, was found abandoned in bondage in his apartment. Had he become de Sade?

One of my former students, Phyllis Rogers, who studied clowns, described going to a pub with a couple of clowns who were dressed in ordinary clothes. One of them tried to pick up a woman at another table when her date was in the men's room. He had forgotten that he was not in costume, and had his friends not intervened, he would have been beaten up when her date returned. Clowns have privileges that others don't. They are sought after by clown groupies wherever the circus is performing: women who want to make love to them in costume. The clowns usually agree, but what pleasure they have is contorted because they do not know—or do they?—who they are at the time. Clowns, at least the American ones Phyllis studied, consider themselves clowns, not people. People are everyone else.

Even their self-denomination does not protect them from the disgust they feel making love to a woman who desires not *them* (whoever they are) but a clown. Once when a clown had a heart attack in the ring, the other clowns ran up to him and began singing "Happy Birthday." When Phyllis asked them why they hadn't rushed to call a doctor, they answered, "That's for people to do. His favorite song was 'Happy Birthday.' " Had they presumed his demise?

Phyllis said that clowns often dress up their guests at the circus as clowns, and the guests, before being led into the ring, are shown themselves in a mirror. The first time Phyllis visited the clowns — to ask if she could study them — they made her up but didn't let her see herself in the mirror before pushing her into the ring. Instead, they gave her a Polaroid picture that was just beginning to develop. It was only when she was in the ring that she saw herself as the clown in the picture. Those first moments in the ring before seeing herself were terrifying, she told me. "I had no idea who I was, what I looked like, how I was being seen. When my picture was fully developed, I jumped up and down in excitement, pointing to the picture and then to myself. 'It's me,' I wanted to shout but didn't. The audience wouldn't understand. They wouldn't even hear me. They just thought I was clowning." When Phyllis took off her makeup, she left a little behind her ears for several weeks until it all rubbed off. She didn't say why. Did it safeguard her from experiencing anew that terrifying moment when she didn't know what she looked like?

We only know ourselves through the eyes — the voice, the smell, the touch — of the other. We are immediately and inescapably implicated in that other. But how do we know what that other sees in us? Can we eliminate our desire from our perception of how we are being seen? However we create the other who observes us, there is stolidity in that other that we cannot mold to our liking. It is that stolidity that anchors our objectification. That is perhaps why I saw myself so clearly on the toy steamroller from Clara's vantage point, even before Clara was there.

I am eleven or twelve years old. My parents have taken me to my first grown-up movie. The hero, at least as I saw him, was a major who had lost his right arm (or was it his left?) in battle. He symbolized for me the grown-up-ness of the film and, I suppose, my own grown-up-ness. I was proud. When we returned home, I went out to play. It was very cold, and there were patches of snow on the lawn that had turned to ice. I began to play the major. I pulled my right arm out of the sleeve of my jacket, letting it hang like the major's, except that he could tuck his loose sleeve into his jacket, and I couldn't because my jacket had a zipper. I stood there for a moment, not knowing what to do next. I wanted to play, but I was too grown-up to play. Just as I was about to slide my arm back into the sleeve of my jacket, I glimpsed my parents looking out the porch window at me. I was paralyzed by embarrassment. In their eyes, I was still a child playing a grown-up. My memory of that moment vacillates between my being able to see myself, as I did in the back garden, but from my parents' perspective this time, and unable to see myself at all — without any vantage point whatsoever. I was a blank. I turned away and tried to sneak into the house and up to my room, but my parents saw me and smiled. Grown-up that I was, grown-up that I wasn't, I managed to contain my tears until I got to my bedroom.

Memories leaping over years fuse, sometimes, perhaps into one of those unknowable but uncannily familiar stories that accompany us and sometimes make their presence but not their content known. Where do they begin? Where do they end?

Memory-time is at once reversible and stubbornly irreversible. We always begin before we begin. Yes, and we always end before we end.

Memories die with death—even when we tell them to others, even when we write them down. They are—in the end—mine, only mine.

III.
THE
RABBIT
SLAUGHTER

I MUST have been five years old, because we had not yet moved from cottage seven to cottage five. Cottage five was much bigger than cottage seven. My parents had to wait several years until one of the larger houses—for some reason the houses were all called cottages—had been vacated through either the death or the retirement of one of the senior resident physicians. Very rarely did they leave for another position. My mother used to say they were more institutionalized than the patients in the hospital. "Institutionalized" was one of her favorite words, and it must have been one of the first words I learned, though I had no idea what it meant other than my mother's disapproval.

My father was always trying to raise animals—rabbits, chinchillas, chickens and ducks, tropical fish, and a canary. They all died, the chinchillas because the room they were kept in was too hot and the tropical fish because the water heater went on the blink and boiled them. The canary just dropped dead one morning. The chickens and ducks stopped laying eggs, and so we ate them. I was ten or eleven at the time and held them tightly as Mr. Axelson, our handyman, cut their throats. Or maybe it was my father who cut their throats. I can't remember. It seems unlikely, though, because my father always wore a suit and tie and never liked the sight of blood. Once the chickens' throats were cut, I dropped them and watched them flutter around, spurting blood all over the cellar floor, before they finally died. I was horrified and fascinated but mainly trying not to throw up. I don't think I was still holding any of them by the time they died and probably didn't feel the sudden weight of lifelessness. That came later, about ten years ago, when Pico, our Bouvier, died in my arms.

But did Phil feel the death of the rabbits he had slaughtered, if it was in fact he who killed them? Phil was one of the patients who worked for us as a handyman when we lived in cottage seven. He stoked the coal furnace, tended the rabbits in the hutch at the bottom of the garden, and did the heavy cleaning, but he spent most of the time in his "office" in a corner of the cellar, reading comic books and drinking coffee out of a bowl he shared with Gargy—a gun-shy Spinone that a hunter had given my father just before I was born. Phil was, as I now remember him, a small, timid man, perhaps in his thirties, who had a lock of greasy blond hair that was always falling over his left eye, causing him to lose his place as he read the comics. He had created his office—sometimes he called it his "hideaway"—by blocking the cellar corner with old, rusted gym lockers that were arranged so that they not only walled him in but also created a "secret passageway" that was closed off by two open locker doors that were hooked together with a chain. I had to know the secret number of knocks for Phil to open the door. The problem was that he kept changing the secret number without telling me, so I usually had to call out, "It's me." "Who's me?" he would ask, adding, "I'm me," and laughed as he unhooked the door. The lockers were filled with the smelly old clothes and raggedy dolls and stuffed animals that he collected. They were headless or missing limbs or split at the seams. "I'll have to call the doctor," he would say as he showed them to me and told me their names, "but you'll have to remind me. I'm always forgetting, and they never cry." I was never sure whether he was pulling my leg or serious.

I loved Phil but was only allowed to go down to the cellar for a half hour before dinner. Phil thought of himself as a scientist and used to explain how things worked, but when I repeated those explanations to my parents, they could barely contain their laughter. Phil's science was his and no one else's. I didn't care. I liked his science and—I remember—kept a chunk of coal that Phil had cracked open to show me a fossil. Phil saw a very rare ancient worm in the coal, but I couldn't see anything. Still, I kept the fossil under my bed until Clara discovered it and threw it away. I wasn't upset. In fact, I preferred reading comics with Phil over listening to his science. He was only supposed to read *Donald Duck*, *Mickey Mouse*, and *Elmer Fudd* to me, but, in fact, he read *Batman*, *Wonder Woman*, and *Superman*. It was our secret, my first real secret from my parents. Phil was sure that if my mother knew (and I suspect she did) he would be fired. So I never told my parents. Clara knew because she was always spying on us, but I don't think she told anyone. There was a conspiracy among the three of us, though Clara did not like Phil and Phil did not like Clara. As it was Sunday, she wasn't at home when I discovered the dead rabbits. They had all been strangled and thrown about the hutch and on the lawn in front of it in what must have been a terrible frenzy.

It was, as I said, a Sunday. My grandparents were coming to dinner, as they always did on Sundays. Just before they arrived, I had gone down to play with the rabbits, and when I saw them, I just stood there immobile, entrapped in so intense a perception that I could feel nothing, neither the horror nor the grief nor even the violence of the act. I had had no experience of death—its finality. Five-year-olds cannot grasp "finality," psychologists say, but this doesn't mean they can't experience it. I did for an instant, and it left its mark. I could not cry. I don't know how long I stood there. I didn't hear my grandparents drive up to the house. I didn't hear anyone call me, though someone must have. I didn't even hear my grandfather's footsteps as he approached me, but I wasn't surprised when he put his arm around me, instinctively covering my eyes, though it was far too late. He didn't say a word. Nor did I. There was nothing to say. He stooped down and touched several of the rabbits. "They're still warm," he said aloud but to himself. "It must have happened this morning." I wanted to touch the rabbits, to feel their warmth, to make them come alive again. I knelt down, but before I could actually touch one—although my fingers were close enough to feel their warmth—my grandfather pulled me away, ordering me not to touch them with a severity I had never before heard. "They may have been poisoned," he said. Holding my hand, he walked me back to the house to tell my parents.

I don't remember much of what happened then. I wasn't allowed into the living room, where my parents and grandparents were talking. I listened at the door until my father suddenly opened it, catching me and sending me up to my room. I don't know exactly what I heard, but I knew then that my mother was sure it was Phil who had killed the rabbits. My grandparents agreed with my father, who said it could have been any of the patients in the hospital, anyone, in fact. I lay on my bed. *It couldn't have been Phil. How could my mother accuse him? He was my friend. He loved the rabbits, and the rabbits loved him.* I knew because I had helped him feed them. He had given them names and talked to each of them as he held out lettuce leaves for them to nibble. They even waited their turn. Phil had a way with animals, my mother used to say. I could hear them nibbling and began to cry.

I'm sorry I never really felt the rabbits' warmth, because then, perhaps, my memory of their contorted bodies, their heads twisted grotesquely, might have dissipated. Dead, they seemed much longer and skinnier than when they were alive. Their fur had lost all luster, and I could practically see their bones through it. But without that warmth, or maybe because of it, my memory of them has remained cold. Sometimes I do see myself looking at them, but that image is not the same as my image of myself in my earliest memories. It is a distancing image — a defensive self-scrutiny that shields me from the warmth I never felt.

My sympathy was with Phil. So was my grief, for I knew that I could never again accept the affection I had had for him. The next morning, I heard my mother and Clara asking each other who could have killed the rabbits. Like my mother, Clara was sure it was Phil. I thought of her as a traitor (though I probably didn't know the word "traitor"). She had betrayed our conspiratorial bond. She said that Phil was sure we would give away the rabbits before we moved, that they would be slaughtered and eaten. He preferred to kill them himself. My mother agreed and used Clara's argument — I was to learn later — when she fought with my father about keeping Phil on. She wanted to dismiss him immediately. My father won, and Phil moved his office to cottage five. Well, not quite, since my mother refused to let him bring his lockers and his smelly old clothes. He did manage to bring a robin's egg blue clothes bag, which he hung from one of the pipes in the cellar in front of the little table on which he had stacked his comic books.

It was never the same for Phil. He stopped sharing his coffee with Gargy and didn't much like talking to me. As he had only one chair, he no longer read the comics to me. He kept telling me how cottage five was dangerous. Five was his unlucky number; seven had been his lucky one. He had seen snakes in the garden, and they were going to get us. They didn't want us there. I told my parents, but they said not to pay any attention to Phil. He was having one of his episodes. He would have to spend a few weeks in the ward, and then everything would be okay. I knew that everything would never be okay, but I didn't say so.

I am not sure if it was the next morning or a few days later that Phil didn't show up. I thought at first that he wasn't allowed to leave the ward, but there was too much whispering going on for me to believe that for long. Something more serious had happened, something children shouldn't hear. Maybe the police had proven that Phil had killed the rabbits. The hospital police had been called in that day to investigate, but, as far as I could tell, all they did was stuff the rabbits into burlap bags and haul them away.

"What's happened to Phil?" I asked my mother.

"He's not coming back," she said.

"Why? He's done nothing wrong. I miss him. He's my friend."

"Yes, I know," she said with forced sympathy. "Wait until your father comes home for lunch. We'll talk about it then."

"No, you won't," I cried, and ran to my room.

I was wrong. My parents told me that Phil had died during the night. "He had a weak heart," my father said.

I didn't believe them. I knew he wouldn't come back, but I didn't believe that he had died.

The next day, a new handyman appeared: Mr. Axelson, also a patient. I already knew him because he had built the bookcases in our old house. He was told to clean out Phil's things. I was ordered not to go near the cellar, but I sneaked through the garden entrance and saw a bottle of strawberry jam fall through the rotted bottom of Phil's clothes bag when Mr. Axelson took it down. The jam splashed all over. It was moldy and filled with maggots. I vomited. When I was older Clara told me that Phil had hanged himself. I had no reason not to believe her, but I preferred to think he died from a weak heart. What other reason would my father have had to tell me, a five-year-old, that Phil was very young to have died of a weak heart?

I'm not at all sure how I understood the slaughter of the rabbits at the time. I've never forgotten it, but I can't say that it has haunted me. I can't say that it traumatized me. It left me with a resonant but unreachable space—the space between my fingers that might have felt the rabbits' warmth and the rabbits themselves. It left me with a longing, yes, if I am honest with myself, to have touched death, the corpse, and the fear, and the desire to overcome that fear which came with the longing. It also left me with the thought that had I been able to touch the rabbits, they would have come to life.

I keep returning to a painting of a French king, touching a man who is covered with scrofula. My mother explained that for centuries it was believed that a royal touch could cure skin disease. I admired the king. How could he bear to touch such a disgusting lesion? Wasn't he afraid of contagion? But he did do it. I am quite sure that I did not think of the dead rabbits at the time, but I wonder if they didn't fuel my fascination. For years I wanted to become a doctor, but after a long and painful struggle I decided against it.

When I told my wife, Jane, about the rabbit slaughter years later, she reminded me of Julian Nibble. Marta had given Julian, a fluffy white rabbit, to our daughter, Wicky (now Aleksandra). Marta was an old peasant who lived with her brother in a single room on the ground floor of a tower in Bonnieux, in the Vaucluse, where we were spending the summer. Marta owned a beautiful *mas* —a farmstead—above the village, which even in those days was worth a fortune, but she refused to sell it despite the many extravagant offers she received. She was childless. Rumor had it that she had an incestuous relationship with her brother. It is true that they shared the same bed. Some of the villagers called her a witch. She would wash the sheets and pillowcases only when the moon was full, because they would be whiter if they dried in the moonlight. Each day we would take Wicky to see Julian, and on her first birthday, Marta gave her a present. It was Julian Nibble, skinned and stuffed with rosemary.

There is a fine line between slaughter and sacrifice. Did Phil sacrifice the rabbits? Was it a private ritual? Can a sacrifice, at least the sacrifice of an animal, be a private affair? I doubt it. Sacrifices require the presence of a group. Poor, gentle Phil, all alone, unable, I imagine, to give to the rabbit slaughter that sacral quality that would turn the rabbits into sacrificial victims. Or perhaps he did, imagining, hallucinating, a public. After all, he was a diagnosed schizophrenic. He was not a Marta, who could never have imagined our upset when she arrived with Julian in a basket. She said that way Wicky would have her friend with her forever. Fortunately, Wicky was too young to know what had happened to her friend. Jane and I did eat Julian. We felt obliged to, for such is the power of the gift, of the gift giver, but it had lost what taste it had. I couldn't even smell the rosemary.

I have seen animals slaughtered, and even more sacrificed. I remember the excitement that surrounded the slaughter of a sheep when I lived on the Navajo reservation. That excitement was coupled with hunger, but, while purely secular, it was some-how celebratory, too. There had been nothing celebratory about my father's slaughtering the chickens. Nor, I imagine, in Marta's slaughtering Julian Nibble. She was far too practical. She may have lived in a world of superstitions, but her act did not rehearse the kind of sacred drama that students of religion and some anthropologists once claimed. Some still do.

Sacrifices are a different matter altogether. I witnessed, and in fact participated in, many of them in Morocco, where I was doing fieldwork with teams of exorcists in the late sixties. I went with Youssef Hazmaoui, my field assistant, to buy a sheep for 'Id al-Kabir, the Great Feast, in which Muslims commemorate Ibrahim's sacrifice of Ismael (Abraham's of Isaac). The market was filled with excitement. Shepherds had brought thousands of sheep there. There was much haggling. Everyone was interested in how much everyone else was paying for a lamb, a sheep, or a goat. It was said that the king would sacrifice a camel. When we brought the sheep back to Youssef's house, his neighbors came out to appraise its size — its cost. I had the feeling that they were calculating the salary I was paying him.

On the 'Id, as we were going to Youssef's for his family feast, Jane and I were taken aback by the blood that was literally flowing in the streets. (Muslims, like Jews, do not eat blood.) We had assumed that when travelers described the streets flowing with blood, they had been speaking metaphorically. Knowing how poor most of Youssef's neighbors were, we felt we were witnessing a gigantic potlatch that extended across the Muslim world and were immediately embarrassed by the thought, since, succumbing to market calculus, we had ignored the sacred quality of the feast.

The 'Id is a joyous event, unlike the sacrifices that were performed at the Hamadsha exorcisms I attended. (The Hamadsha was the name of the religious confraternity to which the exorcists belonged.) There was no joy there, even when the possessing spirits, the *jnun*, had released those whom they had possessed. The sacrifices were weighted by obligation. There was always that sense of imminent danger that accompanies contact with the spirits. Strictly speaking, the ceremonies were not exorcisms but, technically, adorcisms; for rather than ridding the possessed of the malign spirits that had entered them, their goal was to convert the *jnun* into benign, protective spirits. The French classicist Henri Jeanmaire has suggested that exorcisms which aim at the permanent expulsion of the demon occur only when the spirits are considered evil (as in Christianity); when they are considered amoral, then exorcistic rituals seek their transformation, much as the Furies were transformed into the Eumenides in Aeschylus's tragedy. However transformed, the *jnun* were quick to anger and would punish those they protected if the person offended them. They acted as a sort of extrapolated conscience.

The ceremonies were long, lasting well into the night. They were bloody affairs, since some of the men possessed were forced by their possessing spirits, mostly female spirits, to slash their heads with knives (in the past with halberds), to release the heat, the intolerable pressure they felt as their blood—the spirit—mounted to their heads. Women did not mutilate themselves, but they, too, danced wildly in trance, bent over, their hands, their loosened hair nearly touching the floor as they swayed side by side—repeating the same movement, though far more rapidly, with which they washed their floors each morning—until finally they lost control and fell to the floor. I could not help but think that this ecstatic, at times epileptoid collapse was their only respite from the burdens of the cloistered world in which they were imprisoned, if not by their husbands than by the conventions that, unacknowledged by most men, entrapped them as well. The ceremonies were exhausting to watch. Not even the feast that ended them—a meal at which the meat of the goat or sheep that had been sacrificed earlier that day was served—revived me. Though I awoke drained, the Hamadsha who had fallen into trance felt rejuvenated the next day.

As the sacrifices I observed were always performed in the center of a circle of onlookers, I was never very close to them; that is, until I attended a Hamadsha performance at the annual music festival in Essaouira in 2002. Essaouira—a fortress town known as Mogador to the Portuguese, who had built it in the sixteenth century—is one of the most beautiful cities in Morocco. Each year it hosts a music festival at which there is both traditional music played mainly by the Gnawa, a secularized group of exorcists who perform all over the world, and jazz from the United States, Europe, Africa, and Cuba. Since the Hamadsha participate in the opening procession but don't perform (for fear, I suspect, that they might fall into trance, mutilate themselves, and thereby tarnish Morocco's image as a modern nation), I was asked to speak about them to a group of invited scholars—the *côté intellectuel* of the festival—who were to attend a Hamadsha ceremony staged especially for them. Reluctantly I went to the ceremony. I had spent the afternoon talking to a young Hamdushi (a member of the brotherhood) who was disgusted by the secularization and commercialization of the rites. They will anger the *jnun*, he told me with rage, fear, and worry in his eyes.

I found myself sitting next to the sheep that was to be sacrificed. Trembling with fear, its eyes bulging, it pressed itself against me. I had never felt such fear. It took possession of me. I could not distinguish its fear from the fear I was now experiencing. What was even more extraordinary was that when the sacrificer approached the sheep, he, too, began to tremble. It was as though the three of us were caught within the fear. I felt no relief when the sheep's throat was cut, its blood pouring into a pail as it twitched into death. Judging from his expression, I do not think the sacrificer, who had no doubt performed many such sacrifices, felt any relief either. I wondered whether his reaction and, by contagion, mine arose from the primordial danger of having performed a sacrifice for profane rather than sacred reasons. It was a demonstration rather than an offering. Those gathered were an audience rather than participants in an offering and recipients of the blessing — the *baraka* — that the ceremony would normally have conveyed. The Hamadsha who were present were either apprehensive, as was the sacrificer, or disengaged. The few women who danced and fell into trance did so in a desultory manner. As far as I could tell, none were possessed. None of the men danced. Under such circumstances, the death of the sheep was meaningless: a slaughter rather than a sacrifice.

The line between the sacred and the profane is never as clear as we assume it to be. The performance of a ritual in a space that is not demarcated as sacred does not necessarily render the space in which it occurs sacred. Rituals can fail not only in terms of their efficacy — a rain dance that does not bring rain — but also in consecrating themselves, as I believe the Hamadsha ceremony I described did. They lose what self-transformative power they have. But what occurs in hallowed precincts is not necessarily sacred. Cathedrals have often been meeting places for purely secular activities — children playing, dogs running about, women gossiping, and men playing cards — as can be seen in some of the Dutch genre paintings of the 1600s — or meeting places for spies and lovers in countless movies. Still, a sacred precinct can affect the secular. I find it slightly disturbing when the audience applauds after a concert in a church, especially one in which religious music is performed. As I have had no religious training, I might be attributing greater sanctity to a church than does the believer, who by definition responds at least as much to the sacrament as to its location, but the two are hard to distinguish ceremonially. Elation knows no boundaries. Or does it?

IV.

HOME

W HEN I was thirteen, my father died suddenly just as he was about to come home from the hospital, where some calcified lymph nodes had been removed from his chest. He had been shaving...

We had three months to find a house. My sister and I wanted to move far away — to California, to France, to Switzerland, to Manhattan, to Princeton even — but my mother said we had to live nearby to preserve our roots. We moved into a house with a small garden but an enormous stone fireplace, "unusual oak doors," or so the real estate agent told my mother, and a landing nearly as big as a room, where Dusio, our Boxer, kept watch.

Gargy had died by then. My father had run him over in the driveway, while he was sunning. I lay in bed, suffering from rheumatic fever and in far too much pain to get up and see what had happened. I knew — so agonized was Gargy's whelp — but that knowledge, absolute as it was, didn't prevent me from screaming, "What's happened, what's happened?" No one answered. No one heard me. The pain in Gargy's whelp echoed the pain I felt in my legs as I tried to get out of bed and couldn't. My father was so torn, so ashamed, that he couldn't face me until my bedtime. Gargy was my dog. The only picture I have of my father is one in which he is sitting on the ground, holding me, a baby, in his arms as Gargy, a gawky tangle of white legs and a dropping head, presses himself against my father's thigh. Spinones have pink eyes.

We bought Dusio in Italy, in Forte dei Marmi, on my first trip to Europe. My parents had promised to give my sister and me a

Spinone, a replacement for Gargy, when we were in Italy. They had left us at the hotel to see a breeder who was supposed to be selling one. As we were waiting for my parents, we met a man who was walking two Boxer puppies, one older than the other, back and forth in front of the hotel. Someone who worked in the hotel must have told him that we wanted to buy a dog, but we didn't think of this at the time. We were too young. I was eleven, my sister eight.

We told the man about Gargy. We told him that our parents were out looking at a Spinone. He seemed surprised and said he didn't think there were any available in the area. Perhaps we would like to have a Boxer instead. We didn't say anything, though neither of us could stop playing with the two puppies. He told us that he would be passing the hotel just before dinner. My parents came back empty-handed. They knew how disappointed we would be, since we were leaving Italy the next day for France, where there were no Spinone breeders. They were surprised, and I suppose relieved, when we told them we had found a dog, not a Spinone but a Boxer, named Dusio, whom we loved. The man returned with the two dogs, and Dusio, the elder of the two, became ours.

Dusio went mad when we drove past our old house one afternoon, a few months after we had moved. He began attacking deliverymen and had to be put down. I'll never forget his whining in the car that day. His pain, his grief, unlike ours, was raw, defenseless, unmediated. He had been my father's dog.

OUR NEW house never became a home. Clara helped us move in, but it was clear that she was uncomfortable there, outside the hospital. She never came back, and I never saw her again. I missed her, but I was relieved. She was part of a life that had died with my father. Mr. Axelson did come for a few months to build cabinets and do the heavy cleaning, and then he stopped. I never knew why. Perhaps he had gone on a binge. He was an alcoholic. I liked him a lot but never associated him with my father's death.

My mother stopped seeing her friends soon after we had moved to Caldwell. "They'd just be feeling sorry for me," she said when I tried to convince her to see them. She made no new friends. She wasn't prepared for my father's death. Who ever is? My parents weren't particularly close, and I don't think my mother realized how attached she had been to him. She didn't really know what to do with herself. She couldn't admit that she was in mourning. She was, or at least she considered herself, a stoic. She indulged in insights with no one to test them on. Perhaps she didn't want to. Perhaps that was why she dropped her friends. She was far more psychoanalytically oriented than my father. She had been a social worker at my father's hospital when she met him.

The house had been a mistake. It was lifeless, and we were all trapped in that lifelessness—in our, my mother's, moroseness. My sister would shut herself in her room the minute she came home from school, listening to pop tunes and reading movie magazines. I spent most of my own time in my room or in the laboratory I had set up in the basement. My grandmother had given me a Leitz microscope, and I ordered slides and specimens to dissect from the Marine Biological Laboratory in Woods Hole. It was the first time I had ever ordered anything. I made a few friends. One of them, Schulty, had a camera attachment that let him take photographs of what we saw under the microscope. He had borrowed it from his father. Most of the students' social lives revolved around churches, and as we didn't belong to any church, my sister and I felt isolated. School was dreary. I spent the rest of my free time designing houses, but I never thought of becoming an architect. I wonder why. All my designs ended up looking like a Georgian mansion that had become the headquarters of an insurance company. We passed by it twice a week when my mother drove me to an allergist. I had developed all sorts of allergies after my father died, not immediately, but in the summer before starting my new school. The work of mourning—it is endless, unpredictably recursive, Freud notwithstanding, irresolvable.

This was our first move. It took my mother more than a year to sell the house—to the real estate agent who had wanted it all along and was waiting for my mother to lower the price. We then moved to Geneva for us to have a "European education" and lived on the ground floor of a large grand-bourgeois house, off the Route de Florissant, with highly polished floors, a red marble fireplace—Empire, my mother said—French windows that flooded the living room with light, and high walls that surrounded the house and garden. At first I felt closed in by the walls but then I got so used to them, to the sense of privacy, of intimacy, they gave me, that I still miss them, particularly when I visit friends in suburbia, where front lawns put the houses on display.

Then, unexpectedly, my mother decided to move back to New Jersey. She was lonely but wouldn't admit it. I didn't want to go back to America and had to fight with her to stay in Geneva. It was a terrible fight and marked an irreparable break in our relationship. She relinquished only when Mme Briquet, my English teacher, and her husband agreed that I could board with them. Much to my surprise, as if confirming that break, my mother took my sister out of school early to travel through Spain and

Portugal and arranged for me to stay until the end of the school
year at a pension: the Hotel Sergy, where the other guests looked
at me disapprovingly whenever I entered the dining room.

By the time I was a senior at Harvard, my mother and sister
were again in Switzerland, living in a tiny, unhappy apartment in
a building filled with minor bureaucrats from one international
agency or another. I never saw it. Then she was back in New Jersey, where she remained until her jewelry—including my father's
gold watch fob in the shape of a skull with a movable jaw that I
liked to play with when I very little—was stolen. She moved to
Scottsdale, where she lived in the same house until she died. It
was, I believe, the longest she had ever lived in one house—in
a place where she didn't have any roots. I don't think she knew
her neighbors. They were always moving, selling one house for
profit in order to buy another in the hope of selling it for an even
greater profit.

What was she seeking? I often ask myself. A home? She had
become a hermit. She was forty-one or forty-two when my father
died.

Nostalgia is for an absent absence. It requires a forgetting.
What is the "forgotten" that lies behind my nostalgia for where I
grew up before we had to move? I recall the garden, the smell of
the earth, the woods behind the house above the hill where my
father had planted over a hundred dogwood trees, the park we
called "the grove" in front of the doctors' cottages, the wisteria
arbor behind the kitchen where cardinals liked to nest, and the
side gardens, hidden from the street by a maze of bushes that
flowered in the spring, where my parents nurtured a Japanese
maple, where my sister and I caught fireflies and plucked beetles
from the rose bushes, and where an Airedale my parents rescued
from the SPCA dug up a bed of peonies to bury his bones and was

then given to a farmer (so at least my sister and I were told), the herb garden I refused to enter after Clara told me that humming birds were attracted to herbs and could blind you by flying into your eyes, and the chicken coop behind the second side-garden, where the fireplace and the stone picnic table were never used because it was dark, damp, and mosquito-ridden. It was there that the lilies of the valley grew that we weren't allowed to touch because they were poisonous. Clara said that they grew out of Eve's tears when she and Adam were driven from Paradise.

When did I first understand what a home is? I do not mean when I first used or heard the word. You can use a word long before you understand its implications. Do you have to leave home, as the poets say, in order to know it as "home"? Do you have to experience homesickness or relief from familial claustrophobia? I'm not sure. There may be a defining departure or a series of departures or a sudden change of perspective or a series of such changes that create "home."

I am waiting on the lawn near the driveway for a kindergarten friend—I don't remember his name—to get out of the car while my mother is talking to his mother. He doesn't get out. His mother won't let him. Clara is watching from the front door. The garage door is open. Mr. Axelson is working there. He almost never does. He's watching, too. I can't hear what my mother is saying. She is irritated, supplicatory, angrily so. My friend's mother is insinuatingly apologetic. Finally my friend and his mother get out of the car and look around. She holds my friend's hand tightly. He squirms, trying to get loose, but she doesn't let him go. Mother introduces her to Clara. Clara doesn't like her, I can see. "You have a beautiful garden," she says. It is much nicer than hers, I think. "And the house—" Mother interrupts her: "Yes, it is quite nice." But she doesn't invite her in.

My friend's mother drags my friend back to the car as I watch, disappointed, and then in a voice that is loud enough for Clara and Mr. Axelson to hear, she says, "You have to understand. I don't know what goes on here with all—I would be worrying all afternoon." She slams the car door, and as an afterthought, she says through the window, "Maybe sometime in the future," and, without saying goodbye, drives off. "What a bitch," my mother says. Clara and Mr. Axelson are looking down at their feet. "But, Mommy, why can't Eddie"—I suddenly remember his name—"stay?" "It's a family problem," she answers, not knowing, I know, what to say.

But I knew, knew something, something I had never known, that I couldn't put into words, something, whatever it was, that twisted my consciousness around so that I not-quite-perceived that where I lived, what I called, without thought, home could be seen otherwise: with suspicion, as dangerous—as a scary oddity, the reluctant recognition of which provoked my mother's fury, as self-protective as it was protective of me, Clara, and Mr. Axelson, from Eddie's mother. It was "bitch," the word as well as the person, around whom, around which, an embryonic home-consciousness formed.

Rilke wrote at the end of *The Notebooks of Malte Laurids Brigge*, one of my favorite books, that it was difficult for him to be persuaded that the story of the Prodigal Son was not the legend of him who did not want to be loved. (The awkward phrasing is Rilke's.) His parable is obscure, but it refers to Malte's (Rilke's) need to escape vain, self-interested family love in order to become a poet. When he finally comes home, he realizes that his family's love has little to do with him and the transcendent love he seeks. Cloying love—the cloying—we have to escape if we are to become whom we destine ourselves to be.

I was stunned by Rilke's observation, an aside really, that the parable never tells us whether the Prodigal Son ever left home again. I am not sure that once you experience the wrenching departure from home that creates home, you can ever leave it again. So strong is the longing, so insistent the absence, so damning the negation. Though home changes, though we try to re-create it, a moment out of time, we can never succeed, for it is lost in ever-shifting, intangible memories that, however certain they appear to be, are epiphanies and, with time, epiphanies of epiphanies, whose histories are frozen by the paralyzing or, more generously, the defining effect of nostalgia—of the absent absence.

We live in an apartment, which we own and in which we have lived most of our married life. It is our home. Wicky grew up there. But, for me, it is not a house. It is without a garden, detached, a refuge, a place of closed doors. Despite the many years we have spent in it; the improvements we have made; the wall colors we chose; the furniture we bought and inherited; the art we have collected each with its own story; the parties we have given; the neighbors we have come to know; the friends who visited; the love we have made; the arguments we have had; the music we have listened to; the illnesses we suffered; the recoveries; the echoes of lost thoughts, shared and unshared; and emotions, long past, silent but still heard; deep down, I—but not Jane, who likes to nest—have always felt transient. The apartment has no history that preceded us. Yes, we met the former occupants; yes, we heard from the old super that a photographer—"a hippie photographer"—had lived there before them. But that is as far back as history goes, though the building is now over a hundred years old. Houses speak. Apartments don't. There are no ghosts there.

We can only create new homes. They may resonate with our childhood home—positively, like the chimes of a doorbell, or negatively, like the flapping of an unhinged shutter in the wind before it finally falls to the ground, chipped, split, unusable—but they are never the same. Inevitably, we have a different perspective, an observational one: inner, yes, empathetically, like the child's, and outer, like that of the adult, the departed one.

I remember when Wicky was nearly three. We were visiting her godmother in Connecticut, who had a small lake on her farm. I took Wicky on a walk, and, for the first time, she walked all the way around the lake. It was early in the morning and the leaves and the earth were still dew-damp. I was at once proud of her, of her continual chatter, her endurance, as we walked down the overgrown path, and at the same time so overwhelmed by childhood memories of the smell of damp earth that I became obsessed with the idea of moving to the countryside. There she would have the same experiences I'd had—experiences she would never have living in the city. We almost did buy a house I saw advertised in the local paper later that morning. It was an absurd idea, entirely impractical, dislodging Jane, who was in a state of shock. Fortunately, George Devoe, the real estate agent, a grandfatherly man whom we knew, put a stop to our—my—folly before it was too late. Our relief was enormous. I suddenly remembered the joy I had, as a boy, sailing a toy sailboat in the pond in the Luxembourg Gardens. Wicky's childhood was her own, as was and would be her experience of home. It would never be ours but hers, and that would give us pleasures freed from the constraints of irrational repetition.

As strange as it may seem (and it does to me), I cannot help but identify the world of the hospital—of the total institution—with that of a child, with my own childhood world. Both worlds are discrete, turned in on themselves, and detached, like the

detachment demanded by play—a detachment, a separate-
ness, that gives the illusion of independence and the freedom to
ignore, to escape, the constraints imposed, for the young child
by irregular obtrusions of reality, and for the adult by ominous
images of an intrusive reality that he refers to as the "outside
world." The child knows no boundaries; the adult, living in the
confines of a total institution, is so haunted by boundaries that
what lies beyond them can and does, inevitably, take on mythic
dimensions. Unknown? Not really. Dangerous? Not necessarily.
Unprotected to a point, judgmental, alluring, challenging, limit-
ing but filled with possibilities that are lacking, or so it is perceived, on the inside…In its way, it is an intensification of the
fear of the out-framed, the rolling infinitude that leads nowhere
and everywhere, from which we hide in bad faith and seek solace
in the in-framed—the house, the home, the garden, the family,
the country, and, indeed, the psyche. The Germans say *aus dem
Häuschen geraten*—"to flip one's lid," "to be out of one's mind," literally "to be turned out of the little house." The expression may
have come from the French *être un échappé des Petits-Maisons*—"to
be an escapee from the Little Houses"—referring to a former
mental hospital in Paris.

The wrenching that produces "home" also produces an ever-
distancing voice that can at times be imperial in its command of
the past, its objectifications, and the destruction of the animistic
dimension of lived experience. That past, those memories that
are recalled, devoid of resonance, can so easily become the back-
drop, the struts, for what we take to be reality and upon and from
which we act. We write.

My sister hits me over and over again, crying, screaming,
shrieking, "It's not true. It's not true. You're lying. You're a liar."
"No, I'm not, I'm not," I say, at first in a disciplined voice that

surprises me, a coldness that frightens me, and then, since she does not believe me, I shout louder and louder, "I'm not a liar," wishing I were. I look helplessly at Clara, who tries to calm her.

I hear the tension, a crackling in my mother's voice, an unsaid, an unsayable message that lies behind her words. "Mr. Luke will pick you up and drive you and your sister to Dr. della Ragione's. I will meet you there." Her "I" was emptied of all content—just an index.

Was I, was Clara, to call Mr. Luke? He drove my sister and me to school each day. We hated him. He was always spitting out the window and sometimes his spit sprayed on us. I couldn't ask Clara to call. She was in the kitchen, somewhere, anywhere, elsewhere, nowhere. Besides, she didn't like to use the telephone. I didn't have Mr. Luke's phone number. I could have asked the hospital operator. I didn't think to. I had to know more. When we came back from school, Clara hinted that we would have a surprise that day—one that we had suspected. Poppy was coming home. But he wasn't. I knew. I knew. I didn't want to know. Why were we going to the della Ragiones'? They were my father's friends. I liked them. My mother didn't. We always had dinner on Christmas Eve and sometimes on Good Friday at their house. Their Christmas tree was gloomy—just blue lights and silver tinsel. I had to find out. What? To call Mr. Luke? To ask for his telephone number? I had to call the hospital—to ask my mother. She was there. She would still be in my father's room. She had to be. She had to be there.

"I am sorry"—impersonal, devastating, expected and unexpected, hovering in the space between anxious hope and the unsayable, now the said. "Dr. Crapanzano passed away"—died, I heard—"at two-forty-seven this afternoon. His room, the room, is now occupied by another patient."

"But my mother—"

The click. The operator had hung up. The click, not her words, not the unsayable said, was definitive.

I could barely control my tears. I vowed not to cry, not ever. And I didn't, not even at the funeral, though, embarrassed by this, I tried. Mother just coughed. My sister, it had been decided, was too young to attend. Who decided? I'm sure it was a mistake. Death has to be acknowledged. Words are not sufficient. The dead, those close to you, have to be seen, whether in fact or hidden in a coffin. Otherwise, there is too much room for fantasy, especially for a child. I can still feel the cold, the cold of death, unlike any other I had ever felt, as I kissed my father's forehead and smelled the odor of death, of embalming fluids—of a makeup that masked what was already a mask.

As I reread what I've just written, I'm surprised by the clinical tone behind the melodrama. I feel myself falling away from the immediacy of death and the warmth of a home that was not quite yet "home." I am beginning to ventriloquize my later, more mature self, the departed self—the self who returned to the hospital to visit, to help in the laboratory (as I had done since I was twelve), to work there the summer after my first year at college. But I am also voicing what I overheard and was told over the years, most notably by my mother, by Mr. Seachrist, who ran the laboratory and knew more medicine than most of the doctors, by nurses I met, attendants, and patients. I can no longer recall when I first heard whatever I overheard. All I can ask is whose voice am I echoing—and I know that I will never be able to answer with certainty. We have enough difficulty distinguishing our own voice from the voices of the interlocutors who inspire our voice as we inspire theirs. We flee the tyranny of interlocution, to preserve our voice—our sense of self.

THE HOSPITAL was nearly self-sufficient. With the exception of those inmates who were dangerous (there were few of those) or no longer able to emerge from the catatonic depths of their psyches (there were more of them), most of the patients were granted some level of parole — as the staff called it. Some could not leave the wards without supervision; others didn't require supervision but had to remain on the hospital grounds; and still others, such as Mr. Andrews, who delivered our afternoon paper, could leave the grounds provided that they didn't go too far. I am not sure what "too far" meant. Of course, they all had a curfew. If they didn't return before then, they were considered runaways and a whistle would blow, the same one that blew at noon, notifying the police. Mr. Andrews ran away once and was caught on the George Washington Bridge on his way, so he said, to Rockefeller Center to see the Rockettes. He lost his parole, and we didn't get the evening paper delivered until he was granted it again a few days later, probably because the doctors complained about having to drive to the nearest newsstand. It was several miles away.

Mr. Andrews earned money, but most of the patients who had parole worked for the hospital voluntarily and without pay (other than the mandated allowances they received for cigarettes, chewing gum, and other incidentals). They worked on the farm, in the garden, in the warehouses, the bakery, the butchery, the ward kitchens, the electric plant, the laundry, and, of course, for the doctors. We had a large staff: Clara, Phil, and later Mr. Axelson, several gardeners — Orestes, who had a green thumb but planted twigs at the end of each day's work; Ernest, who collected wild mushrooms, which only my father dared eat; Pete, who had the strength of a stevedore and the gentleness of a rabbit, and was diagnosed paranoid schizophrenic; and Mr. Metulowitz, who repaired watches and just about everything else that was mechanical. He made reindeers, elephants, and trees with elaborate branches out of pipe cleaners and the silver paper that lined packs of cigarettes and gave them as Christmas presents. He hadn't said a word for more than twenty years, since he was admitted to the hospital; that is, until my father, much to everyone's surprise, somehow managed to get him to talk again. He immediately lost the aura of mystery that had surrounded him and soon stopped speaking again, though he did manage to tell my mother how sorry he was when my father died. "There was something skeletal about his voice," Mother said. And there was Mr. Swanson, who simonized our car. He was treated with diffidence and was paid for the work he did. I never knew why. The others were just given spending money or presents. I remember going with my mother to the five-and-ten to buy Clara her favorite red Lifebuoy soap and to the local bakery for the end-of-the-day chocolate cookies, which she liked so much. So did I.

We also had an endless series of cooks—they never seemed to satisfy my mother. They were from the outside and were always afraid of the crazies when they first came to work for us. They were given an apartment in the building where the resident nurses lived. There was Miss Abbott, who was fired after my mother discovered her sharpening one of several large boxes of super-sharp German knives. And Elena, who was Hungarian and made delicious strudel but smelled bad. And several Italians whose homemade pasta my father liked but who refused to cook anything that was not Italian. And the wonderful Helen, everyone's favorite, who left us to go home, somewhere in the South, after her husband was killed in the war. We all cried when Helen left. Unlike the other cooks, she sent us Christmas and birthday cards for years. She had taken the blame for an antique lamp I broke when I threw a ball at my sister in the living room. It was to have been our secret, but I couldn't stand the secret, confessed, and was surprised when my parents told me what a wonderful friend Helen must be. They didn't punish me — the worst of all punishments.

Helen was followed by Mrs. Pogel, who stayed the longest and taught my sister and me a little German. She had an enormous collection of postcards, mainly of nineteenth-century German paintings, fields of heather, fairy-tale-looking houses, and of course castles, presumably on the Rhine, which she showed us with a depth of feeling we did not understand. We were too young to know what it meant to reexperience — to experience that which could never be reexperienced but had somehow, desperately, to be conveyed to others, to children even, to my sister and me, to reanimate memories whose referents had not been forgotten but bombed out, burned, obliterated by the war. Mrs. Pogel's son had been drafted and by some administrative accident was sent to fight in the little village in Germany where he had been born and still had family. When the war was over, his mother began stealing sheets and towels to send to her family there, and then, feeling guilty, it was supposed, gave my sister and me extravagant Christmas presents: a scooter for me, a tricycle for her. I'm not sure why Mrs. Pogel left. It was not because of her stealing. My parents felt sorry for her and her family. It may have had something to do with her son, who had been wounded in the fighting, but she worked for us until well after the war ended. We also had a deaf-and-dumb cook, but she didn't work out because, as she couldn't hear the serving bell, she stood in the corner of the dining room watching us eat. And then there was Mary Esther — I still feel the guilt we all felt when she was asked to leave. Mary Esther was black, the best cook of all. She warned my mother before she was hired that she had a problem.

Whenever she touched silver it immediately tarnished. My mother said she would try her out, but in the end let her go. I've often wondered why she hadn't just let Clara set the table.

Everyone was dependent on everyone else at the hospital. Doctors, nurses, and attendants were as dependent on their patients as the patients on them. There was no escape from dependency. None of the doctors I knew, except for the psychiatric residents, ever left the hospital. The residents had their careers in front of them. Even though their departure was expected, it forced the staff to recognize, if momentarily, the loss of possibility that came with their remaining. "Future" would be too strong a word, since they had their dreams, usually revolving around vague ideas of retirement, as did my father, who of course didn't live long enough to retire. Most of the doctors were from the South (why? I don't know) and had served in World War I, which marked them, if only through disciplinary abnegation, an interminable exhaustion, a depletion that left them—I suspected but never knew, since I was too young to know—an encrusted identity. One of them, Dr. Thatcher, preferred to be called Colonel Thatcher.

The hospital added little support to the defenses that protected the doctors from the recognition that, despite their therapeutic pretense, they were by and large simply caretakers. It was not a research hospital, and given the state of psychiatry at the time and the inevitable understaffing, there was little the doctors could do to help the majority of patients other than to make their lives as comfortable as possible, offering them a refuge, a community apart, and making use of the few therapeutic interventions that were current at the time—hydrotherapy, shock therapy (used with far more caution than in most mental institutions at the time), occupational therapy, hypnosis, and brief psychotherapy for the most receptive, who were also the best educated. The doctors would spend hours at staff meetings discussing the diagnosis, treatment, and prognosis, but mainly the diagnosis, of patients. My father said it was a waste of time, a Kraepelinian fantasy. I knew what he was talking about, since I had begun reading sections of Kraepelin's *Compendium* a few months before my father died, whenever I heard my parents refer to a diagnosis I didn't know. I don't want to deny the doctors the satisfactions they had when a patient was cured or when they were able to treat successfully an ordinary or not-so-ordinary illness, which took on, I believe, certainly for my father, far greater symbolic significance than it would probably have had for general practitioners. He was a good doctor, as the nurses told me when I worked that summer in the hospital laboratory.

For the most part, the doctors lost themselves in complaint and gossip, petty affairs and meaningless power games, in the details of family life — they all came home for lunch — or in their collections. Dr. Smith had so fine a collection of Wedgwood that members of the Wedgwood family would visit him when they came to the United States from England. Sometimes, they would come to see the pink Cupid and Psyche that my father had discovered in an antiques shop on Cape Cod. They were unique, made to order for a duchess in the middle of the nineteenth century, and were the envy of Dr. Smith, who offered to buy them from my father so many times that it became a family joke.

Although the doctors' cottages all faced the grove, they were not friends or even particularly good neighbors. My sister and I knew them, of course, but often they would not even say hello when we greeted them. Even though my parents asked him not to, Dr. Sutton, our closest neighbor, used to let his Chow run wild in the grove. The Chow had bitten several of the patients.

The other doctors' children were older than my sister and me, and unless the residents had children, we had no playmates who lived nearby. We were not lonely, since our lives were centered on the patients: those who worked for us, those we came to know, and those we heard about.

I can't say how I saw the patients, other than those who worked for us, when I was little. I didn't really know what a patient was. They were just people who lived on the wards, sometimes did odd things, and needed doctors. When I was seven or eight, or maybe nine, my father would occasionally take me on his rounds. I think my presence, a child's presence, humanized him for many of them. Some were very friendly. Others I knew or had seen around. But there were also the empty ones. I remember them, sitting around the ward lounge or, in the summer, on porches, staring at me in wonderment or, worse, looking past me, as though I was at once there and not there. They seemed less conscious of the nurses and attendants who surveilled them than of one another—a point Michel Foucault missed in his discussion of the disciplinary gaze. However controlling a warder's gaze is, you still know who you are. But the abstracted, incomprehensible, crazed gaze, particularly when it is multiplied, is devastating, like being lost in a nightmare or, in fact, in a hall of distorting mirrors. You don't know who you are. You look away but you still know that *you*—someone whom you do not recognize as yourself—is the object, or perhaps not, of that gaze and of the thoughts and hallucinatory images you can't quite imagine that lie behind or in that gaze. Of course, I couldn't have put it that way then, but I must admit, perhaps because children's primordial sense of identity is far less fragile than that projected on them by adults, to a voyeuristic fascination with those unfathomable looks. When I tell people that I grew up in a

mental hospital, they always ask me, in a disapproving tone — my
poor parents — whether I was frightened, and never quite believe
me when I answer "almost never."

One of the advantages of working for a doctor was that you
were usually given a room of your own in the ward. Clara had a
room, except once, when she had one of her episodes. It was punishing, and even when she recovered, she had to wait a long time
before she got back her room. It had been given to another patient
whom she didn't like. Mr. Axelson had one, too, except when he
went on a binge, and so had Mr. Metulowitz, Mr. Swanson, and
Mr. Andrews. I am quite sure Phil didn't, but he had his "office."
They cherished their privacy — their home within a home that
wasn't and could never be their home. Other patients — I don't
know who they were — built shacks and huts in the woods that
were part of the hospital grounds. When I was older my friends
Freddy and Bob and I would break into them and snoop around,
feeling the thrill — the French would say *jouissance* — of transgression. We never took anything or broke anything and even tried
to cover up our invasion as best we could when we left; that is,
until we were joined by Jimmy, whose family had moved from
the Newark slums. Jimmy went on a rampage, destroying everything that may have been precious to whoever had built the
hut. We couldn't stop him, and never broke into a patient's hut
again. One day, on a self-dare, I went back to the hut Jimmy had
destroyed. Through the window I saw that the mirror Jimmy had
broken had been repaired with Scotch tape. I ran away before I
could see anything else. I would have been happier if the hut had
been abandoned.

I don't think anyone at the hospital was particularly troubled
by free labor, not even the patients. They took pride, so they said
or so it was assumed, in their work. It filled their time, gave them

purpose (how can I say that?), and offered them escape from life on the wards. But, on the outside, there were critics who called it exploitation of the helpless. Three or four years after my father died, several unions began a campaign to end the "slavery" and, as there were no real grounds to argue against them—other than that the work was for the patients' benefit—they won. I remember how shocked I was when I visited the hospital more than thirty years after we had moved. The patients seemed to have lost their spirit; the grounds, which had been the pride of the hospital and the patients who did the gardening, were poorly kept. The farm was closed, and where the dairy had stood, there was now a sewerage purification plant. The picture windows in the lounges in the geriatric wards gave out onto it. The intricate interdependencies that constituted the hospital community I had known and idealized were lost. By that time, most of the patients who would have spent their lives in the hospital were now on psychotropic drugs, if they took them, living in the "outside world"—at home, in halfway houses, or, more likely, on the streets. As I looked at our old house—it seemed much smaller than I'd remembered it—the unkempt gardens, and a couple of old patients, their suspenders so stretched that you could see their stained underpants, leaning against a broken-down wall, staring at me emptily, I asked myself whether the patients (certainly the doctors and staff) were better off when we had been living there. My meditation, embarrassingly, like a memento mori, was interrupted by a hospital policeman who asked me what I was doing there. When I answered that I was on a memory trip and had lived in that house, he looked at me dubiously and asked my father's name. "Never heard of him," he said, and ordered me off the grounds. "We don't want anyone snooping around here. It's private property." He had seen me take some photographs.

The hospital is gone. I discovered this a couple of days ago when I looked it up on the net. It has become, the bloggers have written, the county's "most legendary location, home to escaped lunatics, troubled ghosts, and roving gangs of ne'er do wells," and a daredevil testing ground for bands of teenagers who crawl through the underground tunnels, as Freddy and I had done, that connected the various buildings, and spend nights waiting for scary apparitions in the abandoned wards. One woman actually asked where the dead were buried. It has, in fact, become so dangerous that the police patrol it day and night and arrest anyone they find trespassing. Speculators grabbed up as many acres as they could, at ridiculously low prices, before they were stopped, and much of the remaining land is scheduled to become a public park. Will my father's dogwoods be part of it? Legend has replaced reality, but, I suppose, it also catches the fear that the asylum and its inmates inspired in the local population—in Eddie's mother—and of which I was only dimly aware. It had, after all, been home.

V.
KNOWING
WHAT YOU
DO NOT KNOW

I AM playing on the living room floor in cottage seven. My father is playing solitaire. He comes home from work, listens to the news on the radio, and then plays solitaire. But he is not really playing. He wants something more from solitaire than that. He wants to win. He wants to lose. My mother looks at him from the dining room and shakes her head sadly. Something is wrong. My father hardly talks to me, and when he kisses me good night he is distracted. His lips are dry and cold. I do not understand.

Could I have understood?

The image is fixed in my mind. It recurs from time to time, and, when it does, it fills me with sympathy for my father, and for his shame, which translates into my being ashamed of him. I knew then more than I knew.

How do I write about what I didn't know as a child and yet knew?

I am overwhelmed by similar images—I can't even call them memory-images—that whirl about, resisting any connection, any story, or any determination. The connections, the stories come later, lose the immediacy of the image as it becomes a memory and then a story.

Did my father ever come home from work, listen to the radio, and play solitaire? Did he do it once? Did he do it many times? Usually he came home from work, sat down in his red chair—it wasn't really red, but we called it red—and read the newspaper until dinner.

I don't really know. What I have is the image. I try to make sense of it. It was wartime. The Allies had invaded Sicily. My father was born in Sicily. He had family there but hadn't seen them since he was thirteen and was sent north to boarding school—and was never allowed to come home. He studied medicine at the University of Pavia, but before he had completed his studies, he, like his classmates, was conscripted. As a young medical officer, he was deployed at the Austrian front. I can't imagine what he saw there, what he had to do, what he thought, if he *had* thought. I see his hands, his face, a uniform splattered with blood. The dead, the dying, the wounded, the mutilated, the dismembered, the odor of chloroform, the stink of gangrene, the screams, the groans, and, worst of all, the pleas for help, for morphine, to end the pain. It was the scene of some of the bloodiest battles in World War I. He never talked about it, not even to my mother.

After the war, but before finishing medical school, he spent a year on one of the Italian lakes, probably Garda, in the villa of one of his friends, whose family manufactured sewing machines. They did nothing there, except occasionally sail to the middle of the lake and drop a grenade—my father said "a little bomb"—into the water. One of the crew would then haul in the stunned fish. The violence—he seemed immune to it when he told me the story. It wasn't like him.

Then my father and a distant cousin, more of a friend than a cousin, sailed for America to specialize, but when the steamer stopped in Nice, his friend returned to Florence. His mother was dying. My father wanted to go with him, but his friend said no. From New York, my father wrote to his friend not to come. He didn't like New York. He never felt at home in America. He stayed on because he was opposed to Fascism. Was he? My mother told me it was because of a love affair with a married woman. By then, she was more than bitter. When America joined the war, perhaps even before that, the order came through (from whom I never knew) to dismiss all "enemy aliens" working in the hospital where my father was employed. My father had never applied for citizenship. He would have had to leave the hospital, but he was needed. He got his American citizenship in a day. A few years ago, an old Italian consul told me that he had come across several instances of one-day citizenships at that time.

Did my father want to become an American? I don't know. He was trapped in ambivalence. He was so very much an Italian. He was tied now, legally, amorously, to America. He had married my mother.

The solitaire—he rehearsed his ambivalence over and over again. It wasn't solitaire he was playing. He was soothsaying, predicting through his wins and losses the outcome of the battles that were being fought in Sicily. By the time the Allies moved north, he had stopped playing. There was no need to. The Allies had to win. He had no love of Germany.

It was (was it?) ambivalence, desperation, the shame of a folly that I knew but didn't know as from the floor I watched him manipulating the cards one way and then another, doing, undoing, doing again, in the desire, the non-desire of winning or losing. Did he change his mind, midgame, as to what a win or a loss meant? I don't remember him ever looking at me while he played.

What else did I know then that I did not *know*? There were things that were kept from me, such as the horrors of the war that I knew, without knowing what they were. I must have seen pictures in the paper or in *Life* magazine, or overheard or heard on the radio or from Phil, though I can't remember anything Phil ever said about the war. What did war mean to me then? Clara talked about her brother Gussy, who had been gassed in the war. I didn't know which one; I didn't know if there had been more than one war or whether there had ever been warless times. I knew that Gussy never got better and lived all alone and didn't visit Clara although she always said he was "coming soon." I knew mainly that the war was something you didn't want children to know about, that it was happening somewhere else—in a beyond that was breaking down the way the drum of my steamroller had. A war was somewhere else where steamrollers—and tanks, I knew about them—couldn't go anymore, where people were gassed and couldn't visit their family, and soldiers, like my lead ones—I just remembered them—fell down and died (whatever "died" meant to me) and airplanes crashed. But mainly a war was what children weren't supposed to know about but did. It was dangerous, like going near the TB wards (for those patients who were both psychotic and suffering from tuberculosis). They had a nasty smell, like rotten onions, Clara's underarms when she didn't use Lifebuoy soap, and a bottle of something or other that I wasn't supposed to go near with which my father sometimes washed his hands when he came home from work. It was dangerous. The beyond could be dangerous.

It is nighttime. I hear screaming sirens. It's an air raid. I hear my father groan and get up. He has to go somewhere because he's a doctor. My mother carries my sister to the basement. I follow her. We are sleepy, but I know that we are going to have hot chocolate and marshmallows. We always did during air raids. The phone rings. My mother has to answer it. She hesitates and then reluctantly goes upstairs to the nearest phone. My sister and I want to go with her, but she says no. We are afraid. The phone has never rung before during an air raid. My sister starts to cry. I try to make her stop, but she won't. My mother comes back down. She says, "It was your father. He wanted to make sure we're all right." We are, but I feel something between fear and preoccupation in my mother's words. Years later, I learn that German submarines had been sighted off the New Jersey coast. My father had called to tell my mother that he would probably be out all night.

Knowing now, as I write, what air raids meant in Europe during the war, I am embarrassed by the importance I attribute to the one I am describing—the indulgence—but of course the fear was real for me then. Subjective experiences—the emotions felt—are never relative. Devaluing our own experiences is permissible, so long as the devaluation is realistic and, more important, sincere. There is a delicate etiquette to subjectivity. I remember how outraged I was when I read an op-ed piece by Elie Wiesel in which he assumed a kind of ur-sufferer's right to compare Jewish and black South African experience, as if anyone has that right.

The beyond, the elsewhere, something unknown happening there, the danger it holds, the fear it inspires, leapt into the where-I-was-then. For my sister, and less so for me because I was older, the beyond was fluid, for our boundaries, all of them—personal, interpersonal, ontological—were not yet fixed. They couldn't be contained in our whimsical time and space.

The infant has no beyond, for the beyond loops into the here and now, becoming, almost becoming, one with it and yet, insofar as it allures or terrifies with possibility, it is cleaved—in both senses of the word.

Has the infant become an allegorical figure for me? Does it have any experiential reality?

It is willfulness that turns the beyond into a *beyond*. It is curiosity that creates the unknown and eventually a sense of mystery. Doesn't the uncanny—the *Unheimlichkeit*—the unfamiliarly familiar, familiarly unfamiliar, find its home, its *Heim*, in the cleavage? In the inevitable failure of the beyond to loop back fully into the here and now—into what it is not—thus producing the space-time of inarticulate desire, the presentment of indefinable danger, and the culling of temptation? With the passing of time, we all come to defend ourselves from this if only by giving it a name—the unconscious or the daemonic—or by reducing it, as the Freudians might, to a bodily part (the cleavage) that can never succeed in substituting for it, for the emptiness of that space-time ends only with death.

Wicky is not yet three. She is playing on the floor in her great-uncle Fred's apartment. His wife has just died, and he is in far deeper mourning than I would have ever imagined. Jane and I are trying to pull him out of the downward whirl of his grief but with no success. He cannot escape the darkness in his soul, and we cannot escape its encompassment, as we wait impatiently for another mourner to come so we can leave. Suddenly, with startling effect, Wicky looks up at her Uncle Fred, whom she barely knows, and says—it is a pronouncement—"Life is important," and then, in what seems to me cruel indifference to his insufferable despair, continues to play with her Pooh bear.

Where did these words come from? Neither Jane nor I nor Fred had used them. They were oracular. They had an immediate effect. We were released from the claustrophobia of gloom into which we'd been drawn. Fred offered us coffee that he had prepared and forgotten about, and then several friends arrived and we were able to take Wicky home. Fred died a year later. The coroner's examination took less than five minutes. I was there. He said it was a heart attack, but it was clearly suicide or at least the foreknowledge of that heart attack, if it was in fact a heart attack, and with it, his impending death. His affairs were in order; his will and nine hundred dollars in cash lay on his desk; his collection of Lincoln documents and letters had just been auctioned. His refrigerator was empty except for a bottle of brandied peaches.

Wicky's words seemed to come from elsewhere, as though she were ventriloquizing. Did she understand what she was saying? I doubt it. Psychologists tell us that a child of her age is incapable of abstraction. The more appropriate question is: Did she know what she was doing? What was important to her, I am quite certain, was the effect of her words, though that probably came after she had said them. We assume intention when we speak, and we interpret what is said in terms of intention. What we find difficult to acknowledge is that most of the time our attributions of intention are retrospective. The utterance has already had its effect on us. We are no longer where we were before we spoke or heard what was said. Were Wicky's words more important than her turning back to play with Pooh?

There was a kind of unreflected certitude in her words. They were, as I said, a pronouncement. They did not arise out of puzzlement. So it seemed to me. The ancient Greeks—Socrates—thought that knowledge was recollected. With time, we lose our capacity to recollect. I am only beginning, as I write now, to understand what the Greeks meant. As we forget, we enter a puzzling world—one that demands thought. It is not yet a mysterious world, that comes later, but mystery hovers around puzzlement, like butterflies hovering around a flower.

When my grandson, Garrick, was four, his dog, Wilkie, died. It was his first experience of death. After some embarrassment, Wicky and John, her husband, told him that Wilkie had gone to doggie heaven. I am not at all sure Garrick believed them.

He is exceptionally perceptive. I am sure he recognized their embarrassment—that slight hesitation before an affirmation that does not quite ring true—and of course their sadness. Reference to doggie heaven seemed to arise whenever Garrick missed his dog. It denied what doubt his parents' words evoked. He thought a lot about death, but his thoughts soon changed to beginnings and ends—to the forever. It was about then that he told me, as he had done several times before, that Wilkie was in doggie heaven. This time his words shifted from a declaration to a question. Before I could tell him that his dog was definitely in doggie heaven—and much to my relief, I must admit—he ran off to play with his truck stickers. It was when he learned about infinity a few months later that his puzzlement gradually, poetically, turned to mystery. He said, " 'I love you' plus 'I love you' equals infinity."

Is this a metaphor? Is it an escape from abstraction? Is it a quest for solace in the poetic—a conjoining of the concrete and the abstract?

How can we write about the child's world with words grown so old that they can no longer do justice to their origins?

And yet we do. In their imperfection, in their failure, they resonate with what we experienced or wished we had experienced. Sometimes the line between the two disappears. Imperfection and failure are not without rhetorical force. They call attention to struggle and that struggle places a moral-affective burden on us.

I THINK of Tuhami, the name I gave to Hamadi and to my book about him. I can no longer distinguish between Hamadi, the Moroccan tile maker with whom I met for many hours during the course of my fieldwork in Morocco in 1967 and 1968, and Tuhami, the character whose life we mutually constructed in

our exchanges and I co-opted in writing about him. My empha-
sis on *our* mutual construction of Tuhami's life was met with
considerable critical resistance by some of my anthropological
colleagues—at least those who chose to ignore the anthropologist's effect on any material that he or she collects, or had faith
in a methodology that could avoid that effect. It was an epistemologically naive time. We were taught not to ask leading questions, as if there were any questions that were not leading! My
stress on the role of literary conventions in the formulation of our
field data and in consequence on our interpretation and analysis of that data met with even greater resistance. Were I to have
written Tuhami's life story not as he recounted it—in response to
my questions, his understanding of them, and the relationship he
(and I) desired—but in the life-historical conventions prevailing
in the West, I might have come up with a fine literary biography, but it would have lost much of its cultural specificity and,
more important, Tuhami's own self-understanding. This isn't to
say that my final account was free of literary bias. That would
have been impossible, but at least I was able to call attention to
the formative role of writing in ethnographic description and
interpretation.

Tuhami was in his forties: a very gentle, soft-spoken, immediately likeable, dark-skinned, barrel-chested Arab with a winning
smile except when he was morose, as he frequently was. He once
said, "How can you ever be happy, since you know happiness will
come to an end?" He lived alone in a windowless hovel in the
factory where he worked. He said he was—and he was generally thought to be—"married" to Lalla Aisha, a she-demon with a
camel's foot that she hides under her flowing robes. She haunted
his life, as she did many Moroccans of his background, and prevented him from ever marrying. As such, he posed no threat to

women and was often in their company, entertaining them with his marvel-filled stories. He was an enchanting storyteller.

He told me that after his father died, his mother married a man who so mistreated him that he ran away. A *colon* family, whom I called Jolan, figures in his several versions of what happened to him. They took him in; they gave him work and new clothes, and paid for a long stay in the hospital when he fell into paralytic sadness. He told me that their son, Jean-Pierre, hated him because of the attention his mother gave him.

Mme Jolan's son said there was something going on between his mother and me.

What did he mean?

He thought that Mme Jolan was going to give me one of her daughters to marry. Mme Jolan had given them all Muslim names. They knew how to cook Moroccan food. I left at that time.

(Tuhami stopped.)

Did you ever kiss any of her daughters?

No. (Tuhami was very embarrassed.)

Did you ever want to?

The girls wanted to, but I didn't. I used to take them all over. Once Mme Jolan's sister came to visit. Her name was Sylvie. She had two girls. Both of them were sick. She asked the workers in the factory to pray for them. She promised to give a feast [*sadaqa*] if the girls got better. When Sylvie arrived, Mme Jolan told me to stay around for dinner. I was surrounded by women and spent the evening telling them stories. Then M Jolan came in and asked what was going on. I got up to leave, but Mme Jolan told me to stay. She brought over a table and asked me to beat out the rhythm of a German parade march. I did, and they all laughed. Then they asked me to tell them about Charlie Chaplin. I talked and talked until everyone had fallen asleep. I covered them up and sat down and watched them until morning.

In the morning M Jolan said, "So that is what you wanted." I answered that it wasn't I who wanted it but his wife. Mme Jolan bought me new clothes that day, and I didn't have to work for a month but was paid anyway...[*Tuhami*, 60]

As I read this passage, I'm embarrassed by the insensitivity of my asking Tuhami about kissing the Jolan daughters. He didn't seem to mind, as I recall, perhaps because it gave him an occasion to tell a story that shifted back and forth between reality, or what I assumed was the real, and fantasy. It was a sort of fairy tale, for me a sad one, whether or not there was any truth in it. It reflects Tuhami's misreading of—and his desire for—the Jolans' attention. He was cute. He played the clown, and he enjoyed it. (This, in fact, was one of the few joyous stories he told me about his life.) What he does not mention is that the Jolans never sent him to school or taught him French.

For Tuhami the line between what we call reality and what we call fantasy was blurred. Despite my cautioning readers of *Tuhami* not to rush to psychiatric diagnoses, many of them have insisted on calling him a schizophrenic, referring especially to his relations with Lalla Aisha and the spirit world—and ignoring the complexity of the situation in which he found himself after his father died and his mother remarried; the colonial assumptions of the Jolan family; the role of *jnun* in Moroccan culture and their conventions of storytelling; everything that transpired in the more than fifteen years between Tuhami's experience and our conversations; and, of course, the nature of our own relationship. Once diagnosed, you don't have to think about any of this. Diagnoses can be defensive. They mute curiosity and promote complacency.

About twenty-five years after I saw Tuhami—he died a year or two after our last meeting—I met a woman who had known the Jolan family. I had tried to meet them myself when I lived in Meknes, but that was impossible. M. Jolan and his son were among the few *colons* who were killed during Morocco's struggle for independence. Their workers, whom they abused, detested them, and after Jean-Pierre fired on them and a crowd of other angry workers who had surrounded the Jolans' factory, the protesters captured the two men, threw them into a kiln, and baked them to death. (Tuhami, who at the time was working in a nearby tile factory, was at home sick in bed when they were killed. He told me that had he been there, he would have defended them and been killed, too.) Mme Jolan had moved to France, and the few Jolan relatives who had remained in Meknes were said to be either too fragile or too traumatized to share their memories with anyone. I asked the woman who had known the Jolans about Tuhami. She said that she hadn't known or even heard of him, and after I told her what he said about his relationship with them, she said dismissively, *"C'était impossible."*

Was it impossible? I will never know. Still, I can't help but believe that Tuhami's stories had some source in reality, however misunderstood and embellished that reality was. Is the reality of his experience more significant than whatever truth lies behind those stories? They were aimed at producing an effect in me and on my relationship with him. They were not so very different, in this respect, from Wicky's interjection at Uncle Fred's. But Tuhami's reconstruction of those experiences, however accurate they were, were no doubt a conflation of his desires at the time he was referring to, his desires when he recounted them, and, most poignantly, a nostalgia for a life that in all probability he had never had and never could have had. The nostalgia gave his stories a tragic dimension that extended beyond him to the impoverished, the marginalized, the colonized whose lives edge on impotence and hopelessness. Did he have an inkling of this when he lived through whatever experiences he had in fact had when his father had died and his mother remarried?

At the end of the Algerian War of Independence, in 1962, certainly one of the bloodiest of the anticolonial wars, some sixty or seventy thousand Harkis—mostly illiterate Algerian peasants who had fought alongside the French as auxiliary troops, less for political reasons than in order to survive in a war-torn land—were tortured, mutilated, and killed by the Algerian population at large. When the Gaullist government finally allowed the survivors into France, they were placed in camps, and some remained there for sixteen years, until the last of the camps was closed. I took several of the Harki children (then in their forties and fifties) with whom I was working a few years ago to visit the camps where they had been interned and which were now in ruins or completely razed. As we drove to the camps, they told me—often forgetting that they had already told me—how they and their parents had suffered there. They were herded like cattle, subjected to abusive military discipline and constant humiliation. They lived in close quarters (often at first in tents with complete strangers). They were permitted to bathe once a week—and had to pay for the privilege, and at some camps the rest of the pittance they received from the government ended up in the pockets of corrupt administrators. They remembered the cold winter winds that blew down their tents or swept away the roofs of the barracks in which they were eventually housed; the poor schools and untrained teachers who could only discipline them; and the vacant faces of "troublemakers" who returned from psychiatric hospitals where they had been sent for treatment. However true these accounts were—I have no reason to doubt them—they had become set stories, repeated, at times obsessively, among themselves in conversations, at memorials, and during protests, or as testimony in their demands for compensation, for recognition of the sacrifices they had made for France, and an apology for the lives they had been forced to lead. So repetitive were their complaints that I sometimes lost sympathy with what they had undergone. They were, so I sadly felt, trapped yet again—this time in their stories, which had lost resonance, echoing only the absence of resonance.

And yet, when we got to the camps, the Harki children shook their heads sadly as they looked at the ruins—now empty memory traces. But as they showed me around, several of them began to describe where they had played, who had won a soccer game, where they had crossed a highway to swim in a nearby river, joking about the tricks they had played on their teachers very much the way an adult might show you around a summer camp where he had been sent as a child. It was as though those childhood memories, the nostalgia they produced, overrode, at least for the moment, the pain and humiliation they suffered, the outrage they felt, and the loyalty to France that still tortured them. The reprieve was short-lived. By the time we were driving back to their homes, those moments of nostalgia had faded, replaced by an almost impenetrable, at times suicidal moroseness.

Unlike Tuhami, they were left with little, if any, room to indulge in the playfulness, imaginative freedom, and innocence of childhood. Despite children's inevitable misunderstanding and the puzzlement and mystery it produces, the Harki children knew all too well what they knew, and that knowledge stifled what they didn't know. Tragedy had surrendered to obsession.

VI.
WHEN DID I
FIRST ASK
WHO I AM?

I AM sitting in the back row of my second-grade class. We are having our first test. We may have been tested in first grade, but those tests were not called "tests." Mrs. Blumenthal calls the subtraction we have to do now a test. I stare at the problems. My eyes blur. I can't see the numbers. I get very hot and feel my body as a sticky weight, something that is holding me down, something I can't escape—me. I look around. All the other children are solving the problems; even Rita, the stupidest girl in the class, is writing answers, though they are the wrong ones. Mrs. Blumenthal looks at me and starts to...

I don't remember what happened. I already knew how to add and subtract and even multiply in the first grade, just as I knew how to read. I was the best pupil in the class. My first-grade teacher kept showing me off to the other pupils, and even to Mr. Parks, the principal, when he visited our class. The school was tiny, no more than eighteen children in a class and only one class per grade. We knew all the teachers, and they knew us. I was happy that year.

But something happened to me in second grade. It was not just the word "test" that frightened me. It was me that frightened me. I had lost control of myself (though I wouldn't have put it that way then). I was blocked. I couldn't even read. I was sinking. I used to climb up the path that went through the dogwood grove to the berry garden on the top of the hill behind our house and then sneak into the woods and down, around a couple of boulders into the damp, earthy space they made. I called it the canyon. It was my hideaway. (I used to play cowboys and Indians, sometimes with my sister, sometimes alone, when my school friends weren't around.) I sat on the moss, leaning against one of the boulders, and felt sorry for myself, wishing that everyone in the whole world would disappear. I would stay there until I couldn't stand it any longer. I was bored, bored with myself, and when I was bored, I would always feel a soft pressure just below my temples, like when my earmuffs slipped off my ears, which they often did. I hated wearing earmuffs.

Who was I sneaking away from? No one was there. No one could see me. But I could see myself. How can you sneak away from yourself? You can't, but we do it all the time. Psychoanalysts would relate it to dissociation, repression, and the unconscious. Jean-Paul Sartre would call it bad faith. Had I asked myself the question, which I'm sure I did not, I would have referred to a little soapstone carving of the three monkey-see monkey-hear monkey-speak monkeys, sitting dumbly next to one another, which my father bought for me when I was intrigued by it in an antiques store. I wasn't as interested in its blind-imitation-of-something-you-don't-understand or its see-no-evil-hear-no-evil-speak-no-evil meanings as in the fact that each of the monkeys refused to participate in what was going on by covering his eyes, his ears, or his mouth. I couldn't, but I did, understand why the monkeys refused. Although I was often self-conscious—even paralytically so, the way I had been in Mrs. Blumenthal's class—I had only an inkling of the split in consciousness demanded by self-awareness. When I thought about myself, I would often talk to myself, as I did in the canyon. Though the words I uttered were mine, they seemed, when said aloud, to come from the not-quite-me.

Mrs. Blumenthal called my mother in for a conference, and then she began to give me special reading lessons. She taught me to sound out the words I didn't know, and soon I began to read again and read really well. She didn't help me with arithmetic. I suppose she thought that by working on my reading block, she would break the one I had in math, and she did. I never became a fast reader, and sometimes I blame Mrs. Blumenthal for having made me sound out the words. She was tall and had a big bosom that pressed against me when, sitting on a little second-grade school chair, she leaned over to point something out. I got hot but not the way I did during the arithmetic test. I like to read aloud. I always have to read aloud what I have written; it has to *sound* right. I often read to Jane when she is cooking: Eliot's *Four Quartets*, Merwin's translation of *Sir Gawain and the Green Knight*, *Light in August*, *Absalom Absalom* — we like Faulkner — and, most recently, Ford Madox Ford's *The Good Soldier* and Hawthorne's *The Marble Faun*. Reading aloud, you hear things — subtle changes in the narrator's tone, for example, that reveal tiny but significant changes in perspective, which you can miss when you read silently.

We had a three-volume, leather-bound edition of Shakespeare in the library, which, for some reason, perhaps because it had nine windows that faced the garden, we called the porch. Libraries are supposed to be dark and lamp-lit. After my reading lessons with Mrs. Blumenthal ended, I became interested in real books, not the kids' books we read in school. I tried reading Shakespeare, sounding out the words I didn't know, and I loved those sounds, even when I was reading to myself. I didn't understand most of what I was reading, but that was fine because I could lose myself in the sensuousness of the words. Jane told me that she had done the same thing. For meaning, I used to pore over words in the dictionary that was on the same shelf as the Shakespeare. But even though I sounded out the words, they didn't give me the same pleasure as Shakespeare's. Alone, they lacked the melody that comes with company. I wasn't carried away by them, but I did try to find occasions to use them at dinner, often making my parents smile at my malapropisms. I think "malapropism" was one of those words.

It wasn't until 1202, as Jeffrey Kittay and Wlad Godzich write extravagantly, that prose replaced poetry as the language of truth. That was the year when the Countess of Saint-Pol insisted on a prose translation of the Latin verse chronicle, falsely attributed to the mighty Saracen-killing Archbishop Turpin of *Chanson de Roland* fame. Until then all translations into French had been written in verse. Did truth lose its connection with the sensuous quality of words? Did interlocutors cease to be communicants? Did this turn to prose promote a sense of isolation, alienation, and loneliness?

I remember Wicky, at six or seven months old, kissing her image in the mirror. She tries to caress it, babbling, and then resumes kissing it. I've seen this before, just as I have seen dogs ignore their reflection in a mirror. They do not bark. What was Wicky kissing? Lacan would say her *semblable*, her semblant image, but does she recognize herself in the image? Does she identify with her image? Does she take possession of it? Prepossession is an essential dimension of identifying-with. Or does she simply see a moving body? Are her kissing, babbling, and caressing efforts to control its movement? Or is she simply taking pleasure in the smooth, cool surface of the mirror? Maybe all we can or should do is ask questions. But we don't. We have—we say—an intuitive grasp of the infant's feelings and thoughts, which, as impossible as our attributions may be, seem to satisfy us.

What did I experience when I saw Wicky kiss her image? I smiled. I felt the baby's delight and then her frustration at not being able to reach whatever she saw in the mirror. Was she babbling at her image? Or was she simply enjoying the sounds she was making? When she finally abandoned her *semblable*, she stopped babbling and sank brooding into her body. After a long minute, she began to gurgle, and then, as she tried to reach her toes, to mouth them, her gurgles turned into babbling. I felt an echoing deep inside me, melodic reverberations, that carried me from myself to the baby, to what the baby was doing, and back to myself, not my usual self, but a self I knew so intimately that I could not distinguish it from my intuition of the baby. I cannot say we blended into each other, if only because she was not interested in me. I can't even say I merged with the baby, but with a primordial layer of myself. I was transported. When I awoke from my reverie (I suppose you can call it that) I realized that the mirror glass was not only a barrier but also a protection from whatever lay behind it: the me-not-me, the other-not-other—a space of fascination, the allure of the safely unreachable. This assumes, of course, that, unlike Alice or Jean Cocteau's Orpheus, the baby did not walk through the mirror.

Whatever else it is, the baby's image is fluid, ephemeral, other but not quite other, controllable to a point. It offers no anchorage around which she can find her moorings. She can only gurgle and babble, delighting in the sounds she produces as she hears them, enjoying the lippy pleasure of those sounds, neither outside her, I imagine, nor inside.

EARLIER this summer, in Spoleto, I saw Robert Wilson's play *The Old Woman*. Wilson based it on a book of stories by the

Russian absurdist writer Daniil Kharms. One of the two characters says: "I myself being of extraordinarily lithe body even tried
to kiss myself on my foot. I sat on a bench, got hold of my right
foot and pulled it up to my face. I managed to kiss the big toe.
I was happy. I understood the happiness of others." I was startled. I remembered the memory of Wicky trying to reach her
toe—to bring it to her mouth—and then babbling. I wrote about
that memory a few months ago. The impact of storied memory
extends beyond the story. Memories cannot be contained by the
stories we tell about them. They tumble on. Was Wicky happy?
Was I happy watching her? I didn't think to ask myself. Now I
think I was.

When Wicky was three, her cousin Stephen Shore gave her
a Polaroid camera. A photographer himself, he was interested in
what she would photograph. At first I held the camera, and she
took pictures of wherever she was. But as she grew older and could
hold the camera herself, she began to take pictures of her clothes.
Some of the pictures were quite beautiful, but I don't think she
was concerned about beauty—though Jane and I were—as much
as preserving her clothes (and whatever they meant to her), not in
fact—she did that, too—but in memory; that is, in what was more
substantial than memory but not as substantial as the objects she
photographed. Did the pictures resurrect her clothes? Or Wicky
as she was in the past? Whenever? What in fact was her sense of
the past then? Of time? Of image and object?

SINCE I began studying anthropology in the sixties, theory
in the social sciences and the humanities has been increasingly
dominated by notions of the other, the Other, and Otherness,
which finds its roots, so important to Marx, Sartre, and Lacan, in

Hegel's allegory of the Master and the Slave. Put simply, two individuals (consciousnesses), each discovering their likeness, their desire, in the other, demand recognition by that other. In appraising each other's strength, they become self-conscious for the first time as they view themselves from the point of view of the other, recognizing the other's consciousness of them. They struggle to the death for recognition, but they do not fight to the death, for then there could be no recognition. The stronger enslaves the weaker. There follows a complex analysis of the permutations of their relationship over time. The master becomes dependent on the slave's labor as the slave discovers himself and his power over the master in the products of his labor...

What is striking is the abstraction of the other and, in consequence, the self and the mechanical-aggressive relationship between them. They are governed by desire and fear—the fear of death and perhaps the fear of the desire for death. Hegel never asks how we—how they—know that they desire the same object. He assumes a transparency of motives that we know, and he must have known, is unrealistic. So much of social life rests on misunderstanding other people's motives and intentions. Despite the importance of the body in Hegel's description of the encounter, the body loses its substance, its flesh, in later renditions of the allegory, indeed in Hegel's own understanding. The characters become ciphers, without depth and particularity. Their relationship—dominance and submission—is also without depth and particularity. They override context, with little, if any, creative input, destined to rehearse over and over again their given identity and determinant relationship.

Why has this image of the other—and the self—become so fashionable? Have we surrendered, despite our proclamations of individualism, to cipherdom?

I am in basic training. I am a trooper with a nametag. The sergeant is the unquestionable voice of authority. He orders. We do. Whether we are marching, standing at attention for inspection, on the shooting range, or being chewed out by the sergeant, we have no particularity, though we all try, in our own ways, to demonstrate our particularities, to gain his attention, to ingratiate ourselves, to be ourselves as we were before the initiatory haircut that—so at least I thought—makes us all look the same, despite the fact that some of us are tall, others short, some fat, others thin, some pockmarked and others baby-faced.

We ran the gamut of colors: black, brown, mustard, olive, pink, white, reddish, and yellowish. Nearly all of us developed special relations with one or two of our platoon buddies. Mine was a jazz pianist, a nonstop rapper, who had just cut a record. Our relations with the others in our platoon were impersonal, but we could joke, curse, and occasionally fight with one another.

The sergeant revealed as little as possible about himself. He was power incarnate. His demands were arbitrary, his criticism mordant, and his insults vicious. We were conjoined by our hatred of him, but we did not form a community of hatred nor of respect nor indeed of loyalty to one another or to our country, despite all the "love of country" that was pounded into us daily.

A night or two before our training ended, the sergeant entered our barracks unexpectedly and gave us a pep talk. His voice had changed, saddened almost. I suddenly realized (and I'm sure I wasn't the only one) that after more than two months working with us from four-thirty in the morning until after dark each day, he had, in his own way, become attached to us. He told us that he knew that we hated the army and thought him a power-hungry jerk (or rather some obscene equivalent). He had captured the attention of all of us. And then he told us that the army had given him a life he would never have had and he was grateful for it.

He was a little white guy who compensated for his size with his deep hoarse-from-shouting voice, his strength and extraordinary endurance. He never seemed to sleep. He came from a small town in Texas, he told us, and before joining the army, he had quit school at sixteen (maybe fifteen) and run away to Dallas, where he worked as a shoeshine boy until he was drafted. "Yeah, I didn't want to serve any more than you fuckers [said, this time, with humor]. You're surprised, eh? I served for two years, dreaming about getting out, and then, when I was real short, I suddenly thought, *Hell, what will I be doing on the outside, shining shoes?* So I reenlisted and have served more than fifteen years. Look, had I quit the army, I wouldn't be able to order you guys around. Better than shining shoes, ain't it?" We were silenced, even the crudest of us, looking into our own lives with a seriousness that we had probably been incapable of during the weeks of harsh training. I think, at that moment, many of us, though by no means all of us, recognized that what we had shared brought us together, not as a community but as a collectivity of shared experience, ironically just as that collectivity was about to be broken up as we went off on our separate assignments.

As hard as I try, I cannot remember the sergeant's name.

Did he lose his authority by exposing himself? Or did that authority become greater because of a respect it instilled in us? The play between impersonal and personal authority is obviously far subtler than in rigidly hierarchical institutions such as the army.

STILL in the army, I see a lieutenant at the opera in Frankfurt, where I am stationed. We recognize each other, our common interest in music, but we do not approach each other because enlisted men and officers are not allowed to "fraternize." He walks away, a bit embarrassed, I think. Distance has to be maintained. The next time I meet him, he is conducting an inspection in my barracks. I stand at attention as he eyeballs me for an exceptionally long time. I can't read what he is thinking. His eyes are empty, forcefully so. Then, without looking away, he asks me the serial number of my rifle. I can't remember it. I am not in the infantry and haven't touched it in six months. Still eyeballing me, he sentences me to a day of KP. I'm furious at-him-at-myself for not covering my vulnerability—for the humiliation I felt. A few days later, we meet by chance in the corridor of the office building where I work. "Did you enjoy the opera?" he asks. I stand at attention and say "Yes, sir," cutting off conversation before he does.

My assumption of power—the power of the slave—was not simply a game of one-upmanship but a way to protect my integrity, my sense of self, which, I must admit, was severely damaged by my military service. I crept into a sort of internal exile, which lasted for months after my discharge, and I still find it, fifty years later, difficult to "fraternize" with most of my colleagues at the university. They find me aloof, I know. With colleagues at other universities, I don't have the same problem. I need distance—to fashion the other responsively in my imagination, empathetically, and through what I do in a language resonant with the ever-shifting panoply of affections that extend beyond those, like fear, that are triggered by relations of dominance and submission. The cynicism, masked by claims of realism, that characterizes today's Hegelian casting of the other, is surely defensive, as it is no doubt a reflection of our contemporary social practices.

I had interrupted my studies after graduating from college, at least my draft board claimed I had, and, unlike many of my classmates at Harvard who had continued their studies, I was eligible for the draft. I returned from Vienna, where I was studying, for my draft physical. I had volunteered for six months of active duty followed by seven and a half years of reserve duty. As soon as I was discharged, I planned to go back to Europe to continue my studies for a semester or two and, as there were no reserve meetings abroad, I would be assigned to a control group. It was highly unlikely that I would be called up for reserve duty when I returned to the States. Serving in the army was, as I saw it, a waste of time.

It was at the height of the Cold War, just before the Vietnam War officially broke out, and after a Russian plane was shot down—I believe that was it—the six-month plan was suspended until a couple of days after my draft date. There was nothing I could do. I was caught. I decided to enlist in order to go to the army language school in Monterey. I had hoped to study Japanese, enchanted as I was by Japanese women, or Persian (thinking of my college friend Charam), but was assigned Russian.

It was in Monterey that I realized how corrupt the whole draft system was. One of my classmates, whose father was a well-known Washington correspondent, ended up in a special program. He enlisted for army intelligence and the language school, and after graduating from the language school—that is, after serving for approximately a year and a half—he would be discharged as a commissioned officer and have no active reserve duty, since he would already have been on active duty for at least a year and a half. I was furious. No one had told me about the plan, and I had found no mention of it in any draft literature. He told me that he had learned about it through his father's Washington contacts, and that he was the only one in the program whose father was not in the highest echelons of the Cabinet or in the Senate. There went three years of my life.

In fact, I already knew how corrupt the system was, since my draft board was in a factory town that did not even abut the town where my mother was living when I had to register for the draft. I had never spent more than a couple of months there. By the time I was called up, she had moved twice. It was where all the rich kids lived, and the draft board filled their monthly quotas by drafting them before they drafted the boys in the neighborhood. There was no shame in this. I was told about it, with a huge guffaw, by one of the civilians at the draft center.

A year later, when our car broke down in the middle of the desert around the Salton Sea while three of us were returning to Monterey from leave in Mexico, the garage mechanic asked us why we were in such a hurry. It would take only a couple of days to get the parts. There was a motel down the road, he said, licking his lips salaciously. When we told him that we were worried about being AWOL, he said—I can still hear the mockery in his voice—"Nobody gets drafted here. We cross the border, pick up a wetback for fifty bucks, and give him our social security number. He's happy. We're happy. Got it?"

What is the relationship between contingency and the formation of the self? What is it between outrage and self-formation? It is one of powerlessness, belittlement, humiliation, and the hope you'll get the chance and have the strength to make up for the outrage, the harm done. Contingency marks us. It has no explanation, except, of course, in societies such as the Azande in the South Sudan, which attribute the contingent event to witchcraft and believe they can do something about it. For those of us who do not believe in witches, sorcerers, the evil eye, or an all-powerful deity, we are left with the why. Why me? Why them? Heidegger goes further. He asks the why of the why, but I need not go into that.

Outrage and the anger that sustains it are directed at the perpetrator—an individual, a draft board, a government. They can consume you. I remember reading about an Italian farmer who sold his produce in the Boston market. He was apparently cheated or insulted—I don't remember exactly what happened—by another farmer. His anger was unquenchable. He brooded. He could think only of the insult and the dishonor he felt—the revenge he would like to exact. After many years of his staring hatred across the market aisle at his enemy, his enemy died. You would assume that this would liberate him from his obsession. But, in fact, his anger intensified. His enemy was no longer but his fury remained. He could never get back at him now, not even in fantasy. Death had outwitted him. Soon after his enemy's death, he needed a routine operation—an appendectomy, I think. His surgeon, who had performed the operation hundreds of times, had a premonition that he would not survive. The surgery went well, but the farmer never recovered. He had lost the will to live. His raison d'être was gone.

The case is extreme, but it demonstrates the importance the other can take. In this case, an injury had been done. But often there is no ostensible reason, other than institutional authority, as in the army, the office, or the family, for measuring yourself through the other—others. The idealizations of the other in hero worship, love, and, in the case of belief, a deity are exceptions.

I am just twelve. I'm in my room alone. It is nearly bedtime. I light a candle and pass a pin through the flame several times and then think of all the ways I do not live up to the standards I set myself on my birthday. My standard is Henry. He is in the eighth grade; I'm in the seventh. He's taller than me, handsome, athletic, at the top of his class, and knows how to do things I can't, like driving up and down the long driveway that leads to his house or building a shortwave radio from a kit his father gave him. He has kissed all the pretty girls in his class. I have never kissed a girl. I am not handsome, am a poor athlete, and, though I'm also at the top of my class, don't think much of this, since the kids in my class, unlike those in Henry's, are all pretty stupid except for my friends Freddy and Bob, and Jennifer, who is ugly. I don't know how to drive a car or build a radio. I'm not good with mechanical things. Each time I think of something I did that day—tripping before home base, causing my team to lose, misspelling "prognosticate," being shy in front of the girls who stand around after school, or smelling under my arms, where hair is beginning to grow—I prick my left thigh with the pin and vow to improve. After carrying out this ritual for about a month, I stop suddenly, having realized how dumb it was. Henry would never have done such a silly thing.

I don't remember ever asking myself who *I* was at this time. I wanted to improve. I wanted to be the best athlete in my class. I wanted to swim a mile at the pool. I wanted to learn algebra, kiss Regina and Helene, play jazz on the piano rather than classical music, be the best (rather than the worst) dancer in dancing class, go to the opera—I was too young, my parents said—and go necking at Saturday matinees. I wasn't allowed to go to them. "Only common people let their children go to the movies alone," my mother said.

My parents' friends, my parents, and my grandfather, but not my grandmother, would ask me what I wanted to be. I'd say a doctor. My grandmother would say you have plenty of time to decide.

To want is not to be.

At the end of the school year, Henry graduated. He would have been the valedictorian, but we had no valedictorians. Mr.

Parks did not believe in elevating one student over all the others. I never saw Henry again. My thoughts took a narcissistic turn. I no longer needed a Henry. I began to set my own standards. But they were mediated by the books I was reading — *The Count of Monte Cristo*, *David Copperfield*, and *The Forsyte Saga*. They transported me to worlds where I could play out my fantasies of whom I wanted to be without the interference of reality. Well, not quite. The play of fantasy was no longer child's play. It was serious in its concern and had implications, though I didn't know this at the time.

Still, I didn't seriously ask myself who I was. I was living through the optative as I was living through the real.

A couple of years later, when I was at school in Geneva, I began thinking about myself in French. It gave me an illusory distance. It produced another not-quite-me, sometimes positive, sometimes negative, but in either case, a me I desired to be and knew I would never be. Oddly, there was freedom in this knowledge.

VII.
NUIT
DE
NOËL

ALONG with her other perfumes, my mother kept a thin black bottle on a glass tray on her dressing table. The black bottle fascinated me, not only because it was so different from the other perfume bottles but also because it was called Nuit de Noël. Why would anyone name a perfume "Christmas Night" and bottle it in black? My mother must have told me that the perfume maker had created the scent especially for the woman he loved and gave it to her as a Christmas present, but that wouldn't explain why it was in a black bottle. You didn't wrap Christmas presents in black. All my mother's other perfumes were in clear or etched glass bottles in fanciful shapes. You could see the perfume. How could you tell how much perfume was left in a black bottle? My mother didn't even know if there was any left, because she hadn't been able to open the bottle since she came home from France just before the war started and married my father. When I tried to open it one morning, she ordered me, without explanation, not to touch it. I never did again. It was only after my father died, when we were eating breakfast, that she told my sister and me that she'd finally managed to open it. Before she could stop us, my sister and I raced to her bedroom to smell the perfume. There wasn't much left, but after so many years, at least fifteen, we could still smell the scent. It was beautiful. It had to be beautiful.

There was a mystery attached to my mother's perfume bottle. It stood on the tray like the guardian of a secret that only she knew. It was a fetish—her fetish. Of course, I didn't know what a fetish was then. I have often wondered whether she always could have opened it but never tried. But I did know, even then (whenever "then" was, for my fascination lasted through most of my childhood—which is to say until the bottle *was* opened), that it had something to do with my mother's sadness, with a regret, a moment of past happiness, an abiding nostalgia. Whatever it was, the bottle contained a memory—memories—in an immediacy that destroyed time. It had become a memory-object: the memory itself—a comforting presence, like a good friend, a lover, perhaps, who stood, if "stood" is taken softly, beside her in a time of distress. No words need be said. No story recounted. No images recollected. It just is. Or, given my mother's lasting but inadmissible sadness, a disquieting presence, prolonging the solace that disquiet can sometimes bring, the longed-for sadness, not just the sadness that accompanies nostalgia but also the sadness that bathes us in familiarity and resurrects the forgotten without the pain of actually remembering.

My grandparents did not suffer during the Great Depression. My mother graduated from Wellesley on its eve. From her graduation until sometime in 1937 or 1938, she spent her time traveling in Europe. She did return once or twice to New York, where my grandparents were living and where she earned an MA in French from Columbia and started one in psychology. Occasionally, she volunteered at a soup kitchen. She described the poor who hadn't been so poor before the crash. "They never looked you in the eye. Their eyes had no life. Just filled with shame. Finally, I couldn't stand that shame, those eyes, that obsequiousness. I went back to France."

I never knew what my mother actually did in Europe all those years. Her descriptions of the time she spent abroad were just anecdotes. That, at least, is how I remember them. She never was a storyteller. She talked about the art she had seen—she showed my sister and me postcards—the beauty of Dresden; the lure of Paris, where she seems to have spent most of the time in a series of hotels or apartments; the problems she had crossing the Czech border, how the immigration authorities there smelled of sausages; the Nazis and Italian Fascists, when we were older—their parades, banners, and brutality—the pension where she used to stay in Venice, which had a wonderful library with watercolors by Ruskin—he had stayed there—two of which she somehow came to own. I stayed in that pension when I first visited Venice alone. When I asked about the library, the receptionist said there had never been one, but her grandmother, who was listening, remembered it. Shrugging her shoulders, she said that the American soldiers who'd been billeted there had stolen all the books and pictures. Mostly, my mother liked to tell us about life on the transatlantic steamers she had taken. Her descriptions of those crossings—the clothes she wore, the meals she had, including the captain's dinner and, for some reason I remember this, the hot broth a steward would bring her midmornings as she sat in a deck chair reading—always ended with her saying that all the steamers she had taken had been sunk during the war. She said this matter-of-factly, with what seemed to me to be an almost joyful finality.

Her anecdotes were evasive. There were too many gaps. Of course, I didn't notice this at first, but as I grew older, I began to feel that something important was missing. I defended myself against this recognition by letting my imagination flow, creating an enchanted world that came to have less and less to do with anything my mother said. Her Europe, depleted, became my fairyland—a place of imaginative freedom and escape, even then, from the claustrophobic surround that her repetitive anecdotes produced in me. My sister didn't pay much attention to them.

It was only during the summer before I went to college that I realized what was missing in her stories. There were no people. Whom did she know? Did she know anyone? It was then that she told me about someone she *had* known. It was the only time she ever talked about her feelings, other than being peeved. ("Peeved" was one of her favorite words.) I was playing the piano. It must have been after dinner, because the living room was getting dark. She came in quietly, sat in a chair behind me, listened for a while, and then began to speak. It took me a while to understand that she was talking about a Frenchman, a baron. She had never mentioned him before. She was always ranking people, particularly my father's friends but my school friends, too, in some antedated hierarchy all her own. As she went on, I realized that my playing was giving her a break in the silence of her past. I couldn't stop, because I knew she would then stop talking.

Why didn't I stop playing? It was not just that I was curious. I was, of course. But, as I played, I felt her disappointment, her loneliness, and a mounting anger in myself. Her isolation was an indulgence. She was spoiled. What personal references do we hear when we listen to music? I'm not even sure she was listening to me. The room was soon so dark that I could no longer read the music and had to play the one piece, something by Offenbach, that I knew by heart. I played it over and over, sometimes seductively, sometimes aggressively. My mother didn't seem to notice. She just went on talking. It emerged that she had been engaged to the baron, that just before she was to sail home to tell my grandparents about him, they had traveled to Germany, and from a hilltop—it could have been in Heidelberg, where the baron had studied—they watched, and he praised, a Nazi youth march. My mother said nothing. "I couldn't," she said in a strained voice that carried her fury at him—at herself—her disappointment, her regrets—a termination like a sunken ship. They returned to Paris, and she went home. "I never wrote to him. I never told him why I had left." She got up, saying it was late, and went to her bedroom, closing the door in such a way that I knew she would never mention him again. And she didn't.

Had the black bottle of perfume been a gift from the baron? To say it was would have produced a neat ending, but I knew—I know—better. Or did I? Do I? Yes, it would have produced a neat ending, but with that ending, the black bottle with its sheen of polished onyx would have lost its mystery. Sometimes I do think it was his gift. Then it contains a secret. There is no mystery about secrets when they are known to be secrets—the banality of living with them, her banality. I remind myself that the real mystery is why she waited until my father's death to open the bottle.

Our apartment is filled with the objects Jane and I have collected over the years: the Empire couch we brought back from Morocco, abandoned no doubt by some *colon* in panicky flight to France; the huge, double-faced mask from the Sepik River Jane gave me when I defended my dissertation; the old-master drawings we bought when they were still affordable; a sculpture by Nevelson Jane received when she won the National Book Award; the ex-voto we bought during the Portuguese revolution; the tiny Afrikaner doll—a woman whose face was carved out of a nut, carrying a switch, presumably to whip a restive worker—that I bought when I was doing fieldwork in South Africa; the Chelsea lusterware; a soapstone pot Brazilians cook rice in; the eighteenth-century portrait of a Venetian lady who is wearing Aztec jewelry in her hair that we bought from a neighbor in Italy, an interior decorator, who had bought it for a client who turned out to hate portraits; a deeply cracked wooden head of a marionette from Burma that we have not been able to name. All our sculptures have names: Dorothy for a Baule lady, Ghosty Mummy for a Warega ivory figure—Wicky named her when she was four or five; Housie for a fernwood sculpture from the New Hebrides; Boots for a Senoufo oracle that seems to frighten all our guests; and Gaster for the Sepik mask, in honor of one of my dissertation examiners, whose lips curled just like his. All of the objects have a story of how we found them, but none of them are memory-objects. They do not condense a memory so powerfully that it becomes the memory itself. They can only be listed, as in a catalog.

There is one exception, for me at least, and perhaps for Jane, too. I have never asked her. It is a medieval wooden sculpture of a female saint, probably from the South of France. She is beautiful. She has an aquiline nose, perhaps a little too thin, that reminds me of a nun I must have seen sometime in Paris. She bears the marks of history, not only of great age but of the attempts to destroy her during the religious wars in France. She sits on a shelf in our bedroom, a calming presence, despite her injuries, protecting us by her frank presence—from what I don't know—containing memories, unknown to me, those of her past and of my own, too. It is not because I've forgotten them but because they are situated in that transcending, wordless space of mine-not-mine, in which, like two oceans meeting, the personal flows into the known simply to have existed, somewhere, sometime, elsewhere, in history, we say.

There is nothing religious about my appreciation of the saint. I have no religion. The day I was baptized Catholic was the first and last time I ever submitted to a religious rite. I was three. I had no religious training. My parents were secular without ever bothering to argue their position. My knowledge of Christianity was through art, music, and architecture. It was barely textual, through a couple of Bible storybooks and later through Milton, Gide, Bernanos's *Diary of a Country Priest*, and philosophy. My response was in the main esthetic, if one can ever separate the esthetic from the spiritual.

Do memory-objects have to be beautiful? I'm not sure. Isn't there beauty in objects whose origins lie in pain? Had they no beauty, would they be able to contain and not simply represent pain? We have a drawing of a saint in agony by the Bolognese artist Gaetano Gandolfi. It represents that agony, but it does not evoke it. We do not feel it. It edges on the grotesque. Jane hates it. We are sorry we bought it. At the time, I was taken by the technique. Representations of suffering that do not resonate with the pain we have suffered or the pain we have only imagined, perhaps the more intense of the two, may evoke our sympathy, but the horror they produce in us is rarely long-lasting, rarely transformative. This is why newspaper and magazine photographs of the wounded in war, the dying, and the grieving seldom remain with us. They may inure us to or distance us from horror and suffering. And yet, in good faith, we produce and reproduce them, hoping they will do some good.

Jane and I are in Guyana. It is 1973. The world is in the midst of an oil crisis. Guyana is ruled by one of those brutal dictators whom the United States so often supports—in the name of stability, anticommunism, or, as likely as not, its perceived economic interests. We have been taken over by the minister of the interior, who insists that we fly to a government-sponsored "model" farm deep in the jungle close to where the Jonestown mass suicide later took place. Why, we are not sure. He doesn't seem to be asking anything of us. The fields are overrun by weeds; the dispensary has no drugs; a farmer we talk to has given up his little vegetable garden because he can no longer afford the gallon of gas he needs to run the rotary weeder, which is his only defense against the encroaching jungle. The price of gasoline has gone up four or five cents. Lured by promises of government support, he had moved to the farm with his family a couple of years earlier.

After several days of being flown around the country, we manage to escape from the minister's clutches. Our driver in Georgetown wants to show us how his people, the descendants of indentured laborers brought to Guyana from India by the British, are suffering under the dictator's rule. Forbes Burnham is black. Politics in Guyana are racial. Burnham is supported by the United States because the Indian leader, Cheddi Jagan, is a communist and, therefore, dangerous—another Castro, as Arthur Schlesinger, a former advisor to President Kennedy, described him.

We drive out to a coconut plantation inaptly named Plantation Hope. We are told that Burnham or Burnham's wife, who is hated even more than her husband, owns it. She had all the animals in the Georgetown zoo killed so she could graze cows there to sell milk at an inflated price. The immensely fat manager sits on the upper balcony of the old plantation house, holding a shotgun, as he surveys the Indian workers. He ignores us. Not wishing to offend anyone, I have left my camera in the car. I am not a pornographer of the desolate. We are shown around by a crowd of workers and finally taken to see an old man, who was being forced to work for two months without pay because he had stolen a coconut to feed its milk to a baby whose mother could no longer nurse him. He has not completed his sentence and is now too weak to work. He lies in bed, under a ripped plastic sheet to protect him, as best it can, from the torrential jungle rains that pour down on him through the collapsed roof of his hut. He tells us his story in so tired a voice we can barely hear him and then asks me to take a picture of him. I am stunned. I tell him I have no camera. Our driver looks at me quizzically. I cannot bring myself to photograph such misery. On the way back to Georgetown, I try to explain to the driver why I lied, but he doesn't understand. I can't erase the look of the dying worker's disappointment.

Why can't I take a photograph of misery when I can talk and write about it? Do I distance myself through the insufficiency of words? Or is it the break from time—the immobility of the picture—that prevents me from taking the photograph? There is something obscene about photographing misery, a death-like announcement of the death to come. And yet it can be desired by even the dying. Although my image of the old man is fading, it still has mobility—"vitality" would be too strong a word—that his photograph never would have had. The photograph, Roland Barthes tells us, "repeats mechanically that which can never be repeated existentially." It negates time, I would say, as it serves history.

We have a traumatogenic sense of history and biography, I wrote somewhere, or maybe only mentioned in a lecture; that is, we punctuate the past through pain and suffering. "Whenever man has thought it necessary to create a memory for himself, his effort has been attended with torture, blood, and sacrifice," Nietzsche wrote in *On the Genealogy of Morals*. Whether consciously remembered or buried in the recesses of the mind, traumas become fixations around which life experience, at least a segment of that experience, is configured. Insofar as those fixations are repeated in memory, in flashbacks or action, in replays, or, most devastating, in inflicting the trauma on another, a son or daughter, for example, life loses its vibrancy. They stop time. They lead nowhere. I saw this clearly in my research on the Harkis. They obsessed over being betrayed and abandoned by the French. Many of those I interviewed could refer only to that betrayal and abandonment. Nothing else seemed to matter.

Must we punctuate the past only with pain? Can we orga-
nize it around pleasurable moments? It is probably easier for the
autobiographer to do this than the historian. Would a pleasure-
punctuated life be less vibrant? Would those moments become
fixations, also destroying time? I think of a Brazilian colleague
who spent the happiest years of his life, so he told me once, studying in Paris. Paris was for his generation what Florida's Disney
World is today for many Brazilians. (I am being serious. Formerly
the wealthy would travel to Europe on their honeymoons; their
intellectual life was centered on continental, especially French,
thinkers and artists. Today they fly to Miami for shopping and
fun, exchanging one beach for another.) My colleague studied
under Louis Dumont, a brilliant, cranky anthropologist who felt
his work was neglected. He was right. So great was the influence
of Claude Lévi-Strauss on anthropology, on French intellectual
life, that there was no room in anthropology for another *maître-
penseur.* Dumont sought disciples, and I was told that those who
were wayward were dismissed. My Brazilian colleague must have
been one of the favored. He never stopped talking about Dumont.
He kept a sort of shrine to him in his office. If I remember correctly, it consisted of a signed photograph of the master, several
of his books, also signed, and an empty bottle of Courvoisier that
everyone assumed they had drunk together. There may also have
been a dried flower. This was obviously an exaggerated response
to a period of happiness, if in fact it was as happy as he claimed,
but was its effect on him that different from that of a trauma?
How many troubled marriages survive by dint of an ever-repeated
remembrance of a moment of love? We must not, of course, forget
the element of pain in pleasure and pleasure in pain.

I think of moments of pleasures in my life. They are there, to
be sure, despite what Jane calls my depressive character, but they

are less defined than the painful ones. They seem to flow into and out of the course of life without interruption, unless they are preceded or followed by a painful experience. Tuhami asked: How can you be happy when you know happiness will end?

I am in Vienna, studying. It is a beautiful summer—in contrast to the gray winter and hibernal spring that I was told were unusual. The buildings are also gray and have lost much of their beauty. Even those starkly white buildings such as the ones on the Michaelerplatz, which I pass every day, walking to the university, seem only to make those gray buildings grayer. The war is still in evidence. The walls of the house I live in are riddled with bullet holes. I've spent a grim winter, studying German and German literature, reading Freud in an attempt at self-analysis, which only served to depress me. I am not even sure that the grayness I see everywhere is there. I'm biding time, waiting for the start of my military service. My only relief is the opera and the theater. I remember waiting more than five hours in line for tickets to *Parsifal*, von Karajan conducting. I have made few friends, and those I have faute de mieux. We have so little in common.

But never mind. I'm in love. I met Monika that summer at the university. She is beautiful in a delicate sort of way that contrasts with the coarser looks of many of the other Swedish women who invade Vienna each summer to study German. Monika is younger and less experienced than most of them. She is from Linköping. She has just graduated from high school. There is a freshness about her that I have never known. We spend afternoons and evenings together. I show her Vienna. We walk in the Wienerwald and swim in the pool in Grinzing. We are happy. When I think of that happiness, I remember the smile of an old lady who sees us kissing. It is something she wouldn't have done when she was young, but she is caught for an instant in our affection.

At the end of the summer Monika has to visit her sister who lives in Germany before going back to Sweden. We spend a sentimentally sad day. She worries about leaving me alone in Vienna. I tell her not to worry. I will leave the next day on a hike along the Danube, maybe as far as the great monastery at Melk, and visit the little Gothic churches that line the river. I am dutifully forlorn as I walk from village to village. I know this is a summer romance, but I can't admit it. I return to Vienna and meet some of the other Swedish students. One of them—who was jealous of Monika, I like to think—forces herself on me and kisses me in front of her friends. I write to Monika but she doesn't answer my letters, as she had promised. At first I think it is the influence of her older sister, who is married to a conventional German businessman, and then I become convinced that one of Monika's friends saw me kissing and wrote to her about it. I write again, and there is no answer.

Still, I cherished those moments of happiness. They sustained me through military service. Just before those years in Frankfurt ended, I went to Stockholm on leave, stopping in Copenhagen to visit an old school friend from Thailand, whose mother had married a Danish businessman after she divorced Yawalak's father. I knew Yawalak well. We had lived with the same schoolteachers in Geneva, and later she married a classmate from Harvard who insisted on calling her Inge. One night, her mother showed us pictures from the wedding of her grandmother—a Russian princess who had fallen in love with Yawalak's great-grandfather, a Thai prince training at a military academy in Russia. The pictures were extraordinary. The princess and her entourage took a train as far as Beijing and then as far south as it could go. It was there, in southern China, that her fiancé greeted her with a train of elephants, which carried her to Bangkok. It's hard to imagine the Russian princess's reaction when she saw the elephants.

I tell this story because it must have inspired me to talk to Yawalak about Monika. She used to tease me about the women I dated, and especially those whom I would like to have dated but didn't have the courage to ask out. She always feigned jealousy. Still, I had to tell someone about Monika. I had never mentioned her to anyone. Yawalak's reaction was completely unexpected. She insisted that I stop in Linköping on my way back to Frankfurt from Stockholm. I still had Monika's address but not her telephone number, and we couldn't find anyone with her name in the telephone book. Finally Yawalak and her mother convinced me, but when I arrived in Linköping I couldn't bring myself to get off the train until it started to depart. I jumped off and then felt stupid. What was I doing trying to find Monika after four years of silence? Couldn't I accept the fact that a summer romance was over? Was I, despite my cynicism and worldly pretense, a romantic at heart? Did I have to take every relationship seriously?

I did find Monika's family's apartment, but no one was home. I stood in front of the door feeling foolish and then suddenly I had an insane desire to find her. I rang all the doorbells on her floor. No answer. Just as I was about to leave, a young woman appeared. Excited, I asked her whether Monika still lived there. She smiled. She spoke neither English nor German. I think she was Polish. When she finally understood what I was asking, she pointed to her ring finger, said "Malmö," and smiled sympathetically. She went on to say something I couldn't understand but thought meant Monika was getting married that day. It was probably my fantasy. I always seem to add a melodramatic ending to my stories when I really have nothing more to say. I spent three or four hours waiting for the next train, bored rather than shaken, relieved in a way that surprised me, visiting a reconstruction of Old Linköping.

Ever since my first trip to Europe, when I was twelve, I had wanted to be older than I was, whatever that meant, and therefore ended up feeling younger, and almost always embarrassed. By the time I started school in Switzerland, I was desperate, trying to catch up to myself. I knew too much and not enough. I feigned sophistication, and a worldliness I didn't have, and was a victim of my own game. I never admitted what I was really missing—boyhood. Had that ended with my father's death and the responsibilities my mother forced on me as she assumed them herself? What I liked to think of as my intellectual life was all-consuming. It was defensive then (and probably is today). I had done so little. I couldn't escape my innocence. I longed for experience to erase it.

Isn't the experiencing of something, the doing, immediately cast into a having experienced, a having done—into a realm in which the experience itself dissolves and we are left with an after-image, something no longer ours? We may hold on to it—the way an artist I know, a friend, keeps her paintings by refusing to sell or even exhibit them. The paintings are wonderful. She stores some of them in her studio, others covering her walls, but by now they are no more "hers" than they would be hanging on someone else's wall. They have become memory-objects, like my mother's black bottle of Nuit de Noël, like Monika.

I clung to that brief experience of happiness in Vienna—that image of Monika, the delicacy of our relationship—all through those vacuous years in the army. Our affair was no longer "ours" but mine alone and maybe not even mine. I had no scent to evoke it, other than a faint memory of talcum powder. Then, several years ago, I discovered a long-forgotten photograph of Monika that I had misplaced in a tax file. I only glanced at it, fearing that it would cast away my image of her. It was so precarious. Memory-images are.

VIII.

ECOLINT

I WAS excited when we got to Cherbourg in the summer of 1957, on our way to Geneva, where my sister and I were going to go to the Ecole Internationale. My parents had wanted us to have a European education, and my mother had set her heart on Ecolint—it was the first international school—which she'd read about in France before the war. I've often wondered why we didn't move to Geneva immediately after my father's death. My sister and I had asked to, but of course, my mother couldn't take that seriously. We were children and would have gone anywhere but back to school, where we would have to face our classmates. She was still in a state of shock and perhaps had lost the confidence to make such a big change in our way of life. My father's death was enough. It was she—and not my sister and I—who wanted roots. She was, in fact, more ambivalent about living in Europe than she could admit.

Cherbourg was not the way I remembered it from my first trip to Europe, seven years earlier. Then, sections of the port had still been bombed out, though I didn't notice that at first. I was more interested in watching our car being lowered from the steamer in a net. It seemed so small and yet I was sure it would break through the netting and disappear into the water. The *Roma* was a small passenger ship and really not equipped to transport cars. Ours had been the only one. My father was one of a group of investors who had leased the *Roma* and another steamer to carry pilgrims to Rome to celebrate the Holy Year as Pius XII had declared 1950 to be. My father's interest in Holy Years was entirely financial; he wasn't religious and was, in fact, quite anti-Catholic.

I hadn't really felt that we were actually in France until we stopped at a roadside inn for dinner that first night. It had been a mill and as we waited for dinner, the waiter showed my sister and me how the mill had worked. Everything smelled strange: the odor from the kitchen coupled with the acrid fumes of the Gauloises and Gitanes everyone was smoking, the leaves of the arbor under which we ate, and the waiter's sweat. I had escargot, *truite aux amandes*, and a *mousse au chocolat* that I rushed to finish because my father was getting impatient. We had a long trip ahead, he said, and we did.

The drive took hours. My parents bickered. They had miscalculated the time it would take to reach Paris, and the fog was so thick that it was nearly impossible to see the road. They and Armando—a friend who was driving as far as Stresa with us—decided that the easiest thing would be to follow a bus that seemed headed in the right direction. Its headlights cast a yellow light from side to side, sometimes disappearing as the road curved. Houses, barns, trees, and an occasional wagon left in a field took on strange shapes in the light refracted by that fog. The bus led us out of our way to Rouen before my parents realized their mistake. My mother and Armando wanted to spend the night there. My father insisted that we go on.

By the time we got to Paris, the hotel had canceled our reservations. I was exhausted. I got scared. Where would we find a place to sleep? My sister was crying. The night clerk was particularly unhelpful. He didn't know any hotels that would have a vacancy at this time of the night. "Morning," he said. Finally my mother asked him to call the Royal Monceau, the only hotel she could think of. Raising his eyebrows, he made a reservation. When we got to the hotel, we learned that there were only two suites available. The night clerk hadn't bothered telling us. My parents and my sister shared one of them, and Armando and I the other. I don't remember my parents', but ours had two enormous bedrooms, a dining room, and a living room with a grand piano and a harp. I was so excited I could hardly sleep. Armando and I walked in Parc Monceau early the next morning, while my parents and sister slept, looking at the mansions that backed onto the park. There were some children playing on gravel paths, but no one was allowed to walk on the grass.

We were all sorry to leave the hotel the next day, but it was too expensive to stay. We moved to a cheaper one and remained in Paris for a week. My father and Armando went their way. They weren't sightseers and had business to do. My mother showed my sister and me Notre-Dame, Sainte-Chapelle, the Louvre, the Eiffel Tower, and one of her favorite places — I liked it best — the little Melkite Greek Catholic church, Saint-Julien-le-Pauvre, where the oldest tree in Paris still stands in its close.

It was in Saint-Julien, nearly forty years later, that I lit a candle for my mother, who had just died. Jane and I were living in Paris at the time, when my sister called from Scottsdale to tell me. I wandered aimlessly though the city and somehow ended up at Saint-Julien. I had never lit a church candle, but, daring myself, I did that day. I was self-conscious and felt stupid and superstitious — and waited until the church was nearly empty to light it and then fled for fear of being seen. I learned later that Dante is said to have prayed there.

I hadn't seen my mother in years. I didn't miss her, but to my surprise I felt an emptiness in me and an absence around me that blended indistinct memories, tonal impressions, and a dogged sense of something not altogether irretrievable but not yet retrieved...I suppose you could call them abstract apparitions that asserted themselves unpredictably — around a café that I, perhaps with my mother, perhaps not, had once walked by but hadn't entered, a bookstall along the Seine where I'd spent so much time browsing that I felt guilty when I walked off empty-handed. To stop at the café, to buy a book, or to go into an antiques store that I hadn't entered before would have been an irreverent attempt that day to redeem the unredeemable. There was, in fact, nowhere to go. I returned home exhausted. Jane said nothing. She just glanced at me, acknowledging my state of mind. She had encouraged me to be by myself. I was grateful, but I don't think I ever told her. Death can so easily fold over gratitude.

My most vivid memories of the rest of the trip are of arrivals where we knew people:

STRESA, after a harrowing drive over the Simplon Pass late at night. Much of the road wasn't paved, and some sections were still washed out, or nearly so, by melting snow and the spring rains. My mother had to drive, because my father turned out to be afraid of heights. I felt his fear. I had to conquer that in myself. We were held up at the Italian border by immigration and customs officers who were busy harassing an Egyptian family on their way home. They even deflated the Egyptians' tires. My father was furious and defended the bewildered family, which, of course, enraged the Italian officers, who held us up until Armando bribed them. I think my father's bravado had as much to do with his fear of heights as with helping the Egyptians. We walked along the lake in the morning. I was bored. It was my first experience of the lethargy of Italian resorts. We had a lake fish for lunch, which we were told, and I believed, was the largest anyone had ever caught.

FLORENCE, where we met distant relatives of my father. One of them had the most beautiful house I had ever seen—a converted thirteenth-century mill on a bend in the Arno. It was he who was to have sailed with my father to New York when they were both medical students. My father had discouraged him from coming. He hadn't. He became a ship's doctor, married an Austrian aristocrat, and opened several clinics in the hills around Florence. I felt my father's envy and, worse, his sense of having possibly made a mistake by staying in America. How deep, really, was his anti-Fascist commitment? I was confused by Florence. It was very hot. We spent hours shopping. I loved the Cimabue *Crucifixion* in the Basilica di Santa Croce. It reminded me of home. My mother kept a reproduction of it in a scrapbook along with some other paintings she wanted my sister and me to know. The striped Duomo didn't seem right to me, but I loved the Bargello. It was a real fortress. What I remember most is going with my father's friends to Fiesole for dinner. It got very cold, and my parents made me put on a sweater that belonged to a woman who was with us. I learned years later that she had been unfaithful to her husband while he was a prisoner of war in South Africa. When he came home, he shot her lover. I still associate *"crime passionnel"* — a term I must have heard my parents use that night in Fiesole — with the embarrassment I felt in having to wear a woman's sweater impregnated with perfume that was so strong I was sure everyone in the restaurant could smell it. That's why the waiters smiled at me.

ROME, where we spent a lot of time with my godfather's family. I loved the Colosseum but not the Forum. It was just a pile of rocks. My sister and I watched a couple make love from the window of our hotel room while my parents were out one night. Neither of us knew exactly what was happening, but we were transfixed. My sister told my parents that we had seen a man and a woman go to the bathroom.

AMALFI, where we stayed in a hotel, the Convento di Amalfi, on top of a cliff. You had to take an outdoor elevator to get to it. My mother and sister stayed there while my father and I went by night train to Catania and on to his hometown. He had not seen it in more than forty years.

SICILY. My father stood there looking across a piazza at a very old man, his older brother. He and his brother just looked at each other for the longest time, my uncle suspiciously, my father—well, I don't know how to characterize his look—and then, perhaps more out of embarrassment than recognition, they slowly approached each other and embraced. They had nothing to say to each other. They distrusted each other, of that I was sure, but I didn't know why.

We were staying with one of my father's relatives, a cousin, like nearly everyone I met. He was a doctor who lived in a new house on the outskirts of town. I didn't like him. I didn't like the house. His wife was okay. I liked their feebleminded son least of all. He was in his twenties. His face was unnaturally long, and his jaw jerked back and forth uncontrollably. He was always hugging me, covering me with slobber, grunting words I didn't understand, in a deep, screechy voice. He spent most of his time locked in a play-room in the cellar, but he was always brought up for dinner. I saw his room when his father showed it to us. He wanted to know how it could be improved. I knew immediately: it needed bigger win-dows. But I didn't say anything. I just wanted to get out.

We were sitting at a long, rough-hewed table in the kitchen of a house on one of the family farms. We were going to spend the night there. I was seated in the middle. Everyone was watch-ing me. They always seemed to be. There were so many of them. The cook put a huge bowl of boiled eggs in front of us. There must have been twenty or thirty. She made me crack one of the eggs into the soup we had all been served. No one was eating yet. They just kept watching. I was getting angry. I cracked the egg and a little chicken-like mass splashed into the soup. It was an embryo—tender enough to eat whole. "Eat," someone commanded. I did, and everyone applauded. *Bravo, bravissimo.* I was not squeamish. I would eat anything except peanut butter, which I still hate, though I like peanuts. I was glad I had eaten the egg. I seemed to have passed some kind of a test so I took another egg and another after that. Nearly all of the eggs contained an embryo. When I asked how you knew when they were ready to serve, they told me that only the cook knew, and she wouldn't tell anyone. She had been watching me, too, and shook her head the way old Italian women do when they won't tell you a secret but want to let you know they have one. The cook was not old enough to be a witch, but I was sure some of the village women were.

The doctor took us to see a farm that had been bought by a peasant who had immigrated to the United States and returned with a modern harvesting machine. He was very upset by this. I think he wanted my father to lend him money to buy one for himself. His world—the landowners' world—was crumbling. He used peasant labor, and now a peasant—not even a peasant but a journeyman—was buying up land and farming it with an American machine that in one day could do the work that would take dozens of laborers a week or more. Of course, I didn't understand this then, but I knew I didn't want him to have a harvester.

I was so distracted watching a girl nursing a baby—I had never seen this before—that I didn't see the accident. One of the workers had caught his hand in the harvester. He was carried to the doctor, bleeding badly, moaning desperately, clutching the arm of a man who was walking beside him, grinding his teeth in pain.

I couldn't look at his bleeding hand. My father was shocked when the doctor refused to treat him. "You know when I see patients. Bring him to my office this afternoon," he ordered irritably. "But he'll bleed to death," my father started to say, but before he could finish, the doctor interrupted. "If you give them an inch, they'll take a mile. They'll give me no peace." Without saying a word, my father treated the poor man. He stopped the bleeding and managed to extract some morphine from the doctor, who had his medical bag in the car.

We left that afternoon for Amalfi. I was proud of my father and glad to leave. I knew he would never lend the doctor a cent. There were too many memories between them which were not my own and now some that were.

That trip marked a change in my father. We were all tired. We had been traveling for nearly three months. My father was sad. He was feeling sorry for himself. When we got back to Paris, he wouldn't leave the hotel. My mother didn't know what to do—with him or with us. She knew my sister and I were frightened. She tried to keep us busy, but knowing how sad Daddy felt lay over us like a carapace. After lunch one day she left us at the pond in the Luxembourg Gardens, where we sailed a toy boat we rented from an old man. My sister and I were glad to be alone. I certainly was, though I was scared when our boat crashed into a bigger boy's, but he just laughed, and we became friends, kind of. My mother returned with my father, who smiled for the first time in weeks. I have no idea what she had done to snap him out of his grief. We went to the Café Royal, my favorite restaurant, that evening. I loved the way the candlelight, reflected in the mirrored walls, made everyone, everything, dazzle. I was allowed to have a Chateaubriand, even though it was expensive. It was a sort of celebration for what we couldn't mention: my father's return.

IT IS SOMETIMES difficult to separate relief from regret. I think
that is why I was disappointed when we landed in Cherbourg. We
had spent nearly two years in Caldwell, while my mother was
trying to sell the house. The town was small-minded. The high
school, supposedly one of the best in the area, was deadening.
Fortunately, there were a few good teachers: Mrs. Benson, the
Latin teacher, and Mr. Day, the biology teacher, who had written
our textbook. It had a chapter on evolution but we never got to
it in class, nor, appropriately, did he ever in any of his classes. He
had probably been instructed not to by the principal or the school
board. There were a few other teachers who weren't particularly
good but encouraged the best students. My English teacher used
to recommend short stories in *The New Yorker* for me to read.
Sometimes he asked me what I thought of them. He watched me
at the prom. I was pretty much a wallflower. It was creepy.

My advisor knew nothing about me and didn't even bother
to ask what interested me. He simply wrote out the routine four-
subject schedule—English, algebra, one language (in my case,
Latin), and social studies—and when I asked him if I could take
another language, he said no. It would interfere with my Latin.
That was that. Two weeks later, after I had to stop sports because
of a sudden dust allergy, he agreed to let me take a fifth course but
not French—I would never be able to catch up, he said (despite
my insistence that I already knew some French). He put me into
a general science class designed for the weakest students in the
school. I would have no trouble catching up to them. I did learn
something, but it wasn't science; it was how a class catering to
the poorest students guaranteed their leaving school at sixteen. I
liked the teacher, but after years of teaching general science, she
had been worn down by turning possible success into inevitable

failure. The only specific class I remember was one in which she showed us how Seeing Eye dogs were trained. Her husband was a trainer.

It was there, at that high school, that I experienced prejudice for the first time. True, some of my friends had occasionally called me a "wop" or a "guinea" or "Crappie" with an affectionate aggression that, though it hurt me at first, I could handle. They had stopped by the time I was in the eighth grade, and no one in my new school ever called me names. The prejudice came from a teacher, Mrs. Downes, who taught social studies. No matter how hard I tried, I always got Cs even though I was an A student. Then one day she asked each of us to report on a local institution. She listed them on the blackboard and went around the room asking us to choose one. I knew I would be last and have no choice. I always was. When she got to Mike, who was a troublemaker and one of the worst students in the class, he said he didn't know. She told him to do the psychiatric hospital because his father was an attendant there. He snapped back, "Why me? Ask Vincent." "Why Vincent?" she asked, with unforgettable disdain. "His father was a doctor there." "Is that true?" she asked me in disbelief, and when I said yes, she went on to say, "But he doesn't work there anymore." I suppose she thought he had lost his license or had been fired. "No, he doesn't," I answered. "He died." She didn't say anything; she didn't say she was sorry. But from that day, no matter what I wrote, I always got an A. I learned later from some of the students in the class that I was the only one with an Italian name who ever got an A from her. I was sickened.

I wanted to leave the school, the town, the country, but we were trapped in a house we couldn't sell. I closed up the house when it was finally sold and left the key with the agent, because my mother had to deliver the car to the port the day before the

America was to set sail. I didn't understand why she didn't buy a European car. I think the car represented a home away from home: an identity, those roots she couldn't surrender. Still, the relief she felt—we all felt—was enormous. As the taxi was driving me to the bus station for New York, I saw Maxine on her lawn and waved to her, but she didn't see me. I hardly knew her, even though she lived a few houses down the road from me and had been in my class. She wasn't very friendly. In fact, she had almost no friends. She was Jewish in a town where there were few Jews. For an instant, I regretted not getting to know her. She suddenly seemed interesting, different from my friends. That was my only regret.

My mother drove us directly to Lausanne, where she had rented a small apartment for the summer while she looked for one in Geneva. I went with her; my sister refused. She hated Switzerland because the baker's wife had once refused to sell her croissants until she dressed decently. She was only ten and was wearing shorts and a T-shirt that morning. Switzerland was like that then.

I'll never forget my first day at school. I arrived dressed in a tie and a Black Watch sports jacket. I stuck out like a rube. (The cliché seems appropriate now, though I wouldn't have used it then.) I must have looked stereotypically American. My mother seemed to have lost confidence waiting all those months for our house to sell. She took me to a local department store where she had only bought stockings and Christmas presents for Clara when my father was alive. Now she accepted the salesman's advice, as though he was a world traveler, about the appropriate clothes for me to wear on board the steamer. Aside from the Black Watch jacket, which nobody on the ship seemed to notice, he had convinced her to buy me a midnight blue tuxedo rather than a black one. That was noticed. One of the first things my mother did when we moved to Geneva was to buy me a gray herringbone jacket. But that was after the first day of school. We had never thought to find out what the school's dress code was. There was none.

Ecolint was started in 1924, in the flush of internationalism that followed World War I and the formation of the League of Nations. I was told that two wealthy American women had financed it to compensate for their friend President Wilson's failure to join the League, but there is no mention of them on the school's website. Nor is there mention of some of the near-mythic teachers who had taught there. One was said to have lectured in alexandrines and another to have prepared his history classes as he walked to school, so he could give the historical background to the events he had read that morning in the *Journal de Genève*. Nor, obviously, is there any mention of the role the American and Australian parents played in firing the school's headmistress because, like so many French intellectuals, she was a member of the Communist Party. Later they tried to oust the director of the French side, M. Roquette, but they succeeded only in hiring another director—to balance him, they said—so that while I was there, the school had three directors.

The school was divided into a French side, which prepared you for either the Swiss or the French baccalaureate, and an English one, which prepared you for British university entrance exams or American college boards (today, the International Baccalaureate, which was first conceived of by Mr. Leach, my history teacher). Some students boarded, others were day students, and still others lived with teachers. A few—Rudolph Schmidt, Catherine Anderson, and Mariam Abbebe, among my friends—lived in private homes or pensions. There was very little crossover between the two sides.

I'm in a classroom with fifteen or twenty students. They all know one another. Mme Briquet—she is English—is registering us one by one. She doesn't smile. She asks us what classes we want to take. Occasionally she makes a suggestion, but usually she accepts our choices. Everyone knows what to take. I don't. I don't even know what classes are being offered. There is no list. You are able to take as many classes as you want. I am startled. Maria Bachofen registers for French, German, Spanish, and English as well as algebra and American history. She is Austrian but has lived all over the world. She asks Mme Briquet if she can take a tutorial in Russian. "You'll have to arrange that with Mme Hartoch," Mme Briquet says. I can't believe what I am hearing. I wonder what my high school advisor would say. Other students are registering for three, even four languages. Finally it's my turn. I say English, French, Latin, advanced algebra, American history, and chemistry. I am tempted to add Italian but decide against it. I would just be saying *I can do what you can*, when I'm not at all sure I could. Mme Briquet tells me I should take American literature. She tells all the American students that. I don't want to. It seems ridiculous to come to Switzerland to study American literature, but I agree because I think I have to study it in order to go to an American college.

I am standing in the courtyard, looking around. I see Abbie. She has long brown hair and is dressed like Juliette Gréco, in brown corduroy pants and a loose black sweater. I had been listening to Juliette Gréco all summer on the radio. I knew she was an existentialist, but I wasn't sure what an existentialist was. "That's Abbie," Paul, who has just registered, says. "And that's Marco," pointing to a squat, thuggish boy. "He's Brazilian. He's been here forever. He can't pass his exams. They're going steady." "Is she French?" I ask. "No, she's an American." I'm surprised.

Instantly, Abbie became a model for me. You can be an American without being an American. I never got to know Abbie. Marco guarded her like a dog.

I'm not at all sure why I'd assumed an anti-American posture. I wasn't anti-American. I had no particular opinion at that time. I wanted to be different. I was different. I wanted to escape the closed-mindedness of Caldwell, the prejudice. I wanted more relief than the relief I had already experienced. Just as I was idealizing Abbie, I was idealizing everyone who looked different. I knew I would be disappointed, but I don't think I realized how angry I still was at Mrs. Downes. She didn't really matter. She symbolized the anger, the suffocation, the lame possibility I felt at school and at home. My feelings were all mushed up. I knew vaguely what I didn't want to be but thought I was.

I was immediately taken over by Paul. I liked him. He had a chemistry lab in the basement of his house. I spent several Saturday afternoons there doing experiments, but I soon lost interest. Paul's mother made soggy chocolate chip cookies that reminded me of Caldwell and everything I wanted to forget. Although they had lived all over the world, Paul's family—Paul himself—seemed untouched by anything they had experienced. They seem never to have left suburban Cincinnati or wherever they came from. As I got to know other students whose parents were in the diplomatic corps or bureaucrats in one of the U.N. offices in Geneva, I found that, for the most part, they were as untouched as Paul and his family had been. Their nationality didn't seem to matter. Italian households were Italian, Peruvian were Peruvian, Australian Australian, Japanese, I suppose, Japanese, but I never got to know any students from Japan. The Swiss students kept to themselves. Geneva was, and probably still is, incredibly provincial, despite or perhaps because of all the foreigners who live there.

The students who attracted me were the boarders, living in the school's *internat*, or with teachers. Many of them came from broken or displaced families. I was surprised and, at first, impressed—I can admit this now—by how many came from titled and even royal families. Of course, we all ignored this, but Paul filled me in. He seemed to know their background but had no particular interest in knowing them. Nor did I. What drew me to them, when I was drawn to them, was their fractured perspective. I was looking for the exceptional. I was beginning to realize how deeply I had been affected by my life at the hospital.

Paul told me to drop American literature and take English with Mme Briquet. She was the best teacher in the school. He had registered for American literature because his father, who was in the consulate, was being sent back to Washington in a couple of months and thought it would ease Paul's transition into an American high school. He had lived everywhere but never for long in America.

Paul was right. Instead of reading excerpts of American writers in a glossy textbook, we began reading the Prologue to *The Canterbury Tales* in Middle English. It was magical. It took us three months to get through Chaucer. I had never read so deeply. The English prefer depth to breadth. When I got to college, I was terrified by the realization of how few authors I had studied. I found out later that I had scared some of my friends by how much "philosophy" I knew. I was given sophomore standing on general merit. I accepted it, and that was a mistake.

I took two philosophy courses my second year at Ecolint. One of them was taught by Michel Butor, who had just published his second novel, *L'emploi du temps*. His third book, *Degrés*, was based on the class I took with him. At least that is how I read it. He never knew who was in his class. When I was at Harvard, I went to hear a lecture he gave at Brandeis. He didn't remember me, and that embarrassed me because I had told a couple of friends who went to hear him that I knew him. The rector of the English church taught my second philosophy class. He taught Plato. He said that Plato was the only philosopher he knew well enough to teach. He was substituting for a Guadeloupean teacher who had been fired. We never knew why. Mariam and I ran into him in a smoky student café that winter. When he saw us, he cried out, *"Voilà, mes élèves,"* and tried to hug Mariam, but she managed to squirm free. He was very drunk. Mariam was Ethiopian—my closest friend. She wasn't a tease like Yawalak, but she could laugh at herself as if she were teasing herself. I wished I could, but I didn't have much self-irony.

Two students from the French side and I were having dinner with M. Roquette at a little inn, down the road from school. M. Roquette said it had the freshest trout in the city and that the only way to eat trout was *bleu* with a bottle of Fendant. I couldn't imagine my old high school principal inviting any student to a restaurant. I couldn't imagine him or anyone else in that school discussing the way to cook trout and what wine went best with it.

I didn't know why M. Roquette had invited us. He was telling us how the school got by during the war. He said that it nearly went bankrupt from taking in so many refugee students who couldn't pay, and that after the war, the city of Geneva saved it by buying the land it occupied to pay its debts and then charging it only a symbolic rent. With tears in his eyes, he went on to tell us about a little Dutch boy who had arrived at the school late one night. M. Roquette heard a whimper and a faint knock on one of the French windows in his office. He opened it, and the little boy fell into his arms. He was clutching a piece of balled-up paper. It was a note from one of his former students, a Dutch Jew, asking him to take care of his eight-year-old son. Somehow, the little boy had made it all the way from Holland to the school. He had no memory of how he got there. "He was truly alone with a hole in his memory that could not be filled. What must that be like?" M. Roquette asked us.

It turned out that M. Roquette wanted me to become president of the student body. The presidents were always from the French side, because it was larger than the English side and, despite the school's rhetorical commitment to "international understanding," both sides always voted en bloc. My opponent was American. By that time I was identified with the foreign students, mainly because I'd become an annoying vocal critic of American foreign policy in encouraging the Hungarian revolt and then backing off when the Soviet tanks rolled into Budapest. I won. No one seemed to mind M. Roquette's interference. Several of the Americans — the daughters of army officers serving in the Middle East — called me a communist and a traitor. I was flattered.

It was really after my mother left Geneva that I felt the change in me. By then, I had met Arturo Retti, a Roman student who preferred to be called "Art" because it sounded American. He was a jazz pianist. "Take the 'A' Train" was his theme song. He was a year ahead of me. We met playing soccer and became friends. Arturo lived near the Hotel Sergy, and we would meet most afternoons at a little café around the corner from the hotel, along with Rudolph Schmidt, a South African who carried the *Odyssey* in Greek wherever he went, and Steven Gerig, a mathematical genius who later went to Harvard with me and helped me get through a course on symbolic logic. (It was taught by the worst teacher I had there. Willard Van Orman Quine, the great logician whose class I had wanted to take, was away that year.) We talked philosophy. Rudolph introduced us to Nietzsche and our conversations were interspersed with Rudolph and Arturo's plans to hitchhike across Africa to Johannesburg and catch a whaling boat and with accounts of their tortured love. Arturo was in love with Noi, a beautiful Thai student, whom he eventually married, and Rudolph was besotted by Yawalak. Arturo was an enthusiast, deeply wounded by his father, who lived a perverted life, even by Rome's dolce vita standards, and Rudolph, an inveterate romantic, bathed himself in amorous suffering. Steven and I couldn't compete. We weren't in love; we did not know Greek; we were not going to hitchhike across Africa; and we were not athletes. I wasn't sure I understood *Thus Spake Zarathustra*, which Rudolph insisted I read. He was infatuated with Nietzsche's superman. Neither of them paid any attention to my deficiencies.

Our conversations must have been frightfully sophomoric, but they had a serious effect on me. They opened up a world of possibility I had never imagined—of adventure, literally and intellectually, and, more important, of relationship. They were my first serious friends and have remained so; Rudolph in memory, for he committed suicide while I was still in college, and Arturo in fact. He and Maret, his wife now, visited us last summer in Italy. They live in Geneva. I don't know what happened to Steven. I see Yawalak occasionally. She and her husband, Mitchell, live in Washington most of the year. I saw Noi for the first time in nearly forty years when Jane and I visited her in Bangkok three years ago. She has changed enormously, but she still likes to dance. She used to sneak out of my window at night to go dancing. She and Yawalak also lived at the Briquets'.

IX.
RITES OF
PASSAGE,
RIGHTS OF
RETURN

I DO not remember the first time I heard the expression "rites of passage." It may have been when I was in the fourth grade, though I'm sure I didn't understand its implication, nor, certainly, the longing I came to have, growing older, for guidance, a guide who would lead me through the ordeals of growing into adulthood, which despite all evidence of its advent still seemed impossibly elusive, just around some corner that I couldn't find. It was more than a father I was seeking, perhaps because I had only a faint memory of one — a memory of absence rather than a lost presence. I had lost my father not on the day he died, not at his funeral, not as I watched his coffin lowered into the grave and wondered what would happen to the earth it would displace, but several nights later, when I awoke with the certainty not of his death, that I knew, but of his irrecoverableness.

I am in the cellar. My father is sitting on a Victorian settee that he has brought home, much to my mother's fury, along with two matching side chairs.

I am surprised to see my father. "Daddy," I cry out, "I thought you were" — I stop myself and run to him as he stands up. When I reach out to hug him, when I touch him, he crumbles into a pile, like an anthill, of old, powdery wood.

I didn't crumble but only turned bright red in squelched anger when Miss von Horne, my fourth-grade teacher, accused me in front of the whole class of getting my parents' help when I referred to "rites of passage" and "divination" in a class presentation. She had asked each of us to report on an African tribe. I chose the Watusi because they were the tallest people in the world. I read about their rites of passage and divination in an old book with a red cover and lots of pictures of bare-breasted women that I got out of the public library. "No one your age," Miss von Horne said, "could possibly know what those words mean," and she made me tell the class what they meant. When I did, she pretended to be satisfied, but I knew she thought I was just parroting my parents' words without really understanding them. Why shouldn't I understand them? What did it mean, anyway, to get your parents' help? Of course, I had asked my parents what the words meant, but I had thought about them and prepared the report myself. I had not yet reached the age of irony, for then I would have realized that Miss von Horne's accusation was an embryonic rite of passage from a blind confidence in teachers, even those you didn't like, to serious doubts about their capacity to understand you in your uniqueness and not according to some dictate in a teachers' manual.

Miss von Horne was horse-faced. She probably wasn't that bad a teacher, but I hated her because she was always asking the class about their fathers' war experiences. My father was the only one who hadn't fought. He was too old. I said he had fought in the First World War, but she didn't pay any attention to that. The children in the class teased me, calling me the enemy because my father was Italian. Miss von Horne didn't stop them, but Mr. Parks did when he heard them in the playground and came down and gave us a lecture about our all being Americans.

The war was now on everyone's mind. The enemy was Russia. We had bomb drills where we had to crawl under our desks. Freddy's father laughed when Freddy told him, and Freddy told me. His mother had died when he was in the third grade, leaving his father with three boys to raise by himself. He never accepted anyone's offer of help. He was a proud, bitter man. Freddy said he had a temper. We all knew this, but he used to help Freddy and his brothers make model airplanes. There were certain things, secret things, they could not ask their father. They couldn't ask him about sex; they couldn't ask him about Donna—I think that was her name—who spent a night in his bed and so upset Freddy that he made me meet him halfway between our two houses, which were several miles apart. It was then that Freddy asked me if boys bled the way girls did. I wasn't sure what he was talking about but pretended I did and told him that boys did not bleed with so much authority that I doubted myself and got scared and asked my mother. When she told me I was right, I called Freddy to tell him I had been right, but by that time he had asked Donna, who had laughed at him.

Girls are lucky, I thought when I thought about those things. *They know when they are grown up the way boys don't, but they still go to school.* I could tell when some of the girls in seventh grade had their periods. I could smell it. Once I saw blood dripping down the leg of a girl I'll call Amy, as she was whispering something to Mr. Hilton before he shuffled her out of the classroom to the nurse's office. Amy used to charge the boys a nickel to let them look under her skirt and a dime to touch her. I paid her a nickel only once, and she pulled her vagina open to show me, saying she did it because I was special. I did feel special then—that is, until I learned she said the same thing to each of her customers. I wonder what happened to Amy.

I was one of the first boys in my class whose voice changed. I was in the fourth grade. All the girls laughed at me whenever I spoke, except for Anne Adams, who always ignored me. I liked her, and I liked Regina, who did laugh at me. Anne was the best pupil in the class and, I thought, the prettiest. She left at the end of the year. I missed her. Regina was a flirt. I didn't mind it so much when she laughed at me. Some of the boys called her "Regina Vagina, Vagina Regina" to her face. She didn't seem to mind; she just laughed at them and sashayed off, smiling a smile of arrogant superiority. I wished I could laugh when the girls made fun of me, but I couldn't. I just turned red. I tried not to talk in class, and when I had to, I would whisper. I could control my voice better whispering. But Miss von Horne would always say, "Louder," and I would screech. I thought she said it to humiliate me. Perhaps she did.

I was also one of the first boys to have hair under my arms. That was in the seventh grade, when most of the girls were beginning to have breasts. It was Freddy who made fun of me then, saying I smelled. I was so embarrassed that I tried shaving my underarms and cut myself so badly that I had to tell my mother. She bought me a deodorant. My pubic hair never bothered me. No one could see it but me. It was private. I began to shave after my father died. That was different. I had to learn how by myself, and I did.

None of these changes, not even my first seminal discharges — I didn't know what they were at first — marked me as an adult the way menarche did girls. They were less dramatic. Of course, I never thought that any of the girls were embarrassed by their periods or by their breasts. I didn't think much about how girls felt, except for my sister and then rarely. "Think about how your sister is feeling," my mother used to say. I wonder when I really began to try to feel for them.

What marks a transition may, in fact, mask the absence of a transition. How often have you said "I have changed," only to discover, if you are honest with yourself, that, as sincere as you may have been or thought you were, you have not changed. How many husbands, or wives for that matter, have assured their spouse that they've changed when they haven't? (Why do I focus on husbands?) I have overheard, haven't you, complete strangers assure whomever they are talking to on their cell phones—in the street, in supermarket queues, or in the shadows cast by street-lights at night as you walk your dog—that they have changed, when you know that they haven't and never will. Are we ready to declare them hypocrites, manipulators, or seducers? Sometimes they are. Sometimes they are caught in a moment. How easy it is to deceive ourselves. Are pronouncements of change part of the fabric of modern love? Perhaps a bit of Shakespearean humor is called for.

Why do I immediately associate declarations of change with love? They are subject to an intensity, to entanglements of intimacy, that they do not have on other occasions, as when a worker who is about to be fired for some negligence or other assures his boss that he will change. Under such circumstances, the plea (for assertions of change are always pleas) is pathetic, since there's no doubt as to who has the power. But in marriages, in love affairs, in the relations between parents and children, the structures of power are more complex. A scoundrel assures his wife that he has changed. He puts himself in his wife's power, knowing full well that he has the power, if only by giving the illusion that she has it. (I'll not mention economic and legal considerations. They are obvious.)

Power, the power of convention, tradition, and of stubborn deities, demons, and spirits, is always at play in classical rites of passage. It is that power that fashions indefinite longings, unacknowledged predispositions, and ill-formed expectations into articulate desires and those fears that always accompany and nurture desire. We do our best to ignore those fears or we surrender to them, falling into the inertia of just-doing.

Change is proclaimed where there might not be any change at all.

I am in a forlorn Moroccan village in the fall of 1968. The villagers are excited. The women are preparing a feast, as they did the night before. Most of the men are milling around, deceptively aimless. They are tense, ready to lose their tempers, saying little, and what they say is flat. A few sit along the walls of the houses that surround the village square. They stare at the ground in front of them. They are wan, furtive, buried in themselves, filled, it seems to me, with dread. They are about to reexperience in another—an *ephebe*, a son perhaps—a pain that allures them with the force of ritual as they struggle to obliterate its memory. Rites of passage are never only for the initiates but also for the initiators, those who have been initiated, and even for the indifferent observers. *Do unto your issue what has been done unto you*, I think, playing on Christ's commandment.

Little Labid, dressed in a new white smock and a rough brown woolen *jellaba*, the kind the men are wearing, struts about showing off his new clothes. He is six, maybe seven, seemingly innocent of what is about to happen to him. He is a handsome little boy. His hands have been painted with henna in intricate designs that look like women's facial tattoos, but the women's are an inky blue. He is about to be paraded around the village three times on an old mule that the foreman of the farm in which the village sits has lent his family. The farm has been nationalized, the villagers tell me. "The old French farmer used to give us a sack of flour whenever a boy was circumcised, but now the Moroccan boss expects a sack of flour from us, just for lending us an old mule," one of them says bitterly. "And a bottle of wine," another adds, and they laugh in disgust. They tell me that the French farmer lent them his stallion. They wished it had been white.

The barber arrives. He is late. The musicians and the *shikha*—a female entertainer who usually accompanies him—have already arrived. They are strangers, but the barber is known, since he has performed many circumcisions in the village in the past. The boys who have already been circumcised run away when they see him. Little Labid's father also disappears. "What father can bear to see his son suffer such pain?" I am told. Little Labid, who is no longer allowed to touch the ground, for it will bring him ill luck, is handed to his mother, who stands, her face frozen, in front of the house where the barber waits. She is surrounded by a clutch of villagers; the musicians—a drummer and two oboe players—are behind them. In turn, she hands Little Labid to his uncle, who will hold him during the operation. He draws an old burlap curtain across the door. The villagers are silenced. They are now caught in the irrevocable movement of the ritual.

As Little Labid's uncle tells him to look up at a bird in the rafters, the barber pulls up the boy's foreskin, inserts some sheep's dung between it and the glans, and snips it off in a single scissor cut. He quickly, but with tired efficiency, pushes the boy's penis into a broken egg to which a bit of rabbit dung and henna have been added—to cool the pain. The musicians begin to play. The whining music of the *ghitas*—the oboes—is entrancing. The women of the village begin to dance. Little Labid is bundled up and strapped to his mother in such a way that his penis presses against her sweating back. She dances, at first slowly and then wildly, until he stops crying. He is put to bed in her room, as the dancing continues. The *shikha* takes center stage, dancing so provocatively that the men are embarrassed by their excitement as the women laugh and ululate. Later, she will be visited by those men who can afford to pay her. None of the women seem to mind.

The circumcision ritual is said to declare the boy a man. It is a precocious ritual that can be performed anytime between birth and late adolescence. It is a rite, less of passage—that will come later, with maturation—than of return. Little Labid is taken from the women's world—his mother's care—symbolically declared a man, and then returned to that world. He is destined, I think with an anger that surprises me, to submit his sons to what he himself has undergone.

Is there no escape from the prison house of ritual?

I think of Tom, an Indonesian Catholic who was staying with the Briquets in Zermatt the summer I first traveled around Europe by myself. I met M. Briquet quite by accident the morning I arrived in Zermatt. I had no idea that he and his wife were spending the summer there. Mme Briquet immediately took me in hand, found a cheap room for me to rent, and arranged for me to eat with them and their two boarders. I was relieved. I hadn't realized how lonely I had been in London, where I had gone immediately after saying goodbye to my mother and sister in Paris. They were returning to the United States. I knew no one in London, and discovered only when I got back to Geneva that Yawalak had been living with her cousins just a few houses away from the little hotel where I was staying. M. Briquet promised to take me mountain climbing. Tom, who was rather effeminate, refused, but the other boarder, a high school student from somewhere in the Midwest, was enthusiastic and, unlike me, fearless. Every other afternoon, Tom went to confession. We asked him why, but he just shook his head sadly. Then one afternoon when the two of us had gone for a long walk, Tom told me he went because he couldn't stop masturbating. It was a terrible sin. I was a couple of years older and should have told him it was nothing to worry about and that I did it myself, but I didn't. I think Tom enjoyed confessing more than he did masturbating. He was timid, lonely, and missed a father. He had been sent to boarding school when he was six. After confiding in me, he couldn't look me in the eye and wouldn't go on any more walks with me. I left a couple of days later for Rome.

The ceremonies that we identify with classical — primitive — rites of passage are often lengthy affairs in which the initiates remain in a liminal state between two social statuses, sometimes for months or even years, as in a number of West African societies. They often occur in a surround of danger, of stubborn deities, tyrannical ancestor spirits, demons, and devils. Mutilation is not unusual. Little Labid was protected from the effects of the ubiquitous evil eye and possible sorcery by amulets and phylacteries filled with apotropaic prayers and passages from the Koran.

Our rites of passage are tame by contrast. Symbols of death and rebirth, if they occur, are anemic. Birthdays, anniversaries, graduation ceremonies, marriages, and even funerals are not menaced by breaches of taboo. They may be solemn affairs, but the solemnity, when it is called for, is often forced. They seem to work better when in their joyous phases. This is even becoming true of funerals, now that we say "passed away" and even "passed" rather than "died" and refer to memorials as "celebrations of the life of." Perhaps a bit of danger lies in the word "died." It is too direct for our evasive sensibility. And yet, I feel that our domesticated rites rely for what efficacy they have on intimations of their more "primitive" counterparts. Perhaps it is the contrast between the tamed and the untamed that produces an efficacy that the tamed alone cannot.

Of course, I am speaking from a secular point of view of secular rites. But it is my impression that many of the religious rites of transition are so staged that they dilute, or in fact lose, their spiritual dimension. Some edge on entertainment, for the flock at least. I once attended a baptismal service in an evangelical megachurch in which the baptism itself was performed on a balcony high above the altar under dimmed purple lights to the kind of organ music that always seems to convert the spiritual into the sentimental.

I'm not questioning any believers' faith, and certainly not the experience of the baptism, or the initiates in any other rites, including the secular ones. Nor am I denying an entertainment dimension to the primitive rite or its ability to generate feelings in the participants that seem, at least to the outsider, to conflict with the spiritual or psychological transformation intended by the rite. Indeed, transformation may not be intended. Many rites are purely pragmatic affairs — a sort of licensing. What I miss isn't so much the awe, or the dread or ecstasy, or even the "majesty," of the religious rite, the mysterium tremendum, which Rudolf Otto described in *The Idea of the Holy* — those words seem hyperbolic — than a simple sense of mystery that comes with depth of experience and produces, ideally, a change in sensibility. That may be the most we can hope for in a modernity still tinged by romanticism, and a postmodernity that doesn't recognize the extent to which its play, pastiche, and simulacra are founded on their opposite: the stickiness of reality.

A dream dreamt when I was home, about to go to college. I was caught between two times: the one, ended, in Geneva, devoid of any responsibility, even to myself—for my future; the other anxiously anticipated, though I denied any anxiety. I had no idea what I was going to study; no idea, no idea at all, what I was going to be. The thought of becoming a doctor hung over me. I couldn't admit to myself, or anyone else, that I didn't want to be a doctor, that I had no obligation to be one, that I was clutching at a past, a magical past, that had ended with my father's death. Had he really wanted me to be a doctor? I suppose he had. His grandfather had studied medicine but never practiced it. I was in a state of shock.

When I think back to that August, I remember waiting for my mother outside an administrative building in Newark where she had gone to file some official forms. She had parked illegally and wanted me to watch the car. An elderly lady was struggling up a long flight of granite steps to the building's entrance, carrying a heavy bag. I asked if I could help. She growled a violent "No," and, without even looking at me, said, "Get away, I know your type." I didn't know what to do. I wanted to tell her to go to hell. Did she really think I was going to knock her down or run away with her bag? Who did she think I was? And where was I anyway? I wanted to flee, to go back to Geneva. I also felt ashamed. What an idiot I'd been to ask her.

I am not sure whether I had the dream I am about to describe before or after that. They both marked a transition, without bringing about any ostensible change in me.

I am scrambling through the garden up to my mother's house. It is on a steep slope. I am not following the path but climbing up the terraces. There are many more of them than there were in fact. Finally I get to the rhododendron bushes below the dining room. I smell the damp earth. There must be a lot of earthworms here, I think. I try to look through the dining room window, but it's too high. I pull myself up to the window's edge and peer in. There is a long table, around which a group of men, dressed in blue suits, are sitting, listening to a woman at the head of the table. She is a priestess from somewhere in Asia, perhaps Mongolia. Yes, Mongolia. She has mustard-brown skin and wears a strange costume. The dining room table extends vertically toward the widow, though it is obviously horizontal. I slip down, scraping my hands and knees.

I enter the dining room from a side door (which never existed), and the woman, seconded by the men around the table, invites me in, saying, "We have been expecting you. We have left a place for you." It is at the opposite end of the table from her. My back is to the window. I sit down. I don't know anyone there, but they are all friendly. They are all drinking tea. Someone pours me a cup. It tastes bitter at first and then thickly sweet. I take just a couple of sips. I don't trust it.

The woman is chanting. She stops chanting and says, "You must join us. You are too old to be alone. Do you agree?" "But who are you?" I ask, desperate. "What are you doing in our house? I don't need to join you, whoever you are. Who are you?" "You will know when you join us." "How can I join you when I don't know who you are?" "You are here, aren't you? You scrambled up and peered at us through the window. You didn't have to come in, but you did." There is something hypnotic about her voice. I feel myself drawn to her. I get up, circle around the table, and kiss her on the right cheek. "You see," she says. And I wake up, relieved, strangely so, and different, somehow different without knowing how. It is just a feeling.

I thought of this dream, afterward, as a rite of passage—or, more specifically, as a substitute for a rite of passage I had never had. I am not sure why. There is, in fact, no passage in my dream—only a change in feeling. If anything, it is an initiatory dream and it involves a cult. I am revolted by the idea of being a member of a cult. And yet the dream has affected me deeply. From time to time, often for no discernible reason, it comes to mind, and then I am relieved without knowing from what exactly. I am suffused with a sense of lightness and confidence, and yet filled with sorrow.

Dreams I have had since then often recall that dream. It is a fulcrum, sometimes a font, as when I dreamt of watching myself grow in a few seconds from a newborn baby into a boy with blond hair. I have brown hair. I was lying on a cot, facing the open door of the hogan where I was living on the Navajo reservation. The door framed the dream. When I awoke, I thought immediately of Jung's archetype of the child and recalled in all of its intensity a terrifying vision of myself as a wrinkled, twisted embryo that I had had that spring, the only time I ever took LSD. I was immediately relieved of a burden I had been carrying since then—perhaps without even knowing it. I felt a renewal of possibility…I saw myself leaving the dining room after kissing the Asian woman and slamming the door shut. Had I dreamt this and forgotten it or had I just invented it? It was all too neat. Or was it? Is it?

Now, I was again living between two worlds, that of a student and that of a teacher, but also, and far more important, between being single and being married. I had begun living with Jane that spring. I was in love with her but never thought of our marrying, not at the time. I walked every Sunday morning two miles to the trading post, where there was a telephone to call her, and then back again to my hogan. Those walks—their repetition—were like a ritual. No transition yet, just anticipation of what I couldn't acknowledge.

X.

FROM COINCIDENCE TO CONTINGENCY TO FATALITY

JANE and I are having dinner in New York at the apartment of a woman I'll call Lara. It is unusually strained. Most of the guests know one another, but there are two men, heavyset, in their early thirties, from Turkey or the Levant, whose presence dampens the atmosphere. Though, as far as I know, they are not twins or even related to each other, they look alike. No one has met them before, not even Lara, who has probably been asked by a friend to entertain them. They deal in platinum and rare metals. Before dinner, they tell us about the danger China will pose to the West, to capitalism, since it is the major source of many rare earth metals. They seem pleased with themselves and their information. They say very little at dinner; they are clearly uncomfortable in Lara's presence. They don't know that she doesn't stand on ceremony—which is not to say that she is unaware of her social position as a member of Spain's royal family. She makes use of it, at times thoughtlessly, when it serves her interests. At least the strangers do not use her title. She has placed them side by side at the far end of the table.

I met Lara when I was sixteen. She was awkward, but within a year she had become more confident, assertive at times, but unable to confront her family. Despite the fact that she was quite brilliant, her parents refused to send her to college. Instead, they sent her to a trilingual secretarial school. Her father told me, the only time I met him, "As we were raised to be rulers, we had no other profession. We suffered. I would not want my children to have the same experience." He may have said "kings" instead of "rulers." I said nothing—I was a guest in his house—but I would like to have asked him why he couldn't imagine any profession other than secretary for his daughter. I knew how disappointed she was. The last time I saw her was in Italy, where her family lived; she had graduated from the secretarial school but couldn't take a job because wherever she found one, her mother objected that it wasn't fitting to her status or, if it was, say, a job in an embassy, that she had heard there had been a revolution in that country and their king assassinated. It didn't seem to matter if this was true or not. Hearsay was enough. Their household was very formal at that time. I thought it was less enthralled by princely tradition than tyrannized by the family's indomitably snobbish German governess.

Jane, Wicky, and I are in the Grand Ballroom of the Palace Hotel in Gstaad. It is New Year's Eve. We have been invited by a friend whose husband died earlier in the year. Pat wants to bring her family and a few close friends together. Though there are people from all over the world, many, perhaps the majority, are from the Middle East. Many of the men probably attended Le Rosey, which has a winter campus in Gstaad. I have never seen such an ostentatious display of wealth. Nor has Pat, who is taken aback. I think she suddenly feels poor. I am fascinated by a German woman dressed in a silver dress with a thickly brocaded wire snake climbing up out of her décolletage and emerging from the top of her elaborately twisted blond hair. She certainly makes her presence known. Suddenly all the guests stand up. We do, too, not knowing what is happening. It is Farah Diba, the Shah's widow. It is surreal. Everyone else bows. And I hear, "How the poor woman has suffered. How courageous she is." I have no doubt that she suffered—suffering is relative to circumstance. What offends us is the exaggerated homage paid to her. There is certainly no political consciousness here. Pat never returned to Gstaad. Nor, obviously, did we.

I didn't see Lara again for nearly twenty years; we were never that close. Then, to my great surprise, I ran into her at a party in a rather gloomy Upper West Side apartment. It wasn't hers, but she was living in the neighborhood, a few blocks from us. She had managed to go to Bryn Mawr, where she had met and married an American who programmed computers. Status was his goal. After they were divorced, he wrote a novel of no particular merit, but it earned him a fortune, being the object of one of those crazy Hollywood bidding wars for movie rights. They had two children who were a little older than Wicky. We became friends again and almost bought a farmhouse in Tuscany together, but fortunately we didn't, for a couple of years later we had an irreconcilable falling-out, which at this point I prefer not to describe—perhaps later.

Lara was not herself at dinner, or perhaps she was really, and I didn't know that "self." Halfway through dinner, she turned to me and said tout court, "Mariam is dead." I was doubly shocked—by the news and by the way Lara had told me, as if it were an event of no particular significance. She knew Mariam had been my friend, as she had been Lara's. After the coup d'état in Ethiopia in 1974, during which Haile Selassie died in prison, some saying he'd been strangled, Yawalak, Lara, and I tried to find out what had happened to her and, later, to her two sons. Mariam was one of the emperor's granddaughters, and we knew that most members of his family had been thrown in prison, exiled, or killed.

I DON'T remember when I first noticed Mariam, but I do remember when she charmed me. I was walking back to Mme

Briquet's after school and saw Mariam running down the Route de Chêne to the house where she lived. She was wearing a black cape lined with leopard skin. I was fascinated by her flowing cape, by the leopard skin, its exoticism. I wanted to run down the hill with her, but I just stood watching until I couldn't see her anymore. It was one of those uncanny moments when desire—expectant, undefined desire—coalesces with identity. I was a shameless romantic. I knew it then, and despite my cynicism, I have remained so, though less shamelessly. I can't really imagine what life would be like without the possibilities that romanticism opens. I am not referring to the popular, love-story romanticism that wraps its nature in safety. I mean the coincidence of allure and terror, of an irresistible sense of a transcending yet deeply personal plenitude and with it the pressure of—the longing for—extinction that can be attributed neither to oneself nor to any other graspable source. Once, it was possible to speak of that allure and terror in terms of desire and death, but those tropes have lost their vibrancy though overuse, reluctance, and rhetorical cowardice. My description is no more immune to the loss of resonance—the "im"; the imp—of possibility.

You see, I am not even sure Mariam ever had a cape lined with leopard skin, but I cannot—and do not want to—lose that image of her.

It is odd how iconic representations maintain a life of their own, appearing and disappearing unpredictably. Mine of Mariam represents an impossible possibility, a sense of if-only-I-could-have-done-something-about-it—her death—and a mourning that has grown stronger in the last couple of years as I grow older and feel the diminution not of real possibilities—that of course—but of imaginative ones. I once had the habit, falling asleep, of recasting events in my past. I did not realize that refiguring the past depends on a sense of unbounded future. Such fantasies, perhaps all fantasies, depend on the mergence of past and future, and on the extinction of a present that would otherwise constrict them with a "reality" that we attach, at times quite unrealistically, to the present.

That fleeting image of Mariam, a near fetishistic focus on something that may never have been, the leopard-skin lining, echoes an empty model, that of Arturo's and especially Rudolph's anguished relationships with Noi and Yawalak: an immaturity that I shared with Mariam that year.

Eight Trappist monks are living in a monastery in the mountains in Algeria during the civil war in the nineties. They are alone, desperately so, with their faith, which fails some of them as it sustains others. They are powerless. The local population would defend them were it possible but it is not. Islamists will attack them the next day. They prepare their last supper. They drink champagne, which they have saved for a special occasion, and play Swan Lake *on an old windup Victrola. They wait.*

I am lying in bed, trying to sleep, rehearsing Xavier Beauvois's film *Of Gods and Men*, which I have just seen. I suddenly remember the first time I saw *Swan Lake*. Mariam and I have just finished our final exams. We go to the Parc des Eaux-Vives, my favorite park, which sweeps down to the lake, to see an outdoor performance of *Swan Lake*. Mariam is flying to Addis Ababa the next day. I am leaving for home via Rome. She will be going to the London School of Economics in the fall and I to Harvard. We are sad. We know we will see each other again, but we also know that we will never again have the freedom we have had this past year.

How can I explain that freedom, my tortuous relations with Mariam, her moodiness, suggesting at times that she is drawn

to me and at others that love is impossible? Though she is argu-
ably the most independent of Haile Selassie's granddaughters,
she knows that she will eventually be ordered back home, as her
sisters were. Mariam resisted the emperor once—he wanted her
back in Addis for some celebration or other and she refused to
come, explaining that she would miss her exams. I remember
her anguish and the release, the surprise, she felt when he wrote
back, praising her decision.

We had celebrated the evening she got his letter by going to
one of our hangouts: a large, gloomy café that was almost always
empty. We went there because we had heard that Lenin liked it.
The first time, the waiter had seated us at "Lenin's table." We
knew he was pulling our leg, but pretended he wasn't, and he pretended not to know we were pretending. He was an old man who
listened and once or twice added to our discussions, about the
devastation capitalism, especially American capitalism, would
cause, the horrors of colonialism—the French and the Algeri-
ans were at war—and what could have been, but wasn't, a sensitive topic, the exploitation of Africans by their leaders. I did not
realize at the time how brutal Haile Selassie's regime was, nor, I
think, did Mariam. She had gone to school in England, and when
she went home, she was assiduously sheltered from the misery
that surrounded her. She lived in two worlds, that of the palace
and that of the marginalized. She knew the one intimately and
the other hardly—if at all, abstractly. She was never able to rec-
oncile the two.

I don't think Mariam was bothered by or even acknowledged
this incapacity. But she had a persistent need to render the incon-
sistent consistent, usually by ignoring the inconsistency itself,
and this wreaked havoc on her social understanding. Paradox
gives us little joy. Conflict even less. We live with the illusion

that resolution is possible. It may be ideally, in mathematics, but there is no known mathematical system that can solve the totality of mathematical problems. It is even truer of social and psychological life. We have strategies, often bolstered by the human sciences, to reformulate what we perceive as inconsistencies to fit the narratives of complacent understanding we tell ourselves. Mariam's irony, especially her self-irony, was—must have been—defensive or deflective. But need it be? That is our presumption. That's my point. The human sciences shy away from irony with the rigor of a fundamentalist.

I wonder what the old waiter thought of us. We were an odd couple, an African who spoke with a crisp British accent and had that ironic laugh that made her seem older and more experienced than she was, and, me, a slightly acned American kid—I've never been able to describe myself—who pretended to a sophistication he didn't have and was never sure he could carry it off. Mariam had more confidence; she had no trouble acting her part. It was only when she feigned sexual experience, which I knew she had not had, that her confidence failed her and she revealed her innocence. I was sure she wanted me to be more experienced than I—she—was. She wanted my experience to have come from another woman, and, as it turned out, she wanted her own to have come from another man. It would save our relationship from the embarrassment of inexperience. It would be purer that way.

We've been to the movies. It is late. We stop for a coffee at a café we don't know, a sleazy place with neon lights that turn everyone's face a sickly blue. A couple of hookers are sitting at the bar. One of them is caressing a brute sitting next to her. He ignores but doesn't stop her. She is young, pretty in a sad sort of way, dressed in a bright blue miniskirt before miniskirts are in fashion, and wears dagger-thin heels. Her right leg is twisted back around the base of the barstool. Her eyelashes—I can see them in the mirror behind the bar—are covered with thick blue mascara. Her expression is so empty that I'm not sure she even knows she is stroking the man. Her movements are mechanical. I find them, her emptiness, sexy.

Mariam catches me looking at her. "You should go with her. She's sexy. I'll take a taxi back home," she says, much to my surprise, without any jealousy. "You need to. You must." I am frightened. I have never slept with a whore, with any woman. "No," I say, "I won't let you go home alone." Finally, after arguing, she agrees, provided I return and pick up the hooker. "Hurry," she says, "she won't be here forever." I drop Mariam off. For the first time she kisses me, deeply on the mouth. I take the taxi back to the bar, hoping the hooker will still be there, hoping she won't. She isn't. The next day, in school, Mariam looks at me quizzically but doesn't ask me what happened. I feign experience.

I went back to the bar several times, but I never saw the hooker again. A few weeks later Mariam began ignoring me. When I asked her out she refused. I was sure she was angry at me, despite her encouragement, for sleeping with the hooker. Finally, after several tormented weeks, I insisted that we talk. In a ridiculously formal way—I know it, she knows it—she agrees to meet me for lunch at a café on the other side of town, near the train station, which is known for its steak-frites and mustard sauce. She is cold, businesslike, anxious to get through our meeting. She maintains this posture for the first half of lunch and then tells me she has been going out with an older man, an Algerian, who, she says, had picked her up somewhere *malsain*. She also implies, but never actually says, that she is sleeping with him. I'm devastated, but also so angry that I affect indifference. This hurts her. I am glad.

I have no idea whether Mariam has slept with the Algerian. I don't even know whether there really is an Algerian. I walk all the way across town to Mme Briquet's, passing the bar to see whether the hooker is there. She isn't. I'm not sure if I am angrier with Mariam than with myself for feigning experience, for my innocence. I'm jealous, and this infuriates me. I don't see Mariam for several days. (We have to be at school only when we have classes.) When I do see her again, she smiles, and then both of us break out laughing. One of the teachers who walks by looks at us as if we are crazy. Neither of us ever mentioned our experience-nonexperience again.

After the ballet, we had a tasteless meal in one of those fancy after-the-theater restaurants that face the lake. It is strange; I can remember what we ate —*champignons à la grecque* for me, a *salade haricots verts avec foie gras* for Mariam, white lake fish and mille-feuilles for both of us—but I cannot remember what we talked about. Whatever it was, it wasn't what we were really talking about. We were already missing each other. We drank too much and in the taxi back to Mariam's we had a fight and said goodbye, angry. It was easier that way.

IT'S SUMMER. I'm in London. I've just arrived. I have written to Mariam, telling her I am coming to London. She did not answer my letter. I call the Ethiopian embassy and ask for her address, her telephone number at least. They tell me to write to her at the embassy. I say I am in London only for a few days. They tell me that if I write immediately, she'll get the letter by the end of the afternoon. I don't believe them. I didn't know that there were three mail deliveries a day in London. I buy some stationery and order tea at a Lyons. Three office girls try to flirt with me. I ignore them. They shrug their shoulders. I wish for a moment that I had met them the first time I was in London. I remind myself that I was just sixteen then. I leave for the post office without looking at them, but, hearing one of them call me a toff—I don't know what it means—I turn around. The three of them stick their tongues out at me. I blush and walk out, asking myself why I didn't stick out my tongue at them. They are grotesque; they remind me of Ensor's masked faces. I know I am being pretentious.

By the time I get back to the hotel, there is a message from Mariam. We meet in the morning, go to a Gauguin exhibit, admire a keg he sculpted, and then go to a factory to buy crystal doorknobs for her grandfather. He has seen them in a magazine and said he liked them. One of his other granddaughters, or maybe some other relative, cabled Mariam to buy the doorknobs for his birthday. We enter the shop. It is dusty, Dickensian, and a pale, thin-faced clerk greets us with a superciliousness that parodies itself. Mariam asks to see the doorknobs. He says, "You know they are very dear." Mariam ignores him. She must be used to this, I think. I'm not. With a sigh, he goes into the stockroom and brings out one of them. "Yes, that's the one," Mariam says. "How many of them do you want? One or two? They are a hundred pounds each." Mariam pauses, dramatically, acting, I know, as though she is trying to squirm out of the shop without embarrassment. The clerk is enjoying himself. Finally she says, "Yes, I need fifty-five. When will they be ready?" Instantly, the clerk becomes apologetically obsequious. I am disgusted, but Mariam seems to have enjoyed the encounter. She has changed, I think.

The next day we go to parents' day at a girls' school in the country—I don't remember the name—where one of Mariam's nieces is studying. I notice that all the cars are black, either

Rolls-Royces, Bentleys, or Morris Minors, except for a robin's egg blue convertible. The owner of the convertible and his wife are ignored. I'm told he is a hairdresser, Vidal Sassoon. During an afternoon performance of an excerpt from *The Importance of Being Earnest*, a bee circles around and around one of the mothers' hats. It is straw with flowers tucked in the hatband. I try not to laugh. I catch Mrs. Sassoon's eye. She is also trying not to laugh. Several mothers, not the fathers, look at us disapprovingly. I feel, she must feel, a displaced camaraderie.

We are back in London. I am exhausted, jet-lagged, but Mariam insists that we have dinner together. She says she wants to celebrate but does not tell me what. I think it is just our being together, but I'm wrong. She tells me that her grandfather has invited me to Addis. We could meet in Rome in a few weeks when her classes are over and fly from there. She knows I am planning to spend the summer in Florence. I am excited. I know that Haile Selassie remembers my great-uncle.

BOTH SIDES of my family were connected to the Italian invasion of Ethiopia in 1935. Earlier that year, my father, the man who was to become my godfather, and several other Italian doctors were approached by an Italian envoy, who asked for their support of the invasion. My father refused. My godfather accepted and led, according to my mother, the storming of the Imperial Palace. This seems odd, since he was a doctor. He was a Fascist; he made me read *Mein Kampf* in his study and quizzed me on it. I have often wondered why my father and mother asked him to be my godfather. Was my father more in sympathy with the Fascists than I had assumed? Or was he able to separate politics from friendship? Or was my mother right when she said that he had

stayed in the United States not because he was opposed to Musso-
lini, but because of a love affair? What I do know is that my godfather returned to the United States a lot wealthier than when he
had left, and after the war he moved into an enormous apartment
in the Parioli in Rome, where he was in quest of a titled husband
for his daughter. His wife was a devoted monarchist. My mother
couldn't stand them but insisted I stay with them when I was in
Rome the summer she returned to America. That was when he
made me read *Mein Kampf.*

My maternal great-uncle was one of those family figures who,
even before they die, turn into family legends. He died before I
was born. My father, who had not known him, never mentioned
him, but my mother and grandmother would regale my sister
and me with stories. He was an enormously wealthy man, an
eccentric, who hated lawyers, never trusted doctors, and loved
to philosophize. Early on Christmas mornings he would fill his
Rolls-Royce with baskets of food and leave them on the stoops of
the poor. He was an easy mark. Once he went into a little jewelry
store to have his watchband changed and left an hour later with
a new watchband and more than thirty wedding rings, which
he gave to "the girls" in the office when he heard they were getting married. Apparently, he had accepted the jeweler's story of
imminent bankruptcy and had bought the rings to save him from
it. After he died, a few of the rings were found in his safe-deposit
box. He was, despite his wealth, an ardent admirer of the Soviet
Union. When he was finally able to obtain a Soviet visa, in the
early thirties, he filled his car—another Rolls—to the roof with
soap, having heard that there was a shortage of soap in Russia.
His soap was impounded at the border, and he was then given a
motorized escort to Moscow. The authorities didn't know what
to do with him. He was furious—totally disillusioned with the

Soviet Union—and took the first train to Berlin, telling his chauffeur to make sure he got all of the soap back before driving out. I don't know whether the chauffeur was able to or not.

Family stories such as these are boring to everyone but family members and even to them after a series of repetition. They are a string of anecdotes, tied together, like the events in a picaresque novel, by a protagonist, a cardboard character, who never seems to deepen with experience. Unless they are of some historical importance, they are forgotten with the passage of generations and become empty links in a genealogy, if anyone bothers to construct one.

Though my great-uncle may have been disillusioned by the Soviet Union, he remained a staunch opponent of Fascism and bequeathed ambulances and hundreds of thousands of dollars' worth of medical supplies to Haile Selassie's army. He wrote his will on the way to the operating room. His appendix had ruptured because, mistrusting doctors, he refused medical help until it was too late. Two illiterate orderlies who were pushing the gurney into the operating room witnessed the will. They remembered only his gift to the Ethiopians. After the will was contested again and again, the lawyers, who benefited from it, received the bulk of the estate. I told Mariam about my great-uncle when we were still at school. She told her grandfather, who remembered the gift. She had called him and said I was in London, and he invited me to the palace.

I WAS puzzled. Mariam was well-known in London. She always carried several five-pound notes to pay off the paparazzi who occasionally tried to photograph her in compromising company. It had happened at a club we went to. She didn't want her grandfather to know about the men she was seeing. I don't think that the paparazzi were interested in selling her picture to the tabloids, who also wouldn't have been much interested, since the Duchess of Argyll was providing them with more scandal than they could print. They were simply blackmailing her.

I am exhausted. I have no idea what to say to Mariam's English friends. She insisted I meet them, but I don't understand what they are saying or whom they are talking about. I don't like them. They speak cockney — Mariam tells me it's called "mockney" — but all of them seem to be lord this or that. They play with their titles as they play with their language. I'm the Yank. I'm the boor. They're right. I am a total boor. Mariam sees me as one. I have disappointed her. I want to leave. I insist that we leave. She doesn't have to leave. She shrugs her shoulders apologetically. We leave. I drop her off at the embassy, where she has been staying. She doesn't say a word, not even goodbye. She knows I am leaving the next day. She sends me a postcard from Majorca. She has gone there with one of her lords. There is something final about that postcard. I know I will not meet her in Rome. I will not go to Ethiopia. I'll never see her again, and I don't care. Yes, she has changed.

I'm wrong. Mariam writes to me a year later. She is in New York, studying international relations at Columbia. "When can we meet?" she asks, as though nothing has happened. "I've missed you. I lost your address so I couldn't arrange to meet you in Rome." She's forgotten the postcard she sent me. She is beginning to remind me of Anny, Roquentin's capricious mistress, in *La Nausée*. I wrote my senior thesis on Jean-Paul Sartre's theory of the imagination.

We do meet many times; that is, until Mariam is ordered back to Addis. She is again the Mariam I knew. Everywhere we go people look at us. They are curious. There are no mixed couples, at least not in the places we go. New York was different then. Children surround our table in a restaurant in Chinatown. One of them, who sucks a spoon, reminds me of the kids in a Campbell's Soup ad. Their parents allow them to gawk. Mariam is so annoyed, so amused, that leaning over the table, her left breast presses into a little round bowl of mustard. The children break out laughing. She does, too. This would never have happened in Geneva or London. There we were ignored. Still, she likes New York. She is fascinated by Americans' racism and by their open curiosity. They are always asking her where she comes from; they know she must be special, for why, otherwise, would she be in Chinatown or anywhere else with a white man?

We are driving through Central Park from a fancy Harlem bar, where we have just managed to escape a brawl. We had thought it was a jazz club. There we would have been accepted. A group of drunken men had been talking about us—about my stealing one of their women. The barmaid, exquisite, flirtatious, friendly, curious, told us we should leave. We asked her if there was a back exit. She said no. "Don't worry. I can handle it. I'll call a cab. When I signal, you just walk out real cool. They feel the fear." She flirted with the drunks outrageously. Then she nodded at us, and we left, not daring to look back to thank her.

Mariam pleads with the driver to slow down. She is terrified. I've never seen her like this. I don't understand. He isn't driving that fast. She tells him that she was in an accident that summer, and then she whispers to me that she was the only survivor out of nine. I wonder why she hasn't told me, but why should she have?

Why do I seem to live in a surround of death? My father's, my grandfather's, Rudolph's, later Bill my college roommate's—the autopsies. I suddenly remember an accident I saw in Italy. My father was driving. An overstuffed Topolino—"a little mouse," as the Italians used to call the tiniest Fiat—passes us. The car is straining. I can hear it. "They're crazy," my father says. The car disappears ahead of us, but a few minutes later we turn a bend and there it is, slammed against a wall, crushed. My mother orders my sister and me not to look, but I do and see oranges scattered around an open door. I must have seen more.

The taxi driver asks Mariam where she comes from. It's her accent again. She says, "Ethiopia." He says, "You're Hamitic. You're not black." Neither of us says anything. "Noah's curse," he says, ironically. I suppose he thought he was being kind.

In December 1960 Mariam calls to tell me that she is returning to Ethiopia. I am speechless. I have followed the news of the attempted coup by the Imperial Guard—Mariam's grandfather was in Brazil when it happened—but it has failed and will not affect her.

I'm in Mariam's apartment. The movers are coming in the morning, and she leaves for Addis that night. She is drained. She does not want to leave, she says, but she has no choice. Her grandfather is devastated. The leader of the coup was a street child whom he had taken in, educated, and made a member of the Guard. He must have gone mad, she speculates. "I have to go back to support him. He called me and said he needed me. I never heard him say that before, to anyone." "But you'll come back," I say pathetically. "No, I'll be married. It's been arranged. Maybe one day." We hug, and I feel and she feels a magnetism that draws us apart.

We never even wrote to each other.

AT THE end of dinner, I ask Lara how she found out about Mariam's death. She doesn't answer me. She says that after the next coup, in 1974, unlike her relatives, Mariam decided to stay in Ethiopia—to work on an experimental farm. It saved her life. And then the failing government needed a scapegoat. No doubt she meant to say "scapegoats," or I have misheard her. I was focused on Mariam alone. The farmers were ordered to kill her. They couldn't. They liked her. She was the emperor's granddaughter. They gave her a pistol, locked her in a hut, and said they would burn it down in twenty minutes. Lara didn't seem to show any emotion, saying this. Or maybe I was blinded by my own feelings. Mourning is so personal—or maybe the word is selfish. We take possession of the dead in sadness, remembrance, and story, and as we do, we lose them in that sadness, remembrance, and story.

XI.
THE
THOUGHT
OCCURS

I T ' S T H E beginning of my first semester at Harvard. I've finished unloading the car, and I am about to say goodbye to my
mother, who has decided to drive home that day. We've had coffee at the Pamplona—a little café just off Massachusetts Avenue.
We didn't have much to say to each other. My mother was anxious to leave, and I wanted to unpack. In fact we hadn't had much
to say to each other since I returned from Europe at the end of
July. She was happy to see me, more at least than my sister was,
but I couldn't help feeling that she was still angry about my staying on in Geneva, and even envious. She would never admit that
the choice to isolate herself had been hers or even that it was isolation, but her defenses were breaking down, and she was becoming demonstrably bitter. It was sad to see that, and I didn't really
want to see it. It was a burden I didn't want to assume, and I felt
guilty about that, too.

I also felt isolated, but this was because I missed my friends in
Geneva and had lost contact with the ones at home, with whom
I had never been very close. I saw a couple of them, but we no
longer had much in common. We were going our own ways. My
sister wasn't happy at school and had opted out of any possible
friendships. She criticized everyone she met, mirroring—I hated
to see this—my mother's self-isolation. It was she who, unable
to break away, bore the burden of my mother's depression and

continued to do so until my mother died and perhaps until her own death. I spent the rest of that summer reading—Mann, Toynbee, Kafka, *Manon Lescaut*, Russell's *History of Western Philosophy*, and, in the privacy of my room, *The Rosy Crucifixion*, wrapped in brown paper, which Yawalak had sent me from Bangkok. Even at more than eight thousand miles, she was a tease.

Thank God, I have a room of my own at Harvard. It was my main worry. I didn't want to share a room with anyone. My room is in a building off the Yard that has just been converted into a dorm. It's a corner room on the first floor, one of five rooms in what was once an apartment. Despite its two windows it's gloomy and dusty. None of the other students in the suite has arrived. I wonder who they are.

As I shut the trunk of my mother's car, a green MG (or was it a Triumph?) screeches to a halt. The driver asks if this is Harvard. "I've been driving around this damn city for the last hour trying to find the damn place." Seeing my mother, he apologizes. He is out of the twenties: a shock of blond hair falls over his forehead from under a tweed cap. His tie has blown over his shoulder. He looks fashionably unkempt. I half expect him to take out a pocket flask.

"Say, where do I go from here?" he asks, bewildered. He must have realized that he still has to find his room.

I tell him. He moans, drives off, and, remembering that he has not said thank you, turns around and shouts, "Thanks. We'll see each other, I expect. My name's Eaton." He nearly crashes into a parked car.

My mother laughs. "Nothing has changed since I was in college," she says. She seems relieved. I laugh, too, as Eaton drives by again. He's clearly lost. When he sees us, he shakes his head. "Oh, Jesus," he says.

Yes, I'm at Harvard.

I never got to know Eaton. I'm not even sure I ever saw him again. There were over a thousand freshmen. I thought I was one of them; that is, until I was told I was a sophomore, having been given college credit for the British A-level exams I had taken.

Over the course of the afternoon, my apartment-mates arrive. They are an odd lot. One of them is a loner; he has never lived in the United States although he is American. His father is a businessman in South America. I never get to know him. Two of them are football players from Roxbury. One of them drops out after a few months. Charam, the Shah's nephew, shares two of the rooms with Norman. They have both gone to Le Rosey. Norman's father is a Washington lawyer who has represented the Navajo tribe for years. "The only thing he did for us was to charge us," a Navajo told me years later when I lived on the reservation. Charam's English is, to say the least, limited. We speak French and soon attract a dozen other French speakers who are assigned to Prescott Hall.

Among them was Marcel. He lived in Cuba. Within a week, he seemed to know who everyone was, where they came from, and what their fathers did. Once I caught him looking through my address book. We both laughed. A day or so later, he referred to some of my friends as though he knew them. I liked Marcel, and I still do. He lives in Geneva and, now that he is retired, spends several months in Thailand in the winter. He and his wife play golf. I don't play golf. I don't see any point in spending hours trying to knock a ball into a small hole. I'm too impatient. I don't like fishing either. There is always something else I should be doing. I live under the tyranny of the "should."

Am I being unfair? Why? Marcel is a doting father and grandfather and a loyal friend. Jane and I see him whenever we can. He has never hesitated to help us—or any of his other friends—whenever we need advice and, in Jane's case, background for her European pieces for *The New Yorker*. He has an enormous stock of gossip and possesses more inside information than anyone I know, except for a lawyer in a European branch of one of the big Wall Street law firms who is rumored to work for the CIA.

That "Why?" disturbs me. It has nothing to do with Marcel but with me. When? Then, when I was at Harvard? Or now, as I write? The two moments commingle at times, and separate dramatically at others. Their play reflects the space of what I have written and, more important, an emotional undertow that carries me somewhere I definitely don't want to be. But how do I know that, since I still don't know where I am being carried? This is not casuistry. I think of Magritte's picture of a pipe, labeled *"Ceci n'est pas une pipe."*

I would have felt lost were it not for Marcel, Charam, Miquel (who lived in another dorm, next to Prescott Hall, where Spanish was the lingua franca), and Mitchell, Marcel's roommate, whom everyone in the dorm knew because he woke up screaming several nights in a row. He was Polish. His parents had sent him to live with a peasant family when he was a baby. They were in the Resistance. Unlike most Polish Jews, they spoke Polish without a Yiddish accent and served as couriers throughout the war. When it was over, they—and Mitchell—immigrated to Sweden and then to the United States. He wrote about it in *The New Yorker*. He married Yawalak.

IT IS Thursday afternoon. Marcel and I have gone to tea at Raphael Demos's home. Professor Demos has taught the introduction to philosophy for decades. His specialty is Plato. He is one of the few professors who hold an open house each week. Mrs. Demos serves delicious cucumber and cream cheese sandwiches. The sandwiches are a special draw, given the food served at the Freshman Union. Professor Demos was a kind man, a teacher, whom I came to admire over the years. I was horrified to read Bertrand Russell's dismissal of him in his *Autobiography*: "He worked hard, and had considerable ability. In the course of nature he ultimately *became* a professor. His intellect was not free of the usual limitations." Demos would have been hurt, had he read it, but he died before the *Autobiography* was published. Russell had been his teacher, and Demos often talked about him with affectionate admiration. Russell's superciliousness reminded me of Mariam's mockney-speaking lords.

Paul Grice, the Oxford philosopher who is visiting Harvard this year, is at the Demoses'. I have no idea who he is, nor do I know anything about his philosophy — or that of any of his English colleagues. He describes the seminar he will be giving on causality. I ask him what the difference is between the "cause for" and the "reason for" doing something. He immediately turns the question back to me and goes on pushing me, until, exhausted, I reach a logical high I have never before had. It is my first experience of an Oxford tutorial. The other guests must have been fascinated, since none of them interrupted us. I've no idea, of course, that by giving examples of how the words are used in made-up sentences and conversations, I'm doing British analytic philosophy. Instead, I am reminded of the discussions we had about our weekly paraphrases in Mme Briquet's English class. By the time we leave the Demoses' — we have all overstayed our welcome — the dining hall has closed. Marcel and I and two women who were at the Demoses' with us go to dinner

at an awful Chinese restaurant. One of the women is a ridiculously mannered snob from Philadelphia, and the other is Julie
Martin, who, years later, will introduce me to Jane, when I am in
graduate school at Columbia.

The next day I have to meet the senior tutor in the philosophy department, Rogers Albritton, to arrange for a tutorial. As
a sophomore, I have to pick a major. I have chosen philosophy
without much thought, and this involves finding a tutor. Albritton asks me what sort of philosophy I'm interested in, and when I
say existentialism, I can see a look of disapproval and add "cause
and reasons for." "Of course," he says, "they don't have much to
do with existentialism." "I know," I say without knowing. "I'm
just interested —" Albritton interrupts: "Were you at Professor
Demos's yesterday?" When I say yes, he tells me that they'd discussed the difference between cause and reason that morning in
Grice's seminar. Grice had mentioned our discussion. I am surprised. I didn't think of it as anything more than a word game,
certainly not serious philosophy.

Albritton says he will be my tutor. I am pleased. I liked him
immediately. He is, it turns out, an immensely generous man.
We meet each week for one or two hours. The readings are
in analytic philosophy, logical positivism, and Wittgenstein.
I'm fascinated but miss the passion I've always associated with
"real" philosophy. Throughout the year, we argue about the
degree to which philosophical views are embedded in specific
languages. I insist they are. Albritton is skeptical. At the end
of the year, as if pulling a rabbit out of a hat, he lends me pho-
tostats (there were no Xeroxes in those days) of essays by the
linguist Benjamin Lee Whorf that demonstrated (or at least I
thought they did) how the Hopi language affected perception
and worldview. I have often wondered whether Albritton had

planned all along to lend me Whorf's papers. They have had a lasting influence on me.

THE CLASSROOM at the Graduate Center where I am about to teach is still filled with students asking their professor questions. He looks familiar. I ask one of the students who he is. He tells me, Rogers Albritton. I see that Albritton is now bloated and old. I want to introduce myself. I hesitate. Finally, as he leaves the classroom, I do. He looks at me. Clearly, he does not remember me. I am devastated. He—the way he looked when he was my tutor—is vivid in my memory. I can still recall word for word some of our conversations. I forget that I, too, have aged. It is thirty years since we saw each other for the last time and now I am memory-shorn, stripped of the comfort memories provide me. I feel an intense loneliness and give a boring class. *Who will remember me? And how?* I keep asking myself as I look at the students. They seem so far away, lost somewhere in my elsewhere.

Will anyone I am writing about remember me, remember what we said to each other? Remember the way it was, *wie es eigentlich gewesen*, as the German historian Leopold von Ranke formulated the goal of history? Today, Ranke's quest seems naive—an impossible goal. And yet when I write, as skeptical as I am, I feel a strong desire to get it right. It is, I suppose, a rather selfish desire—to confirm my view of the past, my past, the support that that past gives me. And yet I fear the entrapment of the past, the slippage into fiction. It seems so easy. I also know that we would not know fiction if it were not for our grasp of the real. But is the real the same as nonfiction? I don't think so, for nonfiction also relies on a "real" that, inevitably, is distinct from it. The circularity is exquisite.

But isn't this reflection nothing more than a way of protecting myself from your view, whomever you are, of what happened?

I do know that without the intellectual life I had at Harvard, I might have dropped out. Yes, I had my friends, companions really, "pals," as one of my French friends, Edgar, called them, and most of the time they kept me from thinking too much about myself. But were they really friends? What, in fact, is a friend? None of them were as close as were Mariam, Rudolph, Arturo, Yawalak, and Udo.

Have I mentioned Udo? He was older than I and was studying philosophy in Paris. Noi introduced us. I was more his friend than he mine. Our relationship centered on Noi. He was infatuated with her, and that infatuation—I can't really call it passion—drained him. He was delicate and gave the impression of being overbred, and, coming from the *vieille noblesse*, he probably was. He wrote me two or three times a week from Paris, asking about Noi. He didn't ask me to spy on her. Rather, he seemed to depend on me as someone to whom he could express the pain his infatuation caused him and in which he indulged himself. I was in an awkward position. I knew that Noi didn't share the intensity of his feelings and showed no particular loyalty to him. I couldn't tell him this directly. It would have been too hurtful. I did my best, though, to convey it to him indirectly, but he never recognized what I was trying to tell him—never wanted to recognize it.

I visited Udo in Paris while I was still at Ecolint. It was there that I realized how lonely he was. Whatever he felt about Noi, he needed her in fantasy more than in fact, I suspect—to fill the emptiness he felt. I remember going with him to a lecture given by Merleau-Ponty and how surprised I was that he didn't seem to know any of the other students. We had lunch at the Balzar. It wasn't a student hangout, but the waiters knew him. His letters continued after my return to America. Noi was at Boston University, and I saw her quite often. She simply refused to understand parietal hours and would sneak into my room whenever she was in Cambridge. Once, I was suffering from a high fever. I was nearly delirious. She arrived with orange juice and sandwiches. I must have dozed off, having become the quiet American. I could not have written this to Udo. He wouldn't have understood. Noi returned to Bangkok midyear, and Udo's letters soon stopped. The last ones were about the neurasthenia that he'd decided he had. I never heard from him again.

I didn't feel used. I took a certain voyeuristic pleasure in observing his torment—his inability to reveal himself to me despite his desire to do so. I assumed quite naively that he couldn't find the right words to express his most intimate self. I identified with him. I had the same problem, but I saw mine less in terms of incapacity than as an absence of a sensitive interlocutor. It was a question of contingency I dreaded. At the time, I was taken with what Heidegger called *Geworfenheit*—being thrown into the world. It was one of those concepts such as bad faith, *engagement*, care, and being-for-death that were fashionable in the existential fringes of Harvard's philosophy department. Contingency—that fatal event—could justify just about anything you did or did not do. Potentially everything you did or thought was open to accusations of bad faith. Our psychological understanding blinded us to the ontological conditions of possibility for acting and thinking in bad faith.

No doubt, I am adding a philosophical sophistication to thoughts that I couldn't have had at that point in my young life. It was only when I started to think seriously about myself—actually, when I started conversing with myself—that I was confronted not just with the opacity of the self but with the fact that the core of my self—anybody's self—was unknowable. It wasn't a secret, not even one I kept from myself, for secrets can always be articulated. Otherwise, they would not be secrets. We can name the self, its core, but its contents can be figured only metaphorically and they bear the distortions of that figuration. Lacan refers to the core as a *manque-à-être*, a lack of being. Freud would have understood it in terms of that "unplumbable spot"—the navel—that connects the dream with the unknown. Baudelaire would figure it as a *gouffre*, an *abîme*, an abyss.

> *En haut, en bas, partout la profondeur, la grève,*
> *Le silence, l'espace affreux et captivant...*

> Above, below, everywhere, the depth, the strand,
> The silence, a hideous, captivating space...

> *J'ai peur du sommeil comme on a peur d'un grand trou*
> *Tout plein de vague horreur, menant on ne sait où...*

> I'm afraid of sleep as one is of an enormous hole
> Full of indeterminate horror, leading one knows not where...

Perhaps it would be simplest to relate the core to the impenetrable mystery that creates identity. I image it as a gyre gyring downward.

Why not upward?

DAN AND I were drinking Mosel in a *Weinstube* near the opera house in Frankfurt. It was our retreat—a reminder that there was a world outside the army. It wasn't a student hangout. Those students who frequented it assumed an aristocratic air. They ignored us. Most of them wanted to be seen by the editors and writers who had drinks there. (They reminded me of the young Italian aristocrats who kiss the hands of the women of their presumed class when they meet them, thereby announcing their status and a conservatively noble outlook.) Dan and I talked literature, art, and theater. We talked a lot about the movies. We read journals such as *Filmkritik* that, as philosophically ponderous as their articles were, grounded our discussions. I was not as enthusiastic about them as Dan was, but talking about movies—I refused to use "cinema"—relieved the melancholy Dan affected. That affectation got the best of him. Our conversations usually ended with Dan's collapse of confidence, his sense that he was destined to failure, his sense of impotence, and ultimately his flight from a German student he loved. He couldn't accept her love, for how could any-one love him—a man without a future? I have been using "love," as though Dan used it, but he never did. It would have frightened him. He wasn't romantic enough. He didn't have the requisite energy for love, certainly not for passionate love, or even for utter-ing the word "love." Like Udo, he had diagnosed himself as neur-asthenic—that is, when he didn't think of himself as melancholic. He understood himself, that neurasthenia, in racialist terms. His energy—what little he had—came from his Jewish mother and was quashed by his father's Calvinism. He substituted hereditary taint for original sin and unredeemable inadequacy for guilt.

I never quite knew what Dan wanted from me. Nor did I know what I wanted from him. He didn't seem particularly interested in me. I never told him about Mariam or Monika. He couldn't laugh at himself, as Mariam had. He did not have Monika's fresh-ness. He did not have Udo's withered passion or Rudolph's and Arturo's exaggerated exuberance. What self-irony he had focused so obsessively on his inadequacy that it canceled itself out.

Before he left Germany, Dan introduced me to the student from whom he had fled. We met one afternoon in Darmstadt. Or was it Mainz? She came with two fellow students, supposedly for me to meet but, in fact, as protection from Dan's self-pity. She was a rosy-cheeked, somewhat overweight, uninspiring but energetic woman who spent much of the afternoon talking about the "true" stories she and several other (male) students sold to the *Regenbogenzeitungen* — the scandal sheets — each week. It took them a couple of hours to earn enough pocket money for the four of them. It was a laugh. She had little interest in Dan. I saw no signs of past affection. *Eines kleinbürgerlichen Fräulein.*

Why did I take an interest in Dan? In Udo? Udo imposed himself on me. Dan offered me escape from my buddies. But there was something more: a determination to know somebody from the inside. I wanted assurance that there were men who shared my sensitivity, my self-doubt. I suppose I identified those feelings with femininity, or rather with a lack of manliness. There is a difference. But there was something else I wanted, though I wasn't conscious of it then: the occasion to show strength — to play the man — by preserving an observational distance, or, more accurately, by standing aloof while showing care, or, still more accurately, by assuming power, through them, over myself.

Still, I felt I was missing something essential, which I associated with my father's death. But even then, the association seemed mechanical. What would my father have given me? What could he have given me? What his death gave me was simply the sense that I had missed something and therefore would always be missing something. I was looking for that something in others and, paradoxically, trying to destroy it by knowing it. I wanted to know my self, in an act of consummate bad faith, through the unreachable depth of the other. I wanted a mirror that did not simply mimic me as I moved, grimacing, and winked at myself but one that, quickened in the life of the other, resisted me—my mimicry. Was this the depth I wanted? Or was it parasitism? Of course, I didn't realize then that "depth" was a metaphor and that, as with all metaphors, its object (if metaphors have an object) could never be reached, its intention never achieved. They camouflage the ungraspable and at times simply the inadmissible.

I did not find anyone at Harvard whom I came to know with that longed-for depth. No, that is not quite true. There was Jim Bucciarelli, one of the most patient men I knew, deep, tolerant, a Catholic, haunted by his older brother, who became an Opus Dei priest. Although Jim sometimes asked me to go to church with him, he never insisted. I went only once, to hear Cardinal Cushing speak about Saint Thomas Aquinas. I was disappointed but noticed that when the cardinal began to speak, sunrays suddenly illuminated the saint's image on one of the stained glass windows in the church. *By design*, I thought, *clever, expectable*. Jim hadn't noticed it. Our listening in the dark, as we often did, to the *Saint Matthew Passion* did create a spiritual yearning in me, a sense of the ungraspable—of an infinite absence, as non-being must be. But that yearning did not last. Jim had a quiet, restrained passion, if that is possible, that I cannot help thinking burned so deeply in him that he suffered, soon after he graduated, from a devastating neurological disorder and died in Hawaii. He had lost the ability to write—to speak, to think, as I had known him to do when we spent long nights talking about Kierkegaard, Jim's favorite philosopher, and Heidegger, mine.

My friends at Ecolint, as troubled as many of them were, as in question as their identity was, had a sense of style they didn't question. They may have been mannered, but their mannerism was theirs. They didn't pretend. At least that's how I saw them then. Aside from those of my Harvard classmates who were so wedded to convention (whatever that convention was) that they never questioned who they were or what they intended to do in life, most of them didn't have an assured style. They always seemed to be looking for one, and whenever they thought they'd found it, they tried it on—to often ridiculous extremes—until it collapsed or gave way seriatim to another. Some, I remember, aped what they thought was the style of the Oxford or Cambridge scholar. They wore round horn-rimmed glasses, tweeds, some bespoke from Savile Row, and smoked pipes, demonstrating their depth of thought in long puffs of smoke. There were others—the bohemians—who saw themselves as writers, poets, playwrights, actors, or composers. They were the existentialists, the proverbially anguished or creatively sensitive. There were the playboys, the jet-setters, the "gentlemen," a lot of them from Saint Paul's School, who joined the Porc—the Porcellian Club—sported thin umbrellas with bone handles, and aspired to a career at the Morgan bank or one of the Wall Street law firms; the would-be journalists at *The Harvard Crimson*, many of whom became well-known reporters and editors; the jocks who just managed to pass a gut course, usually in social relations; and the premeds, who had a repertoire of styles that could be reduced to one: getting into a good med school. They always laid the accent on "med." There were those with conventional—that is, Republican or Democratic—political ambitions and a couple of dozen members of the socialist union, who were generally ignored. There were also the slackers, as they would be called today, the defeatists, the nerds. And there were the regionalists, who played up their southern accents, their midwestern provincialism, or even their Boston Irish accents. There were almost no blacks and few Asians at Harvard at the time.

Bill came from Amarillo. He was my roommate for two years. His father manufactured tractors. He arrived in a red Buick convertible. His father wanted him to have a *real* car. I never met his father, but from what I could gather he was a tough-minded Texas businessman. I did meet Bill's mother at graduation. Bill had left us alone. She was a steel magnolia—clearly hard as nails. We struggled to find a topic of conversation. It took an embarrassingly long time. After talking about how expensive the East Coast was and, much to my surprise, how rich everyone seemed to be to her, we ended up talking about roses and rose gardens. I knew next to nothing about roses, besides how to pick beetles off them and the few verses I had read of *Le Roman de la Rose*. But I managed to feign an interest. She told me how relieved she and her husband had been when Bill decided to enter the navy's officers' training program in New London. She never asked what my plans were, and I was just as happy she didn't. I was caught between going to law school and going to New London, like Bill.

If you had met Bill, you would never have thought he was from Texas. He spoke with a slight English accent, though he had never been abroad. (I did detect a slight Texas drawl when he was with his mother.) He bought his clothes at Brooks Brothers, studied English, and eventually joined *The Harvard Advocate*, the college literary magazine, as I did after him. We didn't have much in common, and I'm not even sure that he liked me, but I think both of us preferred it that way. Bill didn't have many friends. He was a voracious, nonstop reader. I remember his reading *War and Peace* in one sitting that must have lasted for more than a day. He never left his chair; he never stopped to eat. I couldn't persuade him to stop, but he did eat a roast beef sandwich I brought him from Elsie's. (Elsie's was just across the street from Lowell House, where we lived, and was known for its roast beef and caviar and cream cheese sandwiches.) He also read *The Canter-bury Tales* nonstop. He never talked about what he read. I have no idea what his grades were, but I do know that he was almost suspended after missing three exams in his junior year. It wasn't that he was unprepared. He was. He simply slept through them in spite of his three alarm clocks ringing. I couldn't wake him. When he received a third warning letter, he resigned himself to leaving, despite my insistence, and that of his friends, that he explain what had happened. He refused, and, without his know-ing it, I told Mr. Perkins, the house master, who called Bill in and must have intervened. Bill never said a word about the meeting.

I don't mean to imply that Bill was incompetent. He wasn't, but he sometimes seemed oblivious to the consequences of what he did or didn't do. He discovered the house secretary's birthday and sent her a dozen roses. He had no ulterior motive. It was just the southern-gentleman thing to do. No one else I knew had ever done this. He was genuinely surprised when we were given the best suite in Lowell House the following year. It was the house secretary who assigned rooms. In his own way, Bill was true to his chosen style.

Poor, poor Bill. What a fool, what a coward, you were. I am suddenly overcome with a furor I didn't know I had—not anger, that I knew I was capable of, but an ontological furor at his betrayal of life. That's not quite right. I would not feel it, I am quite sure, if Bill had committed suicide, but he didn't.

I am driving to Princeton, where I am teaching. I suffer a delayed reaction. I snapped out of a kind of disregard for death. A week or two earlier, I had learned from a former classmate that Bill had died. He was found dead at a drinking fountain in the YMCA at Scollay Square, in Boston. I had heard nothing from Bill in years. One of our classmates told me that while Bill was in the navy, he taught himself Chinese, at first as a gesture of futility and then with fascination, and went on to get a PhD in Chinese and was hired by Ohio State. The first year he lived near the campus, and then he bought a house in the country. By the third year, he had disconnected his telephone so the department couldn't reach him. Needless to say, his contract was not renewed. He moved back to Cambridge, spent all his time in the library, and lived on his diminishing savings and then on his capital. His parents' company had gone belly-up. His father, I believe, had died. His mother was left with her Social Security checks, and Bill became one of those creeps who hung around Harvard Square, drinking watered coffee all night at Hayes-Bickford across from the Yard on Mass Avenue. Unlike the other hangers-on, I am sure he did not approach the students there. Finally, with practically nothing to live on, he moved to a Y in one of Boston's worst neighborhoods, rarely talking to anybody there, except to accuse them of spying on him. He stopped eating, refused to see a doctor—they all worked for the CIA—and died of blood poisoning from an abscessed tooth. The doctor who performed the autopsy said he must have been in unbearable pain for weeks.

When I heard this, I became stone cold. Bill's death was simply a fact, nothing more. I didn't even try to imagine why he had given up so completely. I didn't ask myself if I had ever seen any signs of breakdown. And then, suddenly, in the car on my way to Princeton, I became furious. I was disgusted by Bill's cowardice. "If you want to die, kill yourself," I shouted several times. I could think of no signs of paranoia. The sleep? Who knows? He couldn't wake up. He didn't want to wake up. I imagine him sitting on his bed in the Y, staring at, reading at first, a Chinese manuscript on browning paper, and then seeing blurred characters that became more and more meaningless as his pain increased, until they came to symbolize coded messages that he could not decode, or could decode but knew at some level that he hadn't got it right and never would—that they meant nothing at all.

I remember little of that day in Princeton other than, "Professor Crapanzano, are you all right?" I had lost myself in an erotic delirium, in the middle of a tutorial with a student whose beauty I had never noticed before and never did again. "Yes, yes, I'm okay. It's nothing. It's that I just learned that my college roommate has died." "Nothing?" she says, horrified. "No, that's not what I meant. I'm in shock, I guess." "Do you want me to leave?" she asked. "We can continue next week." "No, let's finish up today. We have a lot to cover." We did.

Why do I associate friendship with death?

I think of Montaigne's friendship with La Boétie. He idealized friendship. He distinguished a friend from an acquaintance. We use "friend" so promiscuously today that we can no longer speak of an "acquaintance" without suggesting a disapproving distance. In the singular friendship Montaigne was talking about, "souls are mingled and confounded in so universal a blending that they efface the seam which joins them together so that it cannot be found." Is this what I mean by a friend? Is this what I have wanted? I think not. I am too skeptical—an odd observation, given Montaigne's skepticism—to think such a friendship is possible. Can it occur only in retrospect, after the friend's death, as perhaps I am refiguring my relationship with Mariam? Does mourning—the nostalgia, the missing, the accompanying regret—elevate friendship to impossible heights? Is friendship, is love, constituted on a longing for the impossible, for what will inevitably end? Montaigne can only attribute his friendship to La Boétie to "some inexplicable destiny."

But, of course, as Aristotle said, we can continue to love our beloved after his or her surcease, which the beloved can no longer do. We can love the inanimate, which cannot reciprocate. Is this why the corpse is so terrifying before it is revivified in memory? Aristotle privileges the lover—loving—over the beloved. The asymmetry that fuels friendship rests on the fact that we can love—we can be friends—with those who do not know that we love them. Loneliness is intolerable under such circumstances. We demand the love—the friendship of the other—through expressing our love (if we dare), for there is always the risk that the revelation of our love will not be reciprocated. It places a burden on the other that, if not immediately accepted, will nullify the possibility of our being loved in return.

We are caught between the timelessness of lovers gazing into each other's eyes and the absurdly short time of hope.

I remember evenings wandering around the Square as if I were a ghostly presence watching other ghostly presences, all of us returning from the library. I had been lonely wandering around Europe by myself, but then I took pleasure in one or another of the characters I had invented for myself, in my anonymity, in the mystery I stupidly imagined I produced. At Harvard I may have been anonymous, but I could no longer create a fulfilling character. Was this growing up? Or was I playing at that, too?

I am invited to a Waltz Evening. A friend of a friend, whom I know only by sight, is driving me. He's helping me with my bow tie. I'm nervous, since I'm a terrible dancer. I don't like cotillions, coming-out parties, or—socially less pretentious—mixers. They're all an artifice, masking the crudest of goals: not sex but connection, not connection but marriage, not marriage but status-determining affiliation and financial benefit. Today, less prone to euphemism, we say networking. And, of course, said then, as now, gold digging. My friend's friend—I can't remember his name — says to me as we walk to his car, "You know, you don't say your name with passion." He repeats it several times with a resonant, albeit incorrect, Italian accent. "You've got to play the role." I don't say anything. He goes on talking about style, my style, his style. I don't think much of it. He knows more about me than I know about him.

What was my style? What were my styles? Was I like everyone else at Harvard? Certainly I was suffering from a lack of confidence. I think of it as an *effritement*. "Erosion" is too strong a word. I saw bravado all over, as well as compensatory shrinkage. Was this the secondary effect of an undergraduate education? Or was it its primary effect? Was scholarship only a cover for pernicious but successful domestication? The thought occurs. Of course, it is not. But the thought lingers.

XII.

DEFLECTIONS

I JUST finished reading Louis Begley's *Memories of a Marriage*. It has led me to reconsider my sense that my classmates lacked a confident personal style. Louis was at Harvard a few years before me. His portrait of his classmates, mediated both by his characters and by his authorial stance, do seem to have a confidence in themselves and their social aspirations, which I recognize but feel was fraying among many of the students I knew. It is certainly true that there were (and no doubt still are) many students who were upwardly mobile and accepted uncritically the values and attitudes of the class they aspired to; that is, as they understood and often misunderstood them with telling, at times comic, results. There were, needless to say, watchdogs who never seemed to miss a faux pas (as they perceived or misperceived it) and could be quite malicious. Self-irony, real or feigned, was one of the few ways to escape their vigilance. I have the impression that the most determined, at least the most obviously determined, of them were from the East Coast, but I may be wrong. I did not know many students from the Midwest, West, or South. Bill was the exception.

My class was at Harvard at the tail end of the fifties. I can't say that we all felt the winds of change. We had to wear ties and jackets to the dining halls, and we read Kerouac. A few played, but only played, the beatnik. There must have been exceptions, but I didn't know them.

Mason was a would-be poet. He had not succeeded in publishing any of his poems, nor had any of my most literary friends, but, unlike them, Mason wanted to be heard. He arranged to read his work in a little café somewhere in Boston where there were weekly poetry readings. Mason was serious. How serious, his roommates did not realize. They were always teasing him, and he responded by teasing himself before they could. He did not play the clown or the self-reflective comedian. He was too serious for that. About ten of his friends went to hear him. Our arrival was, I imagine, seen as an invasion. Jeremy, whose father was a famous Irish playwright, mocked the beat poets who read before Mason in so loud a voice that I left his table and settled in the back of the room. Mason's poems were no better than those of the other poets. The following day a couple of his friends decided to mock the poems they had heard, including Mason's, and read them at the café. I refused to have anything to do with the project. I thought it was snotty and mean. Evidently their reading went better than they had expected. They were taken seriously and amused us the next day by making fun of the regulars who could not recognize the mockery. It was all a joke—a double, a treble joke. But was it? I'm not sure that Mason ever wrote another line of poetry after that. Nor did any of them, all aspiring writers, ever publish anything, as far as I know. Mockery was so much easier.

I met Evelyn at a mixer at Pine Manor, a junior college near Wellesley. I invited her to a friend's party at a beach house in an unfashionable suburb of Boston. I hardly knew her. She was from somewhere in the South, sly, saucy when it suited her, ironically flirtatious, and the sexiest woman I met in college. The party was boring. "So pretentious," she said as the two of us walked along the beach. "Is there a man among you?" she asked, and then kissed me. "And the women..." Her critique was devastating but accurate. "No wonder you're all virgins." We kissed again. "I didn't mean you," she laughed. I had the feeling she was performing a well-rehearsed script, and I told her so. She smiled. My friends made fun of me. "A Pine Manor girl!" I wanted to defend her, but really all I knew about her was her body, and I didn't want to get into that. My friends—I am beginning to wonder why I thought of them as friends—couldn't resist taunting her when she visited me the next week. I admired the way she handled Jeremy, who was the cattiest of them, by flirting with him in so provocative a manner that he turned red and then asking him in "the sweetest voice possible" what was the matter as she stroked his neck. He was speechless. We took refuge in literary gossip. Jeremy, having regained his voice, began to explain our references, as if she couldn't possibly have known them. I looked at her apologetically, and she whispered in my ear—in an exaggerated southern accent—that she was having a wonderful time. I knew she hadn't finished with Jeremy, or any of us. The conversation became more and more pretentious, Jeremy more and more malicious. He began making fun of someone I didn't know whose short story *The New Yorker* had rejected. He recited a few of the worst lines. Everyone laughed except Evelyn. She announced that she liked what she had heard and asked Jeremy if *he* had ever published anything. Without answering, he retorted, "And you?" "As a matter of fact, I spent the morning going over the galleys of a story I wrote for *The Atlantic*." The interminable silence that followed was finally broken when we all laughed at Jeremy. Evelyn got up, smiled at everyone, and said to me, "Let's go to your room."

As I was leaving I heard Jeremy say, "I didn't know *The Atlantic* published bodice rippers." I am being anachronistic. That expression only came into use in the 1980s. Jeremy must have said "true romances" or something like that.

Evelyn was no Cliffy. You—or at least I—hesitated to talk to a Cliffy, even if she was in your class, without being introduced.

A snub was her protection, flirtatious and distancing, preserving a reputation and creating a persona that may have been less desired than forced upon her. There were, of course, exceptions. Gossip prevailed. We all knew who was fast. Those men (as we were called) who didn't have a girlfriend (as she would have been called) were the most dismissive. Obviously, behind all this pretense, gossip, and scorn was a vulgar eroticism and a considerable amount of fantasy fucking. I remember taking a Harvard charter back from Europe. You could literally feel the heat that welled up from behind the brown paper covers of Henry Miller's *Sexus*, *Plexus*, and *Nexus*, which everyone seemed to be reading. (Miller's works were still censored.) I remember the couple sitting across the aisle from me, clearly so content with their summer fling (or was it a romance?) that they required no literary prostheses. What a relief.

I don't mean to imply that there wasn't kinky or even brutal sex around. Owen, for one, announced that he wanted to lose his virginity by sleeping with a dwarf and did. He had read somewhere that dwarfs were oversexed. Then there was Charam, who treated every woman he met as an inevitable lay. He even managed to seduce a telephone operator whom he had met calling information. He was no doubt the most experienced in the class. The Shah's palace, as he depicted it, was as filled with available ("fuckable") women as any brothel. And there were those men who disappeared in the shadows along the Charles River at night. Did they know whom they were meeting? Did they want to know?

When I arrived at Harvard, a feebleminded schoolgirl used to hang around Prescott Hall, offering herself to everyone in sight, until she was taken away by a social worker. A few men had even slept with her. You could tell who they were by their shame-filled eyes. They were ostracized, but I'm not at all sure that anyone in Prescott Hall ever reported them. In my senior year, the woman everyone knew as the "nympho," the wife of a visiting professor, prowled the Square and the Yard and would sleep with any man she met just about anywhere she could. (The fifties' strict parietal hours severely limited her access to any of the houses or freshman dorms.) We dismissed her as a manicurist and made fun of her husband. It was generally assumed that availability was correlated with class, usually determined by the rank of the college a girl went to, and she was treated accordingly.

I remember the shock a friend of mine produced by bringing a townie he had picked up to dinner at Eliot House; that is, until that shock was replaced by genuine puzzlement when everyone realized that he was in love with her. Despite her Boston-Irish accent and working-class dress, she had a natural refinement that many of the most sought-after Cliffies lacked. Needless to say, the do-gooders worried about my friend. What would she do to his future? They barraged him with advice some with rumors of her infidelity and promiscuity, others with her "common" looks — and eventually he dropped her. No one ever thought about her. It was a dreadful time.

Where did I stand?

I was in the midst, part in, part out, of what I was observing, feigning participation some of the time, carried away at other times, never really sure-footed but judgmental.

I'm in the school playground. I'm proud. I've finally managed to hang from my knees on the jungle gym. Walter spits in my eye while I am still dangling. Walter is a bully. He hates me. I can still see his red hair, his orange freckles, his sniffling nostrils, and his wide-wale brown corduroy pants (ripped at the knee) with a clarity that belies nearly seventy years. I thud to the ground and crawl from under the jungle gym, hitting my head on one of the bars. I try to rub away his spit but can't until I begin to cry and my tears wash the slime away. A teacher picks me up and wipes my face with her handkerchief. It is perfumed. She tells me to go to the boys' room and wash my face. When I come out, I watch the kids. Walter is hanging from the top bar. I hope he falls, but he doesn't.

I don't like standing apart. But I always do, except when Freddy and Bob and I sneak into the woods behind the playground to look for a copperhead that Freddy says—but Bob and I don't believe—he saw in the brook that flows past the school. Of course, I am older then—older than when my father used to stop his car in front of the school playground and wave at me. He often did. I would wave back, embarrassed. I didn't want him to see me standing apart. My mother had told me about a boy in a story she had read who always watched his classmates from afar. He became a misfit or a murderer. I don't remember. I have no idea why she told me this story. She sometimes forgot how old I was. But there must be more to it than that.

How can we attribute intention or motives to other people? How do we know? What evidence do we ever have for our attributions? Sometimes we take their word for why they are doing what they do. But why should we take their word? Aren't we being naive? Isn't it possible that their words are chosen to hide their real intentions? But, then again, why shouldn't we take those words literally? Do we ever really know our own intentions?

It is my last class in a seminar on the interpretation of life histories I have been teaching at the University of Paris in Nanterre. It is one of the most memorable classes I have ever taught. One student from the French Caribbean, whom I'll call Nicolette, loves to play, often in an exaggerated and at times irritating way, the part of the poor immigrant victim of colonialism. She has asked to give the last class presentation. I agreed—reluctantly, since I suspected she was up to something. I wasn't sure she would even turn up for the class. She arrived so late that I'd begun to give a lecture I had prepared in case she didn't come.

Nicolette is dressed in a miniskirt and an exceptionally tight sweater. Without apologizing, she crawls under one of the tables that form a closed square and then stands in the middle and peers at us, looking as sexy as possible, embarrassing everyone in the class, including me. Stretching out her leg—tracing a run in its stocking—she announces that she is going to talk about stockings. "Vous savez, les bas," she says, plucking the stocking. She tells us that because she had to attend an inferior colonial school, she failed the math section of the bac and had to repeat the exam in the fall. She and another student, also from the Caribbean, decided to study together, but being poor they couldn't afford to go to a café. "So we go to Le Père Lachaise, you know, the cemetery, to study. Each day, an old man walks back and forth in front of us. We're used to his type. Then one day he says, 'You have a run in your stocking.' 'What do you expect?' we shoot back. 'We're poor students. Stockings cost a lot of money.' The old man walks off and then turns around and says that he'll give us new stockings in exchange for ones with runs in them. Well, what do you expect? We agree. The next day we come back, and there he is with new stockings. He takes the ones we give him and thanks us."

Nicolette pauses for a long time and then asks us to explain what happened. Needless to say, the first response is that the old man is a pervert, a fetishist. Nicolette says no. He never made a pass. Then someone says he was just being kind and asks why we see his behavior as pathological. She is corrected by another student, who says that you still have to account for the fact that he wanted stockings with a run. A few other suggestions are made. Nicolette rejects them. We're stymied.

"It's a riddle," Nicolette announces, and goes on to say that interpretation is always about riddles. We try to solve them with what we think we know — with fashionable theories of interpretation. "You know, Lacan, Marx, Barthes, Lévi-Strauss" — the theorists we talked about in the class. She then tells us why the old man exchanged new stockings for ones with runs. He worked in the cemetery, cleaning tombstones. He used stockings to rub or filter the lye or whatever his cleaner was into the stones. Something to that effect. He had funds to purchase stockings. For years, he had been buying new ones, but when he saw Nicolette's stockings, he suddenly realized that stockings with runs would work just as well as new ones. Nicolette concludes dramatically, "It makes you wonder whether any of the interpretations of why people do what they do that we discussed in class are correct. You see, the colonized, people of color like me, look at what the colonizers, people like you, do as riddles. We can laugh." She breaks out laughing, slides out from under one of the tables, and winks. "Got you," she says.

We all laugh and go to a café to celebrate the end of class. I never get a paper from Nicolette. I learn later that she is an actor. I'm not even sure she ever registered for the class.

I leaf through an old copy of Machiavelli's *The Prince*. His cynicism is uncompromising, almost naively so. He asks if a prince should keep his word. The prince, he tells us, must be like a fox in recognizing snares and like a lion in driving off wolves. He should not keep a pledge if it goes against his interest. He always has "legitimate reasons by which to color his bad faith." He should be a "great dissembler." I have always found something refreshing about Machiavelli's pragmatism. The prince's ambitions are undisguised. He is not bothered by conscience. Advocating hypocrisy (when necessary) exposes the moralistic hypocrisy that is current today in America.

We might easily liken Machiavelli's power-mad prince to a psychopath or a sociopath. I have never understood the difference between them. We live in another age. We have another psychology, another mode of interpretation. The philosopher Paul Ricoeur refers to it as a hermeneutics of suspicion. We are always peering under the surface for "real" motives and intentions. We look for them in the depths of the unconscious the way the shaman sought the source of human affliction in his voyage to the underworld. The deep—the unconscious—is a place of adventure, of mystery and danger. We search it the way explorers searched for the source of the Nile, adventurers for the heart of darkest Africa, Dante for the range of human iniquity in the Inferno, or the cosmologist for the origin of the universe—the deepest conceivable moment of time, before time itself...

I am not suggesting that people didn't question motive and intentions in Machiavelli's world. They certainly did. The Florentines were a suspicious people, and not without cause. But behind the baroque plays of power that they engaged in (as the Italian Parliament does today), they looked for dissembled but not unconscious motives. They assumed a transparency of intention; they were not burdened by the belief that, somewhere in the depths of the psyche, there is a black hole about which we have little knowledge, and over which we have even less control. We sometimes forget that the notion of the unconscious was an invention of the late nineteenth century.

Jane and I are watching the Donmar production of *Julius Caesar*, which has an all-female cast. I wasn't sure it would work, but it does beautifully. It's the first time I have seen a production of the play that captured the depth of the characters and yet preserved its dramatic energy. It also is the first time in years that I am so captivated by a piece of theater that I lose all sense of time. Usually my mind wanders—especially since I started writing this book. Words and gestures suddenly remind me of past events that I haven't thought to include. It is only when Cassius, recruiting Brutus for the cabal to murder Caesar, asks him if he can see his face that my mind slips out of the play and recalls what I've been writing. Brutus answers that "the eye sees not itself." Cassius goes on to tell Brutus that "it is very much lamented / That you have no such mirrors as will turn / Your hidden worthiness into your eye, / That you might see your shadow" (act 1, scene 2, ll. 50–60). And a few lines later, as his seduction continues, he offers himself as Brutus's mirror: "I, your glass / Will modestly discover to yourself / That of yourself which you yet know not of" (act 1, scene 2, ll. 68–70). Before I reflect on these words, I am caught up by the play again.

It is only in the middle of the night, when I awake (as usual), that I think of Cassius's words. No, of course, we cannot see our eyes or our face except in reflection, and then do we really see it? In the mirror, the image is reversed, flattened, and glassy, and—perhaps you are like me—I only glance at myself (except when I am shaving, and then I am focused on the razor). I don't like to look at myself any more than I like to look at my photograph. The relationship between you and your mirror image is in your control. You can smile, grimace, stick your tongue out. The only things you can't change (barring face-lifts, facial reconstructions, scarification, tattooing, and hallucinations) are your physical features. They anchor you, your perduring physicality, and yet reveal changes in you as you age that are beyond your control. But it is not the mirror reflection that interests me. It is Cassius's offering to be Brutus's reflection—an assumption of manipulative power (act 1, scene 2, ll. 41–43).

Late that night, I suddenly realize that theories of self-formation that rely on mirroring mask the interplays of power by which we are fashioned. Narcissus may discover himself in his reflection, but that reflection, his fascination with it, can only draw him into extinction. We put into our mirror image what we take from it. We indulge ourselves in a mystification that denies the self-constituting power of the other. Narcissus can hear only, if he hears it at all, his own echo. But, as any hypnotist knows, when a Cassius presumes to be our reflection, we fall under his sway and either surrender to that reflection or resist it as best we can. Narcissistic desire gives way to the power of the other—the not-I, the not-we, but *the* you. If it were that simple! Brutus gives way to Cassius's power, but is his surrender pure? Does he not surrender, however led by Cassius, to his own desire?

Based on our evaluation of character and circumstance, we also look for dissembling, but since the advent of psychoanalysis, and even earlier, embryonically, in romanticism—certainly in its focus on dream life—we now have a second, motivational, quasi-mystical domain, to which we have only partial access, if any access at all. Put simply, under ordinary circumstances, we evaluate another's (and at times our own) reasons for doing something in terms of character, context, and convention, but when those reasons are obscure, when the behavior being questioned falls out of character and convention, or when it fails to meet our desires, we turn from the ordinary explanations to unconscious ones. There is, as Ronald Laing noted many years ago (in different words, to be sure) a lordly dimension to attributions of unconscious motivation. We cannot divorce it from plays of power and

desire. Within the limits of our realism, discretion, and social etiquette, we may attribute to the other whatever meets our desires,
whether we acknowledge our desires or not, and that attribution,
those attributions foster, in fact or in fantasy, the fulfillment of
those desires.

My friend Olivia comes from an old New York banking family. She tells me that she is in psychoanalysis. Her background is
entirely different from her analyst's. He comes from an immigrant Jewish family, went to a big public school in Brooklyn, and
worked his way through college and medical school. Olivia went
to the most fashionable girls' schools and then to Radcliffe. She
has never worked. She takes singing lessons and writes poetry.
She travels easily between New York and Europe, where she
studies with a voice coach to whom she is devoted. I imagine that
he has made her completely dependent on him. She tells me that
many of her analyst's interpretations make no sense to her. He
doesn't understand her world. She tries to explain it to him, but he
views her explanations as resistance. She is, I should add, no snob.
She asks my advice. I tell her that I can't advise her, though I see a
problem less in the misunderstanding that arises from their very
different backgrounds than in his apparent refusal to reckon with
the differences, instead interpreting them in terms of resistance.
Whose resistance? I ask myself. Can you distinguish between the
patient's and the analyst's resistance? Not easily, I think, insofar
as they are implicated in each other.

I remember the confusion many of the German and Austrian analysts suffered when they came to the United States
just before the war. One of them—it may have been Franz
Alexander—wrote about his misunderstanding of a patient, the
son of a wealthy Chicago businessman, who was struggling, if I
remember correctly, with his career. The analyst assumed that

the problem related to the patient's desire to work when he had no need to, as would have been the case with a young man of similar background in Germany in those days. It was only when he realized that in America the need to work—to prove oneself—was the norm that the analysis progressed.

I'm not convinced. I think that misinterpretations can play an even more important therapeutic role in psychoanalysis than can correct ones (if there ever are any). I am not a psychoanalyst, but as an anthropologist I know that some of my best (to me) insights, as well as those of the people I worked with, arose out of misunderstandings. Olivia and I had a long discussion about misunderstanding in both analysis and everyday life. I have no idea how this affected her therapy, if it did at all.

Might not an anthropology, indeed a sociology or a psychology, focused on misunderstanding be more realistic than one that stresses mutual understanding? I think of a case Susan Falls described in her ethnography of the diamond business. She interviewed, on separate, unrelated occasions, a bride and groom about what they thought of diamonds. The groom said that although he didn't really approve of diamond engagement rings, he gave one to his wife because he knew she wanted one. His wife told Susan that she didn't like diamond rings but wore one because she knew her husband would want her to. Neither ever told the other what they thought of diamonds. I can think of many similar occasions, as I am sure you can. Imagine how the diamond figures in the relationship between the husband and wife. It is more than a humorous story. It is an O. Henry story. Will their marriage last, I ask myself, if there is so little understanding between them? Do they need to confess their dislike of diamonds to each other and then be able to laugh for it to last? Or are they bonded through their misunderstanding—one that preserves their individual identities? How easy it is to allegorize relations.

But what has the assumption of an unconscious done to our social relations, to our self-understanding and that of others, to our attribution of motivation and intention and our sense of responsibility? Does it produce uncertainty, instability, fragmentation, suspicion, possibly a sense of mystery and, I imagine, a desire to control or to be controlled? When you think about it, when I think about it, I find it scary—not just the vertigo it can produce but the submission it fosters to some rigid ideology, constipated religion, or control freak. Think of Patrick Hamilton's play *Gaslight*. The personal and political implications are enormous.

I'm at the Army Language School in Monterey. One of my classmates takes me to Haight-Ashbury to meet an old college friend whom he hasn't seen in several years. We climb up a rickety flight of stairs to reach his room. It is tiny, smelling of stale marijuana, days-old pizza, and exhausted sex. There are bunk beds against three of its walls. Each bed is occupied by a couple or a threesome. None of them are smoking. They are entranced by my friend's friend, Al or whatever his name is, as he pontificates. We sit on the floor. Al offers us an open bottle of warm beer. "That's the last one we got. Don't worry, we're all clean." Everyone in the room repeats, "We're all clean." I don't remember what Al was talking about. It just seemed to be a senseless riff. Someone seconds whatever he says and is seconded repetitively by everyone else, filling the room with a refrain of "Yeah, man. You got it, man." One woman is shouting "amen," as if she is at a Pentecostal revival.

I'm sickened by the veneration shown Al. He seems very ordinary, certainly not inspiring. I can't stand the refrain. I look at the women in the room. They are in various states of undress. One of them catches my eye; that is, if her own vacant eyes can catch anything. A glimmer of erotic interest passes undetected across them as she sinks back into Al's words. I'm hot, so thirsty that I take a sip of the leftover beer and want to retch. I've to get out. I signal my friend, but each time either of us tries to get up and leave, Al orders us to sit down. "Why do you want to leave? You just arrived." "Just arrived" echoes through the room. "Why do they want to leave?" he asks, and his devotees repeat it over and over again. "They don't like us. You don't like us?" Their voices drum. I feel my heartbeat fall into their rhythm. Then, suddenly, everyone is silent. Al speaks quietly, with seeming—therapeutic— concern. He focuses on me. At least that is how I feel it. "You want to leave because you are scared—scared of us, scared of yourself, scared of being like us, scared because you want, really want, deep down, deep, deep down, to be one of us. You love us, man, you're scared of love, scared of being in our embrace, scared of dissolving into one great communal fuck. You want to fuck us all. You're scared of fucking us all." He stops, turns to the woman with voided eyes, and says, "He wants to fuck you, Silvia. I saw it in his eyes. Fuck him, Silvia." "Come on, baby, I won't hurt you. Come to me," Silvia says. I get up. My friend gets up. I start toward the door as Sylvia coos, "Come to me, baby. Fuck me, baby." Al stops her. "Forget it," he orders. "Let them go. They don't like us. They're scared of us. They're scared of themselves. They're scared to fuck. Let the fuckers go back to the base. That's where they want to be. They like the army better than us." As we trip down the stairs, they sing in unison over and over again, "They're scared of us. They're scared of themselves. They're scared to fuck. Go back to the base. Go back to the base." Suddenly they stop, and as we are about to close the front door,

Al shrieks, "Vietnam," and then total quiet. My friend and I walk in silence. Finally he mumbles, "He's changed." We never mention Al again.

We drive back to Monterey that night. I am overcome with anger at Al, at his mindless followers, at my friend for introducing me to him, and at myself for not having told Al off, told everyone off. But what would I have said? What could I have said? Al would have had an answer I could not have challenged. "You don't get it, man, you don't know yourself. You got to know yourself. 'Know yourself,' isn't that what Socrates says? You know about him, don't you, man?" I have a dim recollection of his mentioning Socrates in one of his riffs. Of course, I could have responded in kind, but I didn't, and that infuriates me.

I must have fallen asleep. I hear voices, countless voices, unrecognizable voices telling me what I think, what I really think, what I ought to be thinking, but I can't remember, if I ever really knew, knew in the dream, knew after the dream, if it was a dream, whatever they were telling me. It seemed so nightmarishly real. But it isn't that I don't remember, even in the dream, what they are telling me. What haunts me is that I don't know who is saying it. The voices have become one. I'm suffused by gray images, partial images, skeletal images, each merging into another, never identifiable, never unfamiliar, disembodied—an officiant.

I want to identify her, that officiant, with the Mongolian woman I dreamt about in my mother's dining room. But that would be too neat. Besides, the voices were genderless. They are, I think, the disembodied voices, reduced at times to one, that lie, without identity, behind our interlocutions, changeless and changing, echoing our past, my past, past generations that seep through indirection, through stories, embellished to be sure, counterfeited, assumed, and dismissed but never really lost, framing our futures, my future, in ways that remain unknown until they are experienced—the voice of the future perfect.

That voice, those voices, cannot be confused with the scripts, "the narratives we live by," that are in fashion today in the human sciences, not because those scripts attempt to contain contingency but because the voices sound a particularity, a freedom perhaps, that deflects scriptural orthodoxy. Once, I imagine, the future perfect was assumed with imaginative—prophetic—certainty, but today, with modernity, with the sundering of the self, with the loss of a secure *point de repère*, the scriptural metaphors generated by sociologists and anthropologists, postulated by ideologues, and preached by fundamentalists of one faith or another, have to be seen as pathetic attempts to deny freedom, as illusory as freedom may be, its destabilizing voices. Those shifts in personal style that I observed in my old classmates, as in myself, were attempts to dictate a future perfect. It is the most curious of tenses, rooted in a present that becomes past as it proposes prophetically an event in a future that announces a future beyond that future that renders the event past. Deflections of uncertainty.

XIII.
PERFORMANCE

I'M SITTING in the kitchen rehearsing Peter Quince's lines from the prologue of *A Midsummer Night's Dream*. A group of friends are giving a dramatic reading of the Pyramus and Thisbe play-within-the-play on the front porch of Jill Eikenberry and Mike Tucker's house in the hills outside Spoleto. Jill is Puck and Mike Pyramus. Both of them are, of course, brilliant actors. The rest of us are amateurs. Our dog, Ulie, will play Moonshine's dog. I am ridiculously nervous. I keep rehearsing but am far too tense to get the words out right. Jane tells me to relax—she says I sound constricted—but I can't. I've spoken easily in front of a thousand people, but I haven't acted or even taken part in a dramatic reading since I was in school.

Fortunately, it is a reading. I can remember long conversations while doing fieldwork, but I'm incapable of memorizing written texts. I've often asked myself why. I can improvise, as I do in class, sometimes for three hours. These improvisations are a sort of performance not of another character, but of a not-quite-me, whomever me is. It is the slippage that is important, not from what to what. And I rarely use notes except in formal lectures. The only time I really needed notes was at Wicky's wedding. I ended my speech by reading, first in medieval French and then in English, a troubadour love sonnet. I wanted to remind everyone, including Wicky, of her relationship to France.

My prologue reading turned out to be a success. Several people, including Jane, were surprised at how well I had done. Once I was onstage, if you can call Jill and Mike's porch a stage, I fell

189

into the part. It was such a relief to be over with it and eating pizza from Mike's old bread oven in the garden. Why was I taking this for-fun event so seriously? I wasn't awed, acting with Jill and Mike. They were simply having a good time. Mike hammed up the death scene. Jill, who played Puck, turned herself into a sprite as only Jill could have done. She has extraordinary powers of self-transformation. It is magical to see. We all had a good time except for Moonshine, who had brought a stuffed dog and began to sulk when Joanna, the "director," decided that Ulie would be the dog. Ulie played her part with total indifference.

It was a trivial occasion, but I thought a lot about it—about losing oneself in communal play—in a part. It was something I had clearly missed. Moonshine's reaction was disturbing. He had been too busy brooding to let go. I thought of the transgressive dimension of theater—the escape from self, from the adhesive reality of daily life, the joy and the danger of play. I was reminded of Jane Austen's *Mansfield Park*, in which the preparation of an amateur theatrical by the children of several county families and their friends disrupts their romantic attachments until those preparations are abruptly ended by the sudden return of Sir Robert, the family head, from his plantation in Antigua. I know few better portrayals of the effect of a play on the conventions of everyday life. I was, for the instant, as removed from myself as I was constrained by the script.

The day I deposited my doctoral dissertation, I decided to go to a lecture given by Ernest Nagel in the philosophy department. I had very little contact with other departments when I was at Columbia. Interdisciplinarity was discouraged. When I asked to fulfill one of my archeology requirements by taking a course in classical archeology in the art history department, my request was refused. When I protested, my advisor dropped the requirement instead. I read almost no philosophy in graduate school, nor did I attend any lectures in the philosophy department. My decision to go to the lecture was less about hearing Nagel, whose positivism didn't much interest me, than it was a gesture of liberation from the confines of the anthropology department.

At the end of Nagel's lecture, I had a question but didn't dare ask it publicly. I had become shy. I waited until Nagel was about to leave to ask him. He was interested and wanted to know who I was. I told him I was in the anthropology department. He was surprised and said that I was not going to find much intellectual (or was it philosophical?) excitement there. He invited me to the weekly lecture series in philosophy. I thanked him but explained that I had just deposited my dissertation and was going to teach at Princeton. We walked to the subway stop on Broadway, talking about possible relations between philosophy and anthropology. When we said goodbye, he wished me good luck and said, "You know the scholarly life is very lonely." I have found it so, but I have also been carried away by intellectual excitement, though never at a remove from myself. Teaching is a different matter.

Once, when I was teaching at Harvard, I received a call from Ben Lee, who was a graduate student at the University of Chicago. Ben directed the Center for Psychosocial Studies, which turned out to be the most exciting scholarly center I've known. It has saved me from Nagel's loneliness. Barney Weissbourd, a Chicago lawyer and real estate developer, founded the Center. His Metropolitan Structures was at one time the largest real estate firm in the United States. He entered the University of Chicago at fifteen and three years later, in 1941, graduated with a degree in chemistry. He started law school but had to interrupt his studies for the army. Thanks to Robert Hutchins, the university's president, who took a special interest in those students who were admitted when they were very young, Barney was sent back to Chicago to work on the Manhattan Project. Despite his abiding loyalty to Chicago—he was a long-term trustee—he wanted the Center to be independent of any university. I have always felt that the Center's independence was one of the most important reasons for its success. It wasn't riddled with academic politics. It offered three-year, renewable fellowships to brilliant graduate students and sponsored conferences and small seminars in which scholars such as Jürgen Habermas, Pierre Bourdieu, and John Searle conversed informally with the fellows and a few invited guests. Under Ben's direction and the guidance of Michael Silverstein, one of the most innovative linguists in the country, the Center changed its psychosocial, largely psychoanalytic orientation to a linguistic one, and finally to one that focused on transcultural relations, in which scholars, mainly from China, Russia, and India, met colleagues they might never have known otherwise.

In 1993, the Center held a weeklong conference on the public sphere in Hong Kong—one of the first conferences, if not the first, that brought scholars from Hong Kong, Taiwan, and mainland China together. It was the first time Jane and I had visited East Asia. To our surprise, we loved Hong Kong—a place we had always thought was merely a shopper's paradise. But there was a kind of speculative anxiety there—the city was only six years away from Britain's handover of sovereignty to the Chinese. The reaction, or so it seemed to me, was a pragmatic accommodation that produced an unreal calm. I am reminded of the young reporters and journalism students we met there who, to Jane's distress, saw the career as simply a path to a high-paying job in advertising.

What surprised us most was the presence of thousands of Filipino servants, mostly women, who gathered on Sunday afternoons—their only afternoon off—in the central squares and parks of the city. They seemed lost in a world that offered them nothing more than a minimum wage to send back home. There was nothing unusual about this. It was their number that unnerved us. They seemed alike in servitude. I would like to have talked to them, to pierce their opaque alterity, but there was no one to translate for me. And even if I had found someone, what would I have said? Would my talk have been more than an escape from a reality I would rather not have seen? I didn't feel the same way about the throngs of Chinese people, presumably from Hong Kong, on commuter trains we took or in the workers' suburbs we visited. They were at home, at least it seemed so, though in fact many had emigrated from the mainland, looking for work.

A few years earlier, Jane and I had joined Barney Weissbourd and his wife, Bernice, on a trip to the Soviet Union. It was during the first years of perestroika, and we wanted to make contact with the scholars we thought might be interested in coming to the Center. We weren't very successful. With the exception of one anthropologist who was arrogant and dismissive to the point of sending me back to the hotel in his chauffeured car—the driver told me he was a colonel in the KGB—most of the scholars we met were cautiously indifferent. This may have been because they had never heard of the Center, but to me their response had more to do with years of a resignation that was now disturbed. In time this changed, with the lure of travel and purchases abroad—rather more, I suspect, than with the lure of visiting an American university.

I hadn't been back to the Soviet Union in nearly thirty years when a friend and I took a tour organized by the Austrian-Soviet Friendship Society. We now had interesting contacts, many of whom were dissidents, but I found that, overall, the atmosphere had not changed that much. (Jane, I should mention, had decided to write a piece for *The New Yorker* from Russia; she was far more pessimistic about its future than were her colleagues posted there, who were, perhaps inevitably, caught up in the possibility of change.) We stayed in a nicer hotel than the one on the outskirts of Moscow where I had stayed on my earlier trip but we felt oppressed by the babushkas stationed in front of the elevators on every floor, watching our—and everyone else's—comings and goings. Though I looked for bugging devices in our room, I didn't find any. I actually missed the barracks-like hotel I had stayed in before. There, at mealtimes, I met people who were on other Friendship tours. The Hungarians and Poles were eager to complain to an American about the conditions at home. If I sat with Czechs, they never said a word. If they were East Germans, they would move to another table. Everyone knew that they were being watched.

When we visited Estonia, where we were to meet professors at the university in Tartu, we were able to stay in a private guesthouse that had just opened. Only a few months earlier, no foreign tourists were allowed to spend a night in Tartu because of a military installation nearby. The owner of the guesthouse asked if we would like to meet some of his friends, many of whom were to become high-ranking government officials when Estonia regained its independence. The conversation was fascinating, especially when they asked us how to open a stock exchange. Barney livened up. He was intrigued by the problem and was surprised, as Jane and I were, by how little they knew about capitalism and its institutions. At breakfast the next morning, Barney and I, but not Jane and Bernice, found on our plates a handwritten invitation asking us to become honorary members of the Tartu Businessmen's Club, which had just been founded, perhaps that night after we went to bed. I accepted the invitation, for when would I ever again be asked to be a member of a businessmen's club. Barney said he was honored but refused. Although the owner had asked his advice about managing a hotel, Barney never told him that he owned any hotels—which, of course, he did. In the end, all of us were spooked by the virulence of the Estonian nationalism, especially by their folk dances, which reminded us of Germany in the twenties and thirties.

On our way to the Soviet Union, we had stopped in Prague. The city was subdued, weighed down by the dangers of change; thousands of East Germans were crossing the border in their sputtering Trabants and abandoning them near the West German embassy, where they took refuge before being spirited to the West. Jane and I talked to a number of dissidents, all of whom thought that what was happening in East Germany could not take place in Czechoslovakia. I remember an old man inspecting really just staring at—an abandoned Trabbie. I watched him for maybe five minutes, wondering what he was thinking. He was completely opaque. Finally, he walked to the back of the car, looked at the license plate, kicked the fender several times, and, shaking his head, walked away. For me that image caught Prague moments before the Wall came down.

BEN LEE'S reason for calling was to invite me to a Center meeting on notions of the self. I will never forget our conversation. We talked for several hours about various approaches to the self, the Center's mission, and its (rather Ben's) take on psychoanalysis. It was the beginning of some of the most intense discussions I have ever had with Ben, the fellows, and the Center's guests. I used to attend its meetings three or four times a year, sometimes more. Barney would always be there, sitting in a corner, smoking his pipe. He would rarely intervene. He was a modest, even diffident man. The first time I attended a meeting, I assumed he was a professor. He never asserted himself or indicated that he was the Center's benefactor.

The Center's activities restored my faith not only in the human sciences, particularly in the role that philosophy could play, but also in the value of language-centered approaches to psychoanalysis and anthropology. This is not the place to describe them, other than to say that I began rereading Freud closely, and looking at the way his understanding of the human psyche reflected grammatical structures and context-evoking mechanisms of language. It allowed me to rethink in linguistic terms the relations between theories and methods of interpretation in everyday life, across cultures, and in literary and philosophical understanding. I was, and am still, interested in the way plays of power infect the way contexts are linguistically defined and then subject to interpretation—a kind of loop over onto itself.

I take huge pleasure in these modes of analysis and in considering their social and psychological implications, but I have never wanted to restrict my research to them. I am too nervous, too eclectic a thinker. I enjoy literature (not to mention life) too much to reduce experience to skeletal abstractions that evade the devilish complexities—"the half disciplined chaos," in Melville's words—of human existence.

Understanding is always a process of in-framing and out-framing. What we include is definable, *but* what we exclude from consideration at any one time is so open, so infinite in possibility, that it remains indefinable. In an age of "information implosion," the development of a logic of exclusion is of greater importance than one of inclusion. We can never grasp the wholly outside, but we have to contend with it. Arbitrarily, conventionally, we are forced to limit the indefinable — the out-of-frame. It is here that power enters, authorizing the ways we delimit reality.

BUT EVEN at the Center, I missed communal activities, such as the theater, in which I could lose myself as I did in the sixties.

I and about ten other people are throwing rolls of toilet paper onto the branches of trees that border a potato field somewhere in eastern Long Island. It may have been Water Mill. We are preparing for one of Allan Kaprow's happenings. Unraveled, the paper blows in the wind. Lit that night by the full moon, muted by mist, the streams of paper produce a will-o'-the-wisp effect as dancers in white prance through the woods below them. It is quite beautiful, though it is not as successful as some happenings I have seen, because the audience doesn't participate. They sit or stand at a distance from the performance, turning it into what looks like a staged theater piece. After the performance, we go to Christophe de Menil's house. She and her family have been majestic supporters of the arts. The house is an enormous barn. What I remember most about it is a giant wing chair in which three or four of the women among us sank. I don't think Christophe expected so many of us. I'm not even sure she has invited us to dinner. We are starving. All she can offer us are a few omelets, foie gras, and caviar, which we gobble. I spend the rest of the night talking to Julie Martin about incestuous relations.

For me, the next day is the real happening. Allan has promised the farmer to leave the potato field and the woods behind it as he found them. He didn't realize—nor did any of us—that it is one thing to throw rolls of toilet paper onto trees and quite another to pull down soggy strips of paper now clinging to their branches. It takes us all afternoon, and by the time we finish cleaning up, we are exhausted, less from climbing trees than from laughing hysterically through the cleanup. We are all happy. I have forgotten that I am a student.

There were other happenings that Jane and I went to. In one of Robert Rauschenberg's, Jane was supposed to drive around the floor of the Park Avenue Armory in a car wrapped in a huge plastic bag. Watching her, I suddenly realized that she was being asphyxiated by the exhaust and ran down to the stage, shouting for help, to pull the wrapping off the car. Fortunately, she was fine. This particular happening had been sponsored by Bell Laboratories, which was instrumental in putting scientists and artists together on projects. It was a wonderfully naive time. I miss it, especially in Italy, where a poster for Bob Whitman's happening *Hole* hangs on our kitchen wall. Jane and I run into Bob occasionally. He has lost the spirit of that moment. We all have, I'm afraid.

In *Happenings in the New York Scene*, Allan wrote that "visitors to a Happening are now and then not sure what has taken place, when it has ended, even when things have gone 'wrong.' For when something goes 'wrong,' something far more 'right,' more revelatory, has many times emerged." It is a one-time experience that can be neither bought nor brought home.

Nor can spontaneity last.

A few years ago I received a call from the performance artist (if he can be called one) Tino Sehgal, who had heard a lecture I had given in Berlin at a conference on theater. He was preparing one of his "constructed situations" for the Marian Goodman Gallery, aptly called *This Situation*, and wanted my advice and participation in the performance, in which several people would sit on the floor of an empty room and, according to Tino's random cues, discuss philosophical problems as spectators walked through and engaged in conversation with them. Unfortunately, I couldn't participate in *This Situation*. I had to have a back operation, a belated consequence of a car accident in Spain.

A few years later Tino was back in New York and called to tell me about his new project, *This Progress*, which was going to occupy the entire Guggenheim Museum. It would not be publicized. Visitors would enter the empty museum and be greeted by a nine- or ten-year-old who would ask: *What does progress mean?* As the visitors walked up the ramp that circles the interior of the museum, older children, teenagers, and young adults would replace those who preceded them and also ask what progress means. Finally, older people like me would greet the visitors and talk to them about anything *except* progress or the event itself. After talking to a visitor, the teenager would race up a back stairway to tell us what the two of them had discussed. This was supposed to excite our imaginations when we began our own conversations. Sometimes it did. I thought Tino's project a bit sophomoric but intriguing. I agreed to participate. I did tell him that he was either a fool or a genius. He had no doubt of its success, and it was, much to my surprise, immensely successful. The lines went around the block. Jane waited in line in a snowstorm and could not get in.

I enjoyed *This Progress* for a while, and then got bored. I had a few set themes, most notably the relationship between love and the Internet, which allowed me to compare them. Ever the researcher! Some of the conversations I had were interesting, more were not, but the visitors seemed to enjoy talking about ideas. I did learn that most of the adults stereotyped young people's attitudes toward the net, as if every teenager was a nerd; they did not ask what the teenagers were feeling or missing or whether or not they considered the effects of IT on their lives. With the exception of a couple of real nerds, who simply didn't understand what I was talking about, the young people who visited the museum were sensitive to, at times anxious about, these effects. One elderly lady asked: What has the world become when you have to go to a museum to have a conversation?

I was reminded of a job I had in graduate school, showing apartments in a new building on lower Fifth Avenue. I did this on Sunday afternoons to earn pocket money. I sometimes think I learned more ethnography on those Sundays than I did in class. I was shocked at the sacrifices people, especially from the outer boroughs, were willing to make for a good Manhattan address. Most of the people I showed around wanted conversation more than they wanted an apartment. Some came three or four times. It was not that they were lonely — many came with their families or lovers or friends — but that they wanted time off from what I presume was the humdrum quality of their lives. A few women tried to pick me up. I remember one very nervous married man in his early forties who was renting an apartment for his mistress — he didn't use the word but implied the relationship — and asked if she was worth the rent. What could I say? I had never met the woman or the man's wife. Lillian Hellman's agent sent her to see an apartment there. She was furious. "How could he send me to such a dreadful place?" she grumbled. I agreed with her, but didn't say a word. She was the most impersonal client I met. She never looked at me, not even when she asked me to take her out the back way so she wouldn't have to face "those aggressive agents." I did. She ordered me to get her a taxi and, without thanking me, got in the cab and only looked at me quizzically and then with self-satisfaction when I told her I had liked *The Little Foxes*. I wanted to slam the door in her face but didn't.

FOR ME, the difference between the happenings of the sixties and Tino's "constructed situations" reflects the difference between the two periods. While the happening artists had a strong vision of their projects, they tended to be quite flexible in direction, leaving a lot to happenstance. Some of them were competitive, but they worked in a much more relaxed atmosphere than today's artists. Tino is controlling. He was almost always present at the Guggenheim show. Though he rarely interfered, his gaze was that of an overseer. He stages his situations meticulously, thereby constraining the range of possible responses. His situations are ephemeral. At the Guggenheim, there were no posters, no advertisements, no pictures allowed, and, from what I understand, no signed contract. The situations—more accurately, what transpired—simply fade away. All that is left are memory traces—but not quite, since the *idea* of the constructed situation can be purchased. Impermanence seems impossible in a society that values possession and, at the same time, is cluttered with throwaways.

I think of the beautiful Navajo sand paintings, some of which take hours, even days, to complete and are destroyed within minutes after the patient sits down on them and the singer—the medicine man—chants over him or her, drawing out the curative power of the spirits. Once the ceremony is over, the colored sands, which are considered toxic, infected with the patient's illness, are carried north and buried in the earth. When I first saw a ceremony where sand paintings were made, I was shocked by the destruction of the painting; that is, until I realized that the artistry lay in the making of the painting and not in its final state. For me, the beauty was in the fading—in the sense of time it implied. No doubt the Navajo were concerned primarily with the efficacy of the cure, but they were also attentive to the perfection of the painting. They worry about flaws when carrying out their rituals, and often insert a ritual within the ritual that protects them from the bad effects of such flaws.

Traditionally, the Navajo do not like being photographed. In the ceremonies I attended, they didn't want me or anyone else to take pictures. In more recent years, they have fixed sand paintings onto boards to sell to tourists. I find this sad, in that it destroys the spirit of the paintings and the sense of time that lies behind them. But the artists are shrewd. They reverse the colors of the originals and modify the patterns slightly so as not to profane them. Time is open-ended for the Navajo; they always leave a strand of their rugs untied. Circles are never fully closed. Unlike Western artists, whose ephemeral art is pitted, at times critically, against stop-time—more accurately, the illusion of stoppable time—by creating permanent objects, books, music scores, and photographs, the Navajo, at least traditionally, did not contrast the ephemerality of the objects with a cessation of time. I know I'm not doing justice to the Navajo's understanding of time. My point is that the critique of permanence in constructed situations, happenings, and, more generally, in self-consciously ephemeral art is a response to its opposite, a quest for permanence, which paradoxically valorizes that quest. A parallel would be in the way Dada valorized traditional art by mocking it. Of course, Dada was deliberately iconoclastic.

We are in the kitchen of a tower in Bonnieux, the village in the Vaucluse where Marta gave Wicky Julian Nibble for her birthday. We rented the tower from Julien Levy, one of the most important art dealers in the United States in the thirties and forties. He had dropped out of Harvard in his senior year and moved to Paris, where Marcel Duchamp—he had met him on the steamer on his way there—introduced him to the surrealists. In talking to Jane and me, he played up his relationship with Henry Miller and his crowd with boyish enthusiasm. He had an extraordinary art collection in his house in Bridgewater, Connecticut—a house he never locked, not even when he was away for months. "No one around here would know what to do with the stuff," he told Jane and me when we visited him there. In the early thirties, he returned to America, opened a gallery on Fifty-Seventh Street, in New York, and brought surrealism to America. He organized thematic exhibits there, asking those surrealists who managed to get to the States, often with his help, to paint, for example, a nose. His openings were always a scene. "There was never the kind of opening crowd that paid more attention to who was looking at what than to the paintings themselves. People actually came to see the art."

Julien was a marvelous raconteur. He used to spend hours telling us about the Paris he had known. I remember his creating a history of the Paris art scene in the twenties and thirties based on the affairs of the American lesbian expats living there. I wish I had recorded the conversation. It was more fantasy than reality. Julien himself was a surrealist at heart, who managed to combine an offhand attitude about the art market with an astute business sense. He echoed a moment that was lost, but that came alive for Jane and me when he was visited by painters such as Max Ernst, Dorothea Tanning, and Roberto Matta and their friends, including Balthus's son, Thadée, and his wife, the model Loulou de la Falaise, one of the most beautiful women I have ever seen. Julien would always regale us with stories about them the next day, usually ending with descriptions of their exotically erotic tastes. Whether the stories were true or not didn't matter; Julien was performing. He was in his way an artist, and that summer, with Jane's help, he finished editing a film he had started years before, now in the Museum of Modern Art's film archives, which ended with Wicky's babysitter Penelope entering a *borie*—a stone hut where French shepherds once sheltered their flock—and emerging with a baby, Wicky, a symbol of regeneration. She was barely a year old. Julien said that he preferred Penelope to Jane because she looked more like Wicky's mother than Jane did.

I was enchanted by the world Julien described, though I knew it to be fantastically embellished. I felt that I had been born too late, but I also knew that this sense of belatedness was one of the ways in which I fashioned myself, supporting a romantic melancholy that removed me from the ennui—that's too pretentious a word—of everyday life. It had little to do with the life I was living. I seem to have needed, and still need, to feel myself performing in a counterfactual world. Reality is too much for me (and you?) to handle without fanciful interludes that insinuate themselves into it.

I am interviewing my friend the Italian painter Valerio Adami in a restaurant in Montmartre, not far from his apartment, with its distractingly beautiful porthole window framing Sacré-Coeur. Jane and I have known Valerio and his wife, Camilla, also a painter, for years. Valerio is less well-known in America than in Europe, where his works are in major museums, public buildings, and important collections. A few years before our lunch, he'd had a retrospective at Beaubourg that was the high point of the Paris season. The Adamis live an elegantly urbane life in Paris, Monte Carlo, and on Lago Maggiore. Valerio is perhaps the last gentleman painter.

The Adamis' dinners are famous. Camilla will suddenly throw together a pasta, a *bollito misto*, or a veal *tonnato* and invite *le tout Paris*. There I've met Umberto Eco, Carlos Fuentes, Jimmy Baldwin, Pierre Boulez, Matta, Derrida, Andrei Voznesensky, Inge Feltrinelli, an Indian silk magnate, and curators from everywhere. Though it occasionally gets a bit pretentious, the conversation is always interesting. There is none of the aridity of academic talk. I am surprised at how timid Derrida can be. Eco is expectedly bombastic. Voznesensky is full of himself. I am not sure whether Matta is as confused as he seems. I remember one dinner—not at the Adamis'—where Matta suddenly asked his daughter who her mother was. The daughter didn't seem to mind at all. Dorothea Tanning was sitting next to him, correcting just about everything he remembered. Like his daughter, he didn't mind. He enjoyed the attention.

Jimmy Baldwin also liked to be the center of attention, but, unlike anyone else I have ever met, he had a self-ironic charisma. He seemed to occupy a space that was somewhere between the playful and the serious. Whenever you tried to pin him down, he would slip away. Jane and I liked him immediately. One evening when Wicky was at the Adamis'—she was about twelve—he rapped for nearly the whole evening, focusing his attention on her with his marvelous bulging eyes, flashing the whites as his pupils rolled in tune with his words. Wicky was totally charmed, though I don't think she had any idea who he was. Addressing her alone—the only child—he seemed to have created a pact with her. "We know how absurd they all are." He enjoyed holding his audience captive, as they squirmed, trying to get a word in. I think Wicky was complicit.

Valerio claims to be a traditionalist. "I really do think true freedom comes from the details and not from the openness of the future," he tells me. "It is the adventurous response to the past that gives us freedom, not some futurist illusion." His paintings are a sort of cubist auto-mythology that incorporates some of the most exalted figures and themes of European intellectual history: Nietzsche, Tolstoi, Lenin, Joyce, all fragmented and twisted, Oedipus under an electric light, a naked Prodigal Son playing the violin, Marat, murdered, lying on an ironing board as a woman seems to be pressing him (a play on David's painting *The Death of Marat*), Freud on a train making fish flies, all painted boldly in acrylics. His later paintings are more pensive. The misty beauty—the melancholy—of the Italian lakes haunts him. They contrast with Camilla's, which are political, angry, stormy, and passionate. She has done brilliant series on the horrors of Kosovo.

I ask Valerio whether he has a definite idea for a painting before he starts. I've never really had a chance to discuss his art with him before. He tells me that he begins with drawings, which he "corrects through colors on the canvas," first in aquarelles and then in acrylic. "With acrylic you have to get to the sensual through the complexity of the form," he explains. "It forces me back to a more 'mental' technique, a colder one—I want to call it self-effacing." I think of his corrections as a hardening—a loss of spontaneity. But I say nothing. "I develop my drawings more with the eraser than the pencil. An image makes a sort of trip—one that is already started in the initial image. And at a certain moment, the lines themselves take over. I'm convinced that a drawing isn't mine. It is in my pencil. There is really something transcendent about drawing—a dialectic between emptiness and fullness, the line, the edge, the primary vision, the adventure of a trip that forces you to discover things you never knew, the way the unconscious flirts with consciousness."

How much lighter would our depth psychologies be if we phrased the relationship between the unconscious and consciousness as a flirtation rather than a struggle?

As I was reading Hawthorne's *The Marble Faun* to Jane while she cooked dinner, I was reminded of Valerio's words. Kenyon, an American sculptor living in Rome, is unable to complete a sculpture of Donatello, a young friend, whom he and his coterie liken to a faun. He "gave up all preconceptions about the character of the subject, and let his hands work uncontrolled with the clay, somewhat as a spiritual medium, while holding a pen, yields to an unseen guidance other than that of her own will...A skill and insight beyond his consciousness seemed occasionally to take up the task. The mystery, the miracle, of imbuing an inanimate substance with thought, feeling, and all the intangible attributes of the soul, appeared on the verge of being wrought." Much to his own horror, Kenyon arrives at a hideous image of Donatello that reflects a murderous moment about which he knows nothing.

Gothic imagery and mystical conjunctions aside, I was taken aback by the resemblance to Valerio's description of drawing—of the seemingly independent force of the pencil: "the adventure of a trip that forces you to discover things you never knew, the way the unconscious flirts with consciousness." But the difference is enormous. There is no flirtation between the unconscious and consciousness in Hawthorne. The force is intrusive, brutally so. And so we continue to construe it.

I have been intrigued by how nineteenth-century writers struggled to represent the outside forces that impinged on consciousness and subsequent behavior—before the unconscious was formulated, routinized, and rendered banal. Rather than question the notion of the unconscious and its implications—the dark sources it projects—we tend to attribute the unaccountable in everyday life to an invidious, at best an impish, unconscious. We find it easier to locate the cause of the inexplicable in what is essentially a hypothetical space, as Freud knew, than to accept the mystery that is inherent in social life. Is it so terrifying?

It is a Saturday morning and the Moroccan artist Ahmed El Yacoubi and I are sitting in his studio in the Café La MaMa, which Ellen Stewart, the theater's founder, lends to him whenever he is in New York. He has known her for a very long time. Ahmed comes from Fez, where his father was an herbalist. He left home in his early teens and ended up in Tangiers, where he was picked up by Paul Bowles. He provided Bowles with the material for some of his stories and became a figure in the Tangiers scene of the fifties and sixties. Bowles introduced him to Francis Bacon, who taught him to paint, and Peggy Guggenheim, who collected his work. He, too, was an herbalist, who could make a mild hallucinogen from supermarket spices, and also a brilliant and instinctive cook. It was Allen Ginsberg who introduced Jane and me to Ahmed before I started my field research in Morocco. Ahmed helped me a lot. We became close friends. He was perhaps the most democratic person I have ever met. He recognized people for what they were and not for who they were considered to be. He simply did not understand social distinctions.

I had come to show him the cover of my book *Tuhami*, which was based on one of his paintings, called *The Big Woman*. Ahmed wanted to show me a painting of a woman's face that he had just completed. It had come to him in a dream-vision, he told me. It was

a beautiful face, emerging mysteriously from a shadowing background. Ahmed looked with wonder, as though he was seeing the
work of another artist. He told me that he hadn't painted it; it had
painted itself. Or "she" had painted it. I don't remember his exact
words, but he felt that an uncanny force had moved his hand. I asked
him who the woman was, but all he would say is "It is she," a phrase
that Moroccans use to refer to a spirit—a she-demon, Lalla Aisha
perhaps. I said nothing. The portrait, if you can call it that, reminded
me of Laurel, the woman Ahmed had been living with for several
years and with whom he had recently broken up. I told him what I
thought. As he acknowledged it with his eyes, he shook his head. I
detected a glimmer of fear in those eyes. Laurel would not have had
the requisite force. It had to be "she." Although always potentially
dangerous, as are all the *jnun*, "she"—couched in mystery—protected Ahmed through that mystery. From what? From recognition
and all that lay behind it, I thought, but found the answer flat.

Can we live without that mystery? Or do we prefer to ignore
it? How often do we start a sentence or a story without knowing how it will end? What inspires us? What carries us forward?
Is writing, is speaking, any different from drawing, painting, or
sculpting? Sometimes I marvel at a well-turned phrase that I have
written because it seems to come from nowhere. I never think
that clumsy ones come from anywhere but me.

I have had a misty, recurrent dream before sleep, a dream
of being imprisoned in a dungeon deep in the bowels of a castle
keep. The dreams remind me of an illustration in my copy of *Little Dorrit*. The image, I must admit, offers me a certain comfort
in times of anxiety or duress. Do we not take solace in the unconscious—in that otherness, so we conceive of it, that accompanies
us throughout our lives? Like a double, yes, but also like Robert
Louis Stevenson's shadow.

I have a little shadow that goes in and out with me,
And what can be the use of him is more than I can see.

But can't we see? The shadow is outside us, out of our control, but only to a point. It dances us in ways we cannot dance, in spaces we cannot reach. Does it reflect us? Or do we reflect it? At times, early in the morning, Stevenson's little boy or girl's shadow remains asleep in his warm bed.

XIV.

JANE

THERE are people who reappear, as if by chance, again and again in your life and somehow change. For a while, Julie Martin was one of these people. I first met Julie at the Demoses' Thursday-afternoon tea, where Paul Grice and I had puzzled over the differences between a reason for and a cause. After that, I would occasionally see her in the Yard, and in my second year, when we were in the same tutorial, I saw her weekly. That was the tutorial for which I wrote my final paper on the stare while watching *The Untouchables* in Charam's Eliot House room. Much to my embarrassment, Demos praised the paper, saying I should expand it for publication. I never did. Sometimes Julie and I would have a coffee after the tutorial, but we never became friends.

I forgot all about Julie, until we met by accident in Leningrad in 1961. I was studying in Vienna that year and had made friends with a Belgian student named Françoise, who had discovered an Austrian-Soviet Friendship Society tour to Moscow and Leningrad. It was irresistibly cheap, so I signed on. One member of the group—we were ten or twelve in all—was an American who claimed to be a journalist and thought he knew more Russian than he did. He was caught selling blue jeans in the public toilet at the Kremlin. (Russians, like other Eastern Europeans, were willing to pay wildly inflated prices for them.) He was flattered into signing a confession without understanding what he'd signed. When he told me, I made him report this "confession" to the American embassy. It was Sunday. The duty officer was furious. Since I had accompanied the "journalist" to the embassy,

I became suspect, too. I was told to share a room with the tour leader when we got to Leningrad the next day, and was then followed by a man in a trench coat who was always peering over a newspaper at me. He must have been seeing spy movies. As I was leaving for the Hermitage alone—I wanted to spend more time there than the rest of the group did—I ran into Julie on the Nevsky Prospekt. She was translating at a trade fair. I didn't know she knew Russian and was studying for an MA in Russian studies at Columbia. Our guide, who spoke no English, was even more alarmed than the man at the embassy had been, and he tried to persuade me not to go with her. She was, in his eyes, clearly a contact. The guide was even more distressed when Julie spoke to him in Russian. We caught him signaling my tail.

Within minutes, I found myself followed through the museum by two men and asked one if he spoke English, saying I couldn't understand the title of one of the paintings. It was, in fact, Matisse's *The Dance*. He said no, but was clearly flustered. Although I rather liked being followed, I was worried about Julie. That worry was unfounded. On the other hand, I had put myself in serious jeopardy, having stupidly agreed to leave the country carrying what the journalist said were thousands of dollars worth of Eastern European currency that he had made selling blue jeans in the Eastern Bloc. (He didn't know his money was worthless outside the Iron Curtain.) I had said yes but told him that if I felt in any danger, I would get rid of it. Fortunately, on the night train to Leningrad I'd realized how stupid I was and went from car to car, leaving wads of money in the toilet sinks. I knew that I'd never again have the chance to throw away so much money—any money. I was thoroughly searched as I crossed the border into Poland. Three months later, the journalist appeared at my place in Vienna—he had been detained by the

Soviets—and asked for his money. When I said that it had been too dangerous to keep, he fell into a rage and tried to beat me up.

On leave, just before I was discharged from the army, I met Julie again, walking down the Boulevard Saint-Germain in Paris. She was with her boyfriend, Bob, a lovely man who had been crippled by polio as a child. I didn't tell her I was going to Columbia, but discovered that my apartment was only a block away from hers. I could not avoid her. I had few friends at Columbia, and my friends from Harvard were scattered around the world. Even had they been in New York, I'm not at all sure I would have seen them.

Julie invited me to an open house that she and Bob had every Saturday night at Bob's apartment. It was a way for him to see people comfortably from his wheelchair. He had a beautiful art collection that included Rauschenberg's illustrations for Dante's *Inferno*. I pored over it whenever I had the chance. He went to the auctions at Parke-Bernet and would sometimes buy an entire lot and sell whatever he didn't want to his friends. Jane and I bought three Goya etchings, one of them a vulture gnawing a corpse, which I keep in my study just above an etching—a catalog—of the tortures of the Christian martyrs. They remind me, as if I need to be reminded, of the ingenuity of human cruelty. Most of Bob's guests were writers and artists. It was a relief to escape the academic world.

Julie and her roommates also gave parties, which, sadly, Bob never attended. Most of the guests were students, but there was also an assortment of hippies, peaceniks, and protesters, especially when Julie's younger sister, Amy, and her brother were in town. The Grateful Dead, the Beatles, Ravi Shankar, and occasionally a Bach fugue (after all, a chant of sorts) blasted from tinny speakers as the acrid smell of dulcifying marijuana—a synesthesia that has always puzzled me—wafted through the apartment. Glassy-eyed, orange-and-purple-robed bodies ground against one another, and uptight academics began to dance, unable to catch the rhythm. I was one of them, I'm afraid.

Whenever I think of Julie's parties I remember a beautiful, sharp-featured woman, dressed in tight jeans (for those days) and a tie-dyed indigo blouse that any couturier would have been happy to have designed—and one probably did—which set her apart from all of the other guests, though I imagine she thought she was deep in their spiritual midst. The black mascara she wore dripped artfully, which is to say, with unabashed artifice, down her cheeks in teardrops. The truth is that Julie's parties were on the fringe of flower-power gatherings—what Jane described in her book on Allen Ginsberg as "an amalgamated hippie-pacifist-activist-visionary-orgiastic-anarchist-orientalist-psychedelic underground." Of course, such movements have no center, just greater or lesser marginality from an assumptive center.

I never saw Jane at Julie's parties, but she did come, from time to time, to Bob's Saturday-night salon. I didn't pay much attention to her. I didn't like the men she came with; they seemed out of place even in as bourgeois an environment as Bob's. At first, I found Jane mannered. She had gone to graduate school in English and American literature at Columbia, while I was in the army, and was now writing for *The New Yorker*. She made me realize how much time I had lost in the army—in my indecisiveness. But as I got to know her, I began to realize that under that fragile, exuberant confidence was someone else—someone I wanted to know. We began to go to the movies together, but her world seemed out of reach. I was caught between the desire and the fear of losing myself in her evanescence and, in reverse order, the fear and the desire of finding myself stuck in academic permanence. I was sick of mediating these possibilities, as if they were the only two, through fantasy.

Though I had smoked pot and hashish, I had never taken LSD or any other psychedelic drug. One of Amy's friends, whom I'll call Fiona, convinced me to try some with her. We spent the day together. I didn't realize she was setting me up for a weird trip. We ate pink Twinkies and looked at psychedelic posters in the Village and dinosaurs in the Museum of Natural History. They figured in my early visions. At first, I enjoyed the trip, but it darkened gradually. I saw myself as a shriveled newborn baby, grotesque, but too removed to be disturbing. And then, after I slipped into Fiona's warm, moist, overly moist, vagina, losing myself in her, enveloped in her heat, her womb, she suddenly leaped up, laughing and screaming, ran out of the room, and came back swinging a rusty antique rapier she had found somewhere in Julie's apartment, where we were tripping. She lunged at me, whomever I was for her then. Luckily, she hit a lightbulb with the sword and, shocked by the live wire, dropped it. I grabbed it and fled, leaving her crying.

I had never been so frightened, and that fear canceled whatever effect the acid had. It was the clash of reality and irreality, the powerlessness of being in neither and yet in both, that terrified me far more than a lunging sword. The darkness that followed the splintering bulb, the only light source in the room, hadn't prevented me from seeing and seizing the rapier. It was as though the terror enabled me to see in the dark, when, in fact, I had probably caught it in the split second between light and darkness. I walked up and down upper Broadway until my feet ached so badly that I was forced back into the real world. Not quite: the illuminated store windows appeared a ghastly blue, as if other colors had been extracted. The blue faces of passersby made me wonder if I looked as grotesque to them as they did to me. I stumbled back to my apartment, collapsed on my couch, and fell into a deep, dreamless sleep.

As frightening as that experience was, it seemed to release me from the anguish I had suffered ever since realizing that I was destined—that I had destined myself—to become an anthropologist, whether or not I liked it. Suddenly I saw that whatever I decided to be, it was not a prison unless I made it one. I was "free." Freedom—the word, the concept—brought with it a vision of an existential anthropology, one that focused on the individual caught in his world, the way I was and everyone else I knew was. It was a vision I'd lost in the tedious courses I had had to take. There were no other courses at Columbia then. I can't say that I was happy, but I was excited. Fiona remembered nothing of what had happened. She and Amy went to San Francisco and disappeared into the Haight.

I don't know if my trip had anything to do with my deepening desire to know Jane. I was limited less by shyness than by my inability to change the terms of our relationship. This finally happened unexpectedly. I got angry at Jane and at myself. I had called one night to ask her to the movies. She answered, saying "just a minute," and then forgot I was on the line. I could hear people talking in the background. Jane was having a party. I waited, listening to the chatter, jealous, incensed, torturing myself with all sorts of imaginings, mostly sexual, until I couldn't stand it any longer and hung up, swearing never to have anything to do with Jane again. The next morning, she called to apologize. It was the first time she had ever called me. That Saturday, I met her at Bob's and was indifferent. I spent most of the evening talking to a woman I'd met for the first time and liked. When I asked if she wanted to share a taxi uptown—her apartment was on the way

back to mine—Jane announced that she would join us. I was flattered, amused. I don't remember whether we slept together that
night or a few nights later. What I do remember—an emblem
perhaps of embryonic love—was walking the next morning past
the Cathedral of Saint John the Divine on my way to class. It was
a beautiful spring day. This sounds corny, but it's true. I caught
myself smiling at myself, happy. I felt the warmth of the sun on
my neck and shoulders, and that warmth enveloped me, infus-
ing me with feelings I had never before felt, not with Mariam or
Monika, and certainly not with any of the other women I had
known. I can't call it love. I cannot not call it love.

I've never really been sure what love is anyway. It has too many
meanings, too many tones, objects, suggesting too many relations, sexual ones, erotic ones (they're different), ones of friendship, dependence, and caring, spiritual ones, selfish ones—an
intimate knowing of the intimate that is and has to be edged
with doubt, if for no other reason than knowledge without doubt
would be vacant. "Love" seems to reduce the complexity of any
relationship into a single state of mind that denies as it encour-
ages endless, indeed eternal time—time that risks collapsing into
the habitual, saved and rescued, if at all, only by affection, by a
missing that defies regret, by a range of physical responses, from
passion to the simple need to touch and be touched, to caress and
be caressed, to draw one's lover (that's an easier word) to one's
self and to be drawn by that lover.

I wonder what connection there is between pride and
love—falling in love. I was proud that morning. My pride over-
shadowed my feelings for Jane just as it depended on those
feelings. It wasn't the pride of conquest but it was the pride of
conquest. It was less possessive than prepossessive, anticipa-
tory, of more sex, endless sex, and something more that could

not be known, not yet, if ever—less mystery than the mysterious. (Or have I got it backward?) I was on an adventure that, like
all adventures, would be risky, awkward, foolish, foolhardy, and
extravagant. You see what I mean? How can we speak of love?
What do we mean by love? Why should we ask that question anyway? For me, it's the memory—call it an iconic memory, a feeling memory—of the sun on my neck and shoulders, of an aura,
a flowering (I'm becoming too romantic), an anticipation: the
memory that substitutes for worded love.

Love is an extrapolation of an infinite series of "I love you,"
whether said, unsaid, or imagined at the margins of consciousness. Remember Garrick: "I love you plus I love you equals
infinity."

And Jane?

Neither of us, I imagine, was anywhere near what that memory came to connote for me and could, perhaps, had she had it or
its equivalent, for Jane.

I am sitting in a bar at JFK waiting for Jane's plane to arrive
from San Francisco. She has been gone for more than a month,
while I've been preparing for my orals. She has called me several times a week, described her adventures (that's how, envious, I imagined them). Adventures in Golden Gate Park at the
Gathering of the Tribes for a Human Be-In; or in a hot tub at the
Esalen Institute with Allen, James Pike, the extravagant Episco-
pal bishop who would die a couple of years later in the Judean
desert, searching for the remains of the historical Jesus, and the
Zen poet Gary Snyder; or at a sacred orgy in Marin County, hud-
dled, naked and beaded, in a corner with her notebook, while
the participants sat in a circle chanting, fucked at random, and
shared their "sacred juices" from a silver goblet. Jane said that
the women did not look happy. They looked trapped in a strange,

impersonal choreography, subject to a sternly spiritual dancing master and incapable of pleasure.

Before we moved into a railroad flat that Jane had inherited from two professors who were moving to Nigeria, Jane insisted that we paint it. At first, I thought this was a stupid idea, given that we were going to live there for only eight or nine months. But as we painted, I realized that Jane was right. Painting together, laughing together over an unreachable corner, a splotch in which we saw shapes—probably induced by paint fumes—made the apartment ours. Taking possession, possessing, bound us to a place—not quite a home—that was neither hers nor mine, but ours. The painting was a prenuptial ritual, which we did not recognize as such—the making possible of an "our."

Anthropologists have always focused on the gift exchanges that occur in marriage ceremonies; ideally they balance the two families united by ritual. But the gifts, those that are given to the couple—not to the families, or separately to the bride and groom—are transmuted, in the ideal, into a singularity that enables the *our*. It is the salad bowl, the linen, the cutlery, the bedspread, even the check that conjoins in ways that the exchange of rings, which is subject to the tension inherent in any exchange, does not. It is the odd gift, the ugly vase or, worse, the picture, given by a friend, that neither the bride nor the groom likes but both feel compelled to keep for fear of offending their friend—that, in its own way, is even more binding than the gifts they do like. They are complicit in this and in the embarrassment they share when someone whose taste they admire sees it.

Jane's mother discovered that we were living together. She had driven down from Providence, and, snooping in a closet, she discovered my clothes. It was as if her world had shattered—though not really, since she had known-not-known that Jane had had lovers. But now she was caught between two choices: to convince Jane to leave me or convince her to marry me. She didn't want to interfere and, actually, did her best not to. Of the two choices, the second was, for her, the worse. She didn't really like me. I was still a student, not financially secure, and would never earn enough to satisfy her daughter's needs.

JANE SEES me waiting for her at the exit gate. She smiles, waves—a hesitance, a slight flush, a reddening that never becomes red but lingers, downcast eyes, a furtive glance, a "hi," constrained, slightly nasalized...I had read somewhere that psychoanalysts can tell when their patients are concealing erotic fantasies by a sudden nasalization of voice. A hug—slightly forced, an escape from embarrassment. I say, without reflecting, let's have a drink. Jane agrees.

I can't convince her that I'm not jealous of him, them, whomever. I'm not angry at her. I'm envious of her—her experiences. She would have liked me to be jealous. I refuse the anger, the jealousy, but not the envy, and delight in the refusal.

I didn't yet know the intensity of Jane's empathy when she is working on a story. She dissolves into that empathy, that empathized world, and though she remains an acute observer—perhaps this is her strength—she observes from within and emerges only as she writes. Writing—the extraction—is for her self-torture. She is a punctilious, an obsessive editor, as anyone who has ever worked with her on a manuscript bemoans. Immensely competent on a story, she becomes, writing it, helpless, dependent, lost in herself, and though she does not acknowledge this, takes refuge in a stultifying domesticity. She rearranges the kitchen, straightens the pictures, and begins to cook. Once she has finished the story, she can laugh at what she couldn't acknowledge while she was writing.

As our trip to Morocco approached, Jane began to talk about getting married. I was horrified. I didn't—and still don't—really believe in marriage. I find the state's sanctioning love obscene. We began to bicker. I mocked Jane's desire as bourgeois. She announced that she wasn't going to Morocco unless we were married, that the Moroccans might make problems for us if they discovered we weren't. I couldn't believe that I was hearing this from someone who had spent so much time with the most promiscuous of hippies who had never had a problem in Morocco. One evening, she had dinner with a former lover who had come to New York from Bermuda, ostensibly on business. I didn't mind, but by the time she returned, hours late, I was jealous for the first time and furious at my jealousy, even though she swore they were now just friends. I was convinced that Jane had stayed out late on purpose—to incite my jealousy and thereby confirm my love. We fought, and the next morning, still fuming, I said, "If we are going to go on fighting, we might as well be married." I wasn't serious, but Jane took it as a proposal. I laughed.

We decided to appease her mother by marrying in Providence. Jane and Allen were planning to drive to Lowell, Massachusetts, to see Jack Kerouac. Allen suggested we spend the night at Jane's mother's house; he wanted to be one of the witnesses at the wedding. We asked Jane's mother to be the other, but she refused. Still Allen charmed her, and that night, when I sneaked into Jane's bedroom, we joked about her mother's preferring Allen to me. She had insisted, for propriety's sake, that we sleep in separate bedrooms.

Our aborted elopement turned the privacy of marriage into a family affair. We were to have a proper wedding with cherry blossoms and magnolias at Jane's uncle Josselyn's house in King's Point, on Long Island. I agreed; that is, until Josselyn asked me to lunch and tried to convince me to have a Jewish wedding. He wasn't particularly religious but was an ardent supporter of Israel and had been bar mitzvahed at the age of forty or fifty. I refused, saying that as a nonbeliever, I felt that a Jewish wedding, any religious wedding, would be, well, "blasphemous." He had, finally, to acquiesce. Jane and I were relieved.

Jane's insistence on marriage before leaving for Morocco, I came to realize, reflected her anxiety about living there for a year or, as it turned out, more. William Shawn, the editor of *The New Yorker*, told her to write something there — to find a story she wanted to tell. He was a flexible editor, who had complete confidence in his writers' choices and rarely, if ever, interfered with them. His was a writer's magazine, he said. Jane was relieved, but not entirely. She asked me if she could talk to Margaret Mead about fieldwork. Mead agreed. I'll never forget her expression when she met Jane. It was clear that she'd stereotyped Jane as a Jewish princess who would never adjust to field conditions. In the event, Mead wasn't much help. She knew very little about Morocco and told Jane that she would probably have to wear a veil — an absurdity in a country that had had, and still had, a little more than a decade after independence, a large French population. I attributed Mead's suggestion to ignorance, but now as I write, I think she was probably trying to scare Jane. She was wily.

Mead and I shared a taxi to Columbia. She made it clear, without saying it, that I was making a mistake. She asked if we were going to have a big wedding. I told her that it would just be family, and that Jane's book publisher, Charles Duell, and his wife, Ruth, were giving a party for our friends later in the week. Detecting (or perhaps encouraging) my embarrassment, she told

me that since a wedding was a ritual, I should take an anthropological perspective. And then, grasping my thigh—the only time
she had ever touched me—she said that my hair was too long
and made me look balder than I was. She congratulated me for-
mally as we left the cab. Freud saved me. In mentioning my bald-
ing, Mead had touched my sorest point, as she must have known
she would. I defended myself by taking her observation, indeed
her order to cut my hair—she could be imperious—as an act of
symbolic castration. She respected my intelligence but not my
independence. I was one of the only male students at Columbia
who worked with her and earned a doctorate. The others were
so devoted to her research—to her—that they never managed
to graduate. She was always careful to find them jobs that she
thought were "suitable," as she told me once.

Jane and I had argued and were not speaking to each other
before our wedding. I had seen an exhibit of Redon drawings and
wanted to give her one as a wedding present. We arranged to
meet at the gallery an hour before it closed for her to choose the
one she most liked. I hoped it would be one of those I liked. That
evening, the gallery was sending the unsold drawings back to
Paris. Or was it London? Jane didn't arrive in time. She and her
mother had been at Tiffany's, looking for china. I was furious.
What was I doing marrying someone who forsook a Redon for a
Tiffany dinner service? It wasn't like her. That I knew. Or did I?
We had similar taste in art, though she didn't at all appreciate my
predilection for the grotesque and the cruel. It was her mother's
fault, I thought, evading the fear of bourgeois entanglement. I
took the trappings of bourgeois culture for being bourgeois.
Jane was to prove me wrong. But, in the days before our marriage, she had become closer to her mother than she had been,
enacting a primordial attachment to her, her maternal line, to

her perpetuating that line. I wished Jane's father were still alive. I felt caught in, and at the same time excluded from, that women's world.

On our drive to Josselyn's, we got stuck in a Puerto Rican Day parade, which forced us to leave the highway in Queens. We were completely lost. A policeman stopped us when I drove through a yellow light. "What's your rush?" were the first words out of his mouth. "Are you late for a wedding?" I said yes. He thought I was being snide, until he looked in the car and saw Jane dressed in what was discreetly but clearly a wedding dress. "You're serious," he said, broke out laughing, and escorted us to the road to King's Point. He wished us luck and drove away, not knowing that he had broken the tension between Jane and me. We were again speaking and were eased into our roles by a joint that Jane's cousin Stephen gave us. He had easy access to pot; he was photographing Andy Warhol's factory for a Swedish publisher.

I went through the ceremony dutifully, and was surprised to discover that I was deeply moved by it. Oddly, I could not remember the moment between our taking vows and exchanging rings. Later, I came to realize that, as in any rite of passage, there is an exquisite moment of being-in-between, a moment when you are no longer what you were—a bachelor—and not yet what you are about to become—a husband. Can any of us really remember this no-longer but not-yet moment? I don't think so. I still don't. In Morocco, I recognized that rites of passage (like the Arab circumcision ceremony) are precocious, announcing a change of status but only projecting the changes to come in relationship and identity. It is that precocity, the contradiction between a proclaimed reality and "actual" reality, between a punctuated moment and the flow of time—the time of transition—that gives the ritual its efficacy.

XV.

INTERPELLATION

L AST WEEK, I was leaving a meeting at my local community board—we were fighting the expansion of a rapacious private school in the neighborhood—when a man in a yarmulke accosted me. I recognized him from the meeting. "Are you Jewish?" he asked. "No," I said, and then irritably, "Why do you ask me?" Instead of answering, he demanded to know what I did. I told him I was an anthropologist. "What's that?" And before I could answer (or walk away), he wanted to know if that had anything to do with religion. I shrugged. "Do you write about Jews?" he asked. I realized then that he was a simpleton, and, more kindly, I told him no, but that there were anthropologists who did, and said good night firmly.

Walking home, I wondered what the man had wanted. Why was he at the meeting? He didn't live in any of the buildings involved in the protest. Why was I so irritated? I thought of similar occasions. Once, a young Lubavitcher, recruiting in front of the Plaza, had asked if I was Jewish, and when I said I wasn't, he apologized. Much to his surprise, I asked him why he had apologized. After an awkward moment, the two of us had a fascinating discussion on being an outsider on the inside or an insider on the outside. I don't think he had ever had as long a conversation with a non-Jew. I was saddened by that. I liked the man. I understood, at least I thought I understood, the reasons for his isolation—self-imposed for obvious historical reasons and imposed by acknowledged and, worse, unacknowledged prejudices. Of course, I had to recognize the by-now clichéd stress on the sense of belonging that characterizes ultra-orthodox communities. However real their sense of community is, it is also deflective. Can communities like those—which foster dependency and cohesiveness to such an extent that the self loses itself in the collective—be open to the views of the outsider? Is closure a necessary condition for their existence—for the identity of their members? Is this an essential characteristic of exclusivist religions such as Judaism, Christianity, and Islam? Is it a consequence of considering one's people chosen or singularly possessed of truth? Although the long history of Jewish persecution can account in part for closure, closure cannot be reduced to a defense against prejudice and persecution.

I am interviewing a professor of theology at a conservative evangelical Bible college in Los Angeles. We are talking about Wittgenstein. It is part of my research on literalism as a prevailing cultural style in America. The professor has not read Wittgenstein. He has heard that Wittgenstein was an atheist. I acknowledge that this is true but that there was also a significant spiritual, if not mystical, dimension to his life. The professor is surprised. I can see a gleam of interest in his eyes, but it quickly disappears as he tells me, not unsympathetically, that Wittgenstein did not know Jesus. I am used to those dismissals by now.

Are they so very different from those of my opinionated colleagues?

Later that afternoon I am talking to John, a student at the Bible seminary. He is less tolerant than the professor. He tells me that Christians, that is, evangelical Christians—evangelicals tend to preempt the word "Christian"—can never and ought never to befriend non-Christians. I am shocked by John's vehemence. Seeing this, he adds that they might work with non-Christians in a friendly way, but that isn't the same as friendship. Still perceiving my shock (somewhat feigned, I admit: I have heard this many times, though rarely with the same vehemence), John says that he cannot accept the two degrees of separation advocated at Bob Jones, the most conservative of the evangelical universities. There, you can't even be friends with Christians who befriend non-Christians. When I ask John why, he tells me that the non-Christians will have a corrupting effect on the Christians. *But are they not protected by Jesus, by their faith in Jesus?* I am tempted to ask, but I already know the answer. He will refer to Satan.

The Fundamentalist Christians I worked with always asked me at our first meeting if I was reborn. They were almost always friendly, though I also knew that we could never be friends; our views of the world were too radically different. But was this true? I have friends who are Muslims and Hindus. And I knew that the evangelicals I'd met were committed to helping me with my research, if only because they saw this as Jesus's plan for bringing me to their faith. As good Calvinists, they were committed to witnessing—converting—non-evangelicals like me.

A Brazilian colleague has taken me to a favela in Rio to attend an evangelical church I have heard about. I want to contrast it with the churches I studied in America and, earlier, in South Africa. The service starts at nine at night, but my colleague insists that we arrive at the favela at six. She tells me that a friend who will introduce me to the preacher wants me to come early. I assume that he has arranged for me to interview the preacher, but, when I arrive, he shows us around the favela instead, introducing me to his friends, among them a lot of ten- and eleven-year-old boys. They call me a gringo and laugh. I laugh, too. Then, once when we have walked the muddy streets of the favela, he takes us to the church. We are very early. Only a few old women are there. A half hour later, he and my colleague decide to leave. I feel stranded but am determined to stay. I wait another hour for the service to begin. The church is tiny, but the preacher has a loudspeaker that fills the room as he shouts into a microphone. Many people drop notes into a clay pot near the altar. The preacher picks them out, one by one, reads them silently, and then asks us to pray for the person who has left each note. We never know for what or for whom we are praying.

The shouting gets so loud that I decide to leave before the service ends. I have a throbbing headache. I walk through the empty streets to a steep flight of stairs that lead down the mountain to the *asfalto*, the asphalt, which is how the favela dwellers refer to the city below. Starting down the stairs, I see the little boys I have met earlier. They are now carrying semiautomatic rifles. I'm scared. Clearly they are working for a drug lord, but they greet me with smiles as they call me gringo. I laugh with relief. I have been interpellated. I am safe. When I get down to the *asfalto*, I find myself in a desolate, utterly empty square. Now I am not just scared but terrified, completely disoriented, panicked. Rio is a notoriously violent city, especially at night. How am I going to get home? I assumed that I'd find a taxi, but there are none. I miss the little boys with their machine guns. Then I see a policeman and call him. He runs away. He is afraid of me. I call once again, but he has disappeared. It's a dangerous neighborhood. I start running—anywhere—without knowing where I'm going. Finally, I see a taxi. The driver slows down, appraises me, and then stops. I sink into the seat exhausted and dream all night of the din in the church, echoing louder and louder.

Jane and I invite the French writer Nathalie Sarraute and her husband to dinner. She is giving the Gauss lectures at Princeton. I drive her back and forth. We are nervous. We feel very young. We invite Hugh Nissenson and his wife, thinking Nathalie would like to meet another novelist. Hugh describes how he was bullied in Central Park, during the war, because he was a Jew. Nathalie looks disgusted. He tells her how guilty he feels, not living in Israel. Tartly, which was not her way, she says, "Well, why don't you move there?" Hugh is at a loss. "You wouldn't understand," he says finally. "You have to be Jewish to understand the torment." Nathalie answers, "I am Jewish, but I have rejected that." Hugh is shocked. "But how can you reject that? You can reject the beliefs, but you can't reject the identity." "Why not? I have the freedom to choose," she says. "Were I to accept what you call my identity I would be a racist. That I reject." Hugh is speechless. He sulks. Nathalie, supported by Sartre's existentialism—Sartre was her friend—rests her case. Jane and I try to change the subject.

Nathalie's position was ridiculous, but I admired it. It took courage. Should principle succumb to social etiquette? To prejudice? To absurd, racialist constructs of identity? To apostrophe and interpellation?

Freddy and I are walking in the woods. I must be ten or eleven. He says that his father thinks my mother is Jewish. "Is she?" I say no, but I'm not sure. It has never occurred to me. No one has ever talked to me about religion. That night I asked my mother if she was Jewish. She said no and asked me why I wanted to know. I told her that Freddy's father thought so. I was bothered by her answer. I can still see her lips quiver. It was only after my father died that she told me that my grandmother came from a German Jewish family that had immigrated to the United States in the 1840s and that my grandfather's background was more obscure. His grandfather, a Russian Jew, had run off with a Tartar dancer and was disinherited. He moved to Saint Petersburg, lived an "unconventional life," whatever she may have meant by that, and became a Nihilist. Then she said that when my grandfather came to the United States, he a joined a Russian Orthodox Christian monastery somewhere in upper New York State, remaining there for several years, and eventually entered the University of Pennsylvania medical school and became a dentist — under the pressure of an older, far more practical, brother who had settled in Philadelphia, years before my grandfather arrived in America by way of Berlin and Paris, where he had gone to continue the studies of Oriental languages he had begun at the university in Saint Petersburg. It was only after he died that my grandmother discovered he had been a lay brother in the monastery. He left some money to the monastery, but, as it no longer existed, it took her lawyers a long time to find the proper beneficiary, if they ever did. They did meet an ancient monk who remembered my grandfather. He said he was a deeply spiritual man and a devoted Christian. This seems odd, since, like my parents, he and my grandmother were so ardently secular.

I was thirteen or fourteen when my mother told me about my Jewish ancestors. I asked her why she had never told me. She hesitated for a long time and finally said — stuttered really — that she didn't want my sister and me to bear *that* burden, that it was she who had insisted that we be baptized, since, so she'd said, she had been foolish enough to think that the Germans might win the war and wanted to protect us. I was even more shocked by this. I had always thought of her as rational, but I was wrong. Over the years, she began to talk about being "tainted" by her Jewish blood and attributed her self-imposed isolation to bad blood. I thought her a coward. She neither accepted her identity (whatever she thought it was, and that probably changed over time) nor rejected it, as Nathalie had done, however unrealistic her rejection was. Rejection always involves acknowledgment.

My mother didn't consider herself an anti-Semite. She had contempt for just about everyone, and Jews were no exception. As I was growing up, I fought her contempt, though at times I still catch myself echoing it. It doesn't seem to come from me. What I didn't understand—or refused to admit—was my mother's self-contempt. Did she herself acknowledge it? I'm not sure. Did she discourage it in my sister and me? I never remember her doing so.

I never asked my mother why she had waited until after my father had died to tell me this.

I have never considered myself a Jew any more than I consider myself a Christian, Italian, or even white. I have been moved, at unpredictable times, by the beauty of Christian ritual, especially by the music, but not by its theology. Unlike Nathalie Sarraute, I do not think of this as exercising my freedom of choice. I'm too cynical for that—or perhaps indifferent. I will not, of course, be believed. I will probably be seen as defensive. I admit to a perverse delight in contemplating the contortions produced by the paradoxical nature not of social life in its immediacy, but of our attempt to rationalize rather than indulge ourselves with irony, joy, or sadness in the absurdity of our constructs of social reality. It isn't existence that is absurd but our view of existence. Existents simply are. Our folly is to assume they are identical with their representation. That's the danger.

JANE AND I have just been married. We will be moving to Morocco in the fall. We want to rent a house in Rhode Island, in Little Compton, for the summer. We find one. As Jane is inspecting the kitchen, the real estate agent calls me aside and asks if my name is Italian. I say yes, and she says with relief, "Then you are not Jewish." I want to laugh—laugh, not cry. A punch, a stab aside, how else can one react? The Nazis were defeated a few decades earlier. What's the point?

Why didn't my father object to my baptism? I doubt that he shared my mother's delusion. Or did he? He was, as I've said, not a religious man. I have no proof of this other than what my mother told me. That is not quite true. He never talked about religion. He stipulated in his will that he be buried in a non-sectarian cemetery.

I return home from school several months after my father's death. My mother is white with fury. I know no other way to describe it than with this cliché. "Read this," she says, handing me a letter on thick, creamy paper: an attestation with the papal seal. It announces that the Pope has delivered a mass for my father. "How did this happen?" I ask. "I don't know," she says, "but I have my suspicions." "I have my suspicions" is one of her favorite phrases. "They must have paid for this. They never approved of me." She doesn't tell me who "they" are. There isn't time. She grabs the letter and the attestation from me and rips it to shreds in so decisive a manner that all reference to it ceases. "The effrontery, the insult" are her last words on the papal mass.

My father was sent to a Jesuit school. A second son, he was destined for the Church—to keep the family's property intact. Apparently, at least so goes the family story, he had no idea that he would be entering the priesthood until he learned it from my grandfather's mistress. Call her Teresina. She had been jilted, and in an act of terrible vengeance, Teresina seduced my father, calling him "my little priest," and told him. He was thirteen or fourteen. With all the bravado that must have resulted from bedding Teresina, he told his father that he would never be a priest, and in the course of the fight that followed, he yelled that he had slept with her. My grandfather exploded. "You will be a priest or a cobbler." Stubbornly, my father repeated, "I will never be a priest." "Then you'll be a cobbler." My father left the room without answering, and the next day was sent to apprentice with the local cobbler, who, while embarrassed, could not refuse my grandfather's command.

When my mother told me the story, I was the same age as my father had been when Teresina seduced him. I don't think my mother realized this. I didn't until now. I was jealous and ashamed of my innocence. I imagined Teresina as a savage beauty of tempestuous, operatic passions and wild, insatiable sexual prowess. In fact, she was probably an overweight peasant who had lost her figure by the time my grandfather left her for a younger woman. But I didn't want to admit this.

I don't know how long my father apprenticed with the shoemaker. I doubt if it was more than a month or two. The family was in disgrace, but no one could stand up to my grandfather. He was a notoriously willful man. As it happened, it was one of my father's Jesuit teachers who intervened and negotiated a peace. My father was to surrender his inheritance, and in return my grandfather was to pay for his education through university. He was to be sent north to a boarding school. I believe it was the school D'Annunzio attended in Prato. My father said something to that effect when we visited Vittoriale, the poet's villa on Lake Garda. Anti-Fascist, but ambivalently so, he was an admirer of D'Annunzio.

My father never saw his father again. They never wrote to each other. The rupture was complete, but it left traces. I remember asking my father a few months before he died about a thin black scar on the palm of his right hand. I had never noticed it before. "It's nothing," he said, making a fist, and then, after a pause, "I cut myself when I was a 'shoemaker.'" Surprised, I asked him *when* he had been a shoemaker, but he changed the subject. My mother, as her bitterness grew, insisted that my father had come to the United States to specialize mainly to extract as much money as possible from my grandfather. I don't believe this. He was, as I remember him, a willful man, and he often lost his temper, but he wasn't petty and vengeful. By then, of course, he had been drained of ambition — by precocious and not so precocious displacements. I don't want to blame his exhaustion — his *appauvrissement* — on the traumatic effect of a long-past seduction and ostracism. Italians tell me it is an old Sicilian story and dismiss it with a laugh.

Sometimes I envy those who believe. When this happens both shame and guilt humble me, substituting, I suppose, for the humility and piety I should be feeling...

Should I be?

What should I be feeling?

Can there be faith without constraint — the ubiquitous *should* that opens up the space of its transgression.

That *should* precedes the Law.

It is so much easier to speak of the Law than of the pre-legal, the pre-nomic *should*.

And the transcendent?

Jane and I often go to a Lutheran church a few blocks from our apartment to listen to the Bach cantatas that are performed on Sunday afternoons at five. The music transports us. Sometimes, not always. I sense those moments in her as she does in me. But that experience resists description. It is the ethereal, the transcendent, and that emptiness, positive at times, negative at times, that demands filling — a wordy filling that destroys it. Once, sitting in that church, listening, distracted, to Bach's music, I realized that whatever it is that we call transcendent or ethereal is a field of struggle between self-preserving inarticulateness and self-destructive articulateness — between that emptiness and God, deity, spirit, the myriad population of figures and characters, indeed emptiness itself, with which we populate it: words, sometimes heartfelt, sometimes sufficient unto themselves, mostly blemished, through overuse — through use.

XVI.
IS FORGIVENESS
POSSIBLE?

J ANE and I were having dinner at Benno Schmidt and Helen Whitney's house in New York with the historian Peter Gay and his wife. Benno was president of Yale at the time. In the middle of dinner, Peter announced with evident satisfaction the recent discovery that the deconstructionist literary critic Paul de Man, who had taught at Yale, had written articles for the Belgian collaborationist newspaper *Le Soir* when he was starting his career. Benno was stunned. His immediate response was fear of the reactions it would produce at Yale. Since becoming president, he had been attacked by members of the faculty and some students for not being "fully committed" to Yale—which seemed to involve his spending weekends with Helen at their home in New York, where she was a well-known documentary filmmaker. Scrutinizing Benno's every move had become a faculty obsession. One anthropologist told me he kept a record of how many nights a week Benno spent in New Haven, in the president's house. Helen and Benno were not fans of deconstructionism, but it was Peter who immediately related what I think he called the moral vacuousness of de Man's thought to Nazism. He ignored me when I said I had never heard an echo of anti-Semitism in anything de Man had ever said to me, and that many of the writers and philosophers he admired were Jewish. He had been one of my teachers at Harvard. I would have gone on to ask why no one was particularly concerned about Mircea Eliade's unapologetic support of Romania's anti-Semitic Iron Guard, whose virulence is said to have shocked even the Germans, but it was clear that no one wanted to hear what I had to say.

THE REACTION to de Man's articles spread across the academic world and made the front page of *The New York Times*. Interviews were conducted and misquoted, speeches were made, essays written, and books published on the subject. They all focused on his purported anti-Semitism. In fact, only one of the two hundred articles he had written for *Le Soir* was explicitly anti-Semitic, though others could be read as such. The scholarly reactions questioned the relationship between de Man's apparent silence about those articles and his literary theories. They were concerned with, among other things, the ways in which rhetoric masks meaning and meaning rhetoric, and in consequence the impossibility of interpretive certainty. It was later discovered that de Man had been anonymously denounced while teaching at Harvard and had sent a convoluted letter to the Society of Fellows there, explaining that he had written for *Le Soir*; that he had stopped when the Nazis "no longer allowed freedom of statement"; that after the war, like everyone in Belgium, he had been subject to "a very severe examination of his political behavior" during the war and furnished with a *certificat de civisme* to the effect that he was "cleared of any collaboration." He concluded angrily and pathetically: "To accuse me, now behind my back, of collaboration, and this by persons of a different nation who cannot possibly verify and appreciate the facts is a slanderous attack which leaves me helpless." His life was scrutinized. It was found that he was involved in fraudulent business practices after the war and that he had married his second wife while still married to his first, who, with their two children, was living in

Argentina. Mary McCarthy, who had met de Man soon after his arrival in the United States, when he was working at the Doubleday bookstore in Manhattan, was impressed by his knowledge of literature and helped him obtain a teaching position at Bard College, his first in the country. Mary once told me that while he was still at the bookstore, he would give her books that he clearly couldn't afford on his salary. Smiling, she said nothing more, but I think she was flattered by de Man's evident attachment. She didn't know about the *Le Soir* articles.

De Man's collaborationist sympathies and morally dubious opportunism are reprehensible. But the public discussions of the relationship between his egregious views and his scholarly work, though potentially significant, added little to anyone's understanding of that relationship. Many of the responses to de Man's collaborationist writings, particularly among his conservative critics, were themselves morally questionable, given that they reduced de Man's immoral acts and sympathies to opportunities for expressing academic disagreements, jealousies, and trivial politics that had little if anything to do with his views. For some academics, they were transparently careerist — a way to get on the tenure and promotion bandwagon, by writing for or being quoted in the popular press. There were others who felt genuinely disappointed, hurt, and even betrayed by him. I can understand the disappointment and the hurt but not the betrayal. How had he betrayed them? Why did they expect him to confide in — that is, confess to — them? Is confession necessarily a proof of collegiality or friendship?

Jane asked me what my response would have been had de Man confided in me. It was, of course, impossible to know — at least without also knowing the circumstances and the manner of that confession. Would I have stopped him? It has been said that de

Man once tried to tell a senior Jewish colleague at Harvard about his work for *Le Soir*, but the colleague wouldn't listen, saying he was interested in de Man's scholarship, not his personal life. No, I'm sure I would not have stopped him. I would have been surprised and disappointed by what he had to say, though perhaps not as much as many of his colleagues, if only because I've met Germans, when I lived in Germany, who spoke honestly about their past, some self-critically, some dishonestly, and others neutrally or apologetically. More than a few — this in a dive in Frankfurt, popular with the old noncoms in Hitler's army — indulged in drunken diatribes, blaming American Jews for Germany's defeat. There was no point in arguing with them. I've often wondered if their children became Nazi skinheads.

I might have argued that de Man's articles were harmless, given what was happening in Europe at the time, but that would not have been an excuse. There were obviously Belgians who would have refused to write for *Le Soir* had they been asked. What is stunning was de Man's opportunism. I would have let him talk, but I would like to have seen him squirm. This reaction troubles me, since de Man — the de Man I knew — was likable and I liked him. I suppose it's possible to justify his acts on the grounds that he was young and inexperienced. He was in his early twenties when he wrote the articles. I am loath to offer him this way out, but still uneasy about not taking into account his age. I mustn't forget the Belgians of his age who fought in the Resistance. Like most Americans (and despite my skepticism), I value personal growth, encourage change, if only on pragmatic grounds, and respect conversions when they appear to be sincere. There are, however, acts that preclude consideration of growth, change, and conversion. They stop time and with it possibility. The actor's identity is fixed forever and is, as it were, confined to the evil he has committed. Were de Man's articles, opportunism, and silence of this magnitude?

As I was reading André Gide's *The Counterfeiters* late last night, I was startled by this observation made by one of the characters — Edouard, for those of you who know the book: *"A présent, peu s'en faut que je ne voie dans l'irrésolution le secret de ne pas vieillir."* Edouard has come to understand irresolution as the secret for not growing old. Gide's convoluted French sentence is impossible to translate adequately into English, but perhaps because of this, it captures the irresolution to which he is referring. Is my hedged response to Jane's question a response to aging? Or is it simply a symptom of the professor's proverbial inability to come to a firm decision, since he or she — since I — tend to see too many sides to a problem? Or are any of us in a position to judge de Man?

Professor de Man and I are walking around Harvard Yard. I took his course on Valéry, Rilke, and Yeats the previous spring. It was magical. His readings had a philosophical depth I had never imagined possible. He was not yet a deconstructionist. Rather he was deeply imbued in Hegel, the phenomenologists, and Heidegger. His approach and increasing popularity among students infuriated several of his senior colleagues and, a few years after I graduated, led to his moving to Cornell and then to Yale, via Johns Hopkins and Zurich.

I had discussed my senior thesis with him at the end of that semester; he suggested that I write about the relationship between Baudelaire's symbolism and Henri Bergson's approach to consciousness, matter, and memory and offered to direct my thesis if the philosophy department agreed. They didn't, I had just learned, because "literature wasn't philosophy" and because no one outside the philosophy department could direct a thesis there. They had looked through the department's archives.

Besides, I was told, no one in the department then had the expertise to direct it. When I told this to de Man, he laughed. It was expectable. Though John Wild taught courses on existentialism and Paul Tillich on Schelling, the department was so dedicated to Anglo-American analytic philosophy that they didn't even offer a course on Hegel! De Man suggested that I write on Sartre and the imagination and agreed to guide me informally, which he did. We met two or three times a month, almost always walking around the Yard, talking less about Sartre than about other French philosophers who were barely known in the United States: Léon Brunschvicg, Jean Hippolite, Alexandre Kojève, Jean Wahl, Gaston Bachelard, and Maurice Blanchot, among others. He became more than a mentor—a friend. Sometimes he seemed to be talking about himself but in so abstract a way that I was never sure.

On one of our walks, de Man seemed particularly troubled. He began talking about the impossibility of apologizing for something if you had no platform from which to do so—no one with the authority to receive your apology. Was he talking about himself? How could he apologize? How could he confess? To whom? On what occasion? Where? We indulge ourselves in confession, taking—at times naively—what is confessed as an accurate account of what was actually experienced and is now felt. Despite their admiration for the silent hero (though rarely the silent heroine), Americans seem to be uncomfortable with an etiquette of silence. Silence suggests a secret and a secret suggests shame, and shame suggests guilt.

I am not justifying or condoning de Man's silence or Eliade's, or that of countless other collaborators and Nazi sympathizers, many of whom continued to teach after the war, in Europe and the United States. I am simply calling attention to some of the obstacles that preclude revelation and perpetuate silence. We have to consider them when we judge someone's silence—or inaction—the way we also have to recognize how these obstacles are used to justify silence and inaction, keeping the delinquency—the evil—alive to haunt the perpetrator and his or her children.

Gunther is having a drink in our living room. Jane met him two or three days earlier on a flight back from Amsterdam. Every seat on the plane was taken, most by black Muslims who were coming home from a pilgrimage to Mecca and had transferred in Amsterdam. Jane was sitting on the aisle beside a couple who had just been married in Mecca. The couple had met for the first time at their wedding. At least that is what the bride told Jane before her husband attacked her, pinching, slapping, and jabbing her with his elbow. The woman was terrified and did nothing to stop him. Her lack of response must have enraged him, because he reached over her and began to pinch Jane. Jane called the steward and asked to be given another seat. He said there were none. The other pilgrims did nothing to stop the man. Finally, Gunther, a German sitting a few rows behind Jane, offered to exchange seats with her. At the end of the flight she thanked him and asked him home for drinks. She did not expect him to accept, but a few days later he did.

Gunther tells us that he frequently comes to the States to buy small factories, particularly in the South, for businesses that want to avoid the high cost of German labor. At the time, the mark was particularly strong, and Gunther seems less bothered by the exploitative dimension of his business than with America's indifference to its workers' welfare. Neither Jane nor I say anything. The conversation shifts to the war. Gunther says that a Jewish family lived, hidden, in the apartment next to his family's and that his mother and father helped them, as best they could, by buying their food and warning them whenever the SS swept the neighborhood. One day, Gunther's father heard the Gestapo climbing the stairs. He wanted to warn his neighbors but, fearing that he would be caught, did nothing. He had to protect his wife and children, including Gunther, who was a baby. He was haunted, Gunther tells us, by his silence—his inaction. It is clear to Jane and me that Gunther is also haunted by it—perhaps because it saved his life. Jane and I have the impression that his father never blamed his family. We cannot ask him. We barely know him.

I have often wondered why Gunther told the story. Was it because we were strangers? Did he tell it to others? To friends? I certainly didn't feel that his confession was obsessive. It couldn't even be called a confession, for confession implies an assumption of responsibility, and Gunther, though responsible—in saving him, his father condemned their Jewish neighbors—he was not responsible. He was caught in his father's assumption of responsibility—in a justification that, strictly speaking, was uncalled for. His father had no choice. He couldn't sacrifice his children, his wife, or perhaps himself. Is that the rub? His own fear of death. Or is it? Perhaps. More likely that would diminish him, and diminished he could not assume responsibility for what he was not able to do. What must have troubled him was doubt: Had he miscalculated? Had he had time to warn his Jewish neighbors? Could he have hidden them safely after all in his apartment? I imagine those possibilities, acknowledged or not, troubled Gunther as well. But any doubt Gunther may have had wasn't directed toward himself but toward his father. He made no mention of doubting his father's story, but the silence of no-mention is inevitably a mention.

The inheritance of a responsibility that you are not responsible for is terrible. To speak of guilt, shared, inherited, singular, or collective, is, I suppose, a way of simplifying the dynamics of responsibility: an evasion of responsibility, cast back to an origin—original sin, Oedipal guilt—that deflects responsibility to a mythic event, as in the Bible, or to what we take to be an inescapable psychic dynamic. Evasions such as these are, in the theological sense (and in the psychological one, too) indulgences. Put in theological terms, they require a redeemer—a role that humans can never assume. We can listen, as Jane and I did to Gunther, but while we could feel for him, while we might even point out the dynamics of his position, his inevitable, inescapable, entrapment, we could do nothing more. Nor, for that matter, could a psychoanalyst. An analyst cannot "redeem." He can only listen and occasionally intervene, offering an interpretation (reinforced by his professional status) that, as illuminating as it might be, more often than not merely recasts the rawness of responsibility as the solidity of shame and the imperviousness of guilt, the comfort (and the pain, too) of abstraction, conceptualization, and a storied fatality that transforms the particular into a communicable generality. We can deal with it as such, or think we can. And we do, some of the time—in mysterious ways that, despite our psycho-mechanics, bypass our understanding.

Paul de Man, if I remember correctly, gave greater weight to the absence of a platform than to an interlocutor empowered to accept an apology, offer forgiveness, and relieve him of whatever burden he carried. He was, I think, too much of a realist to believe that such an interlocutor existed. Were he to find one, he would have had to surrender his silence—the silence imposed upon him by "circumstances," the absence of a platform for which he could take no responsibility—and what respite that silence gave to him.

There are, of course, socially condoned platforms from which to confess both publicly and privately. They, too, are not without moral implication. I think of being "born again"—by the convenience of suddenly discovering God, however sincere that discovery may be, and confessing to Him and His flock, as the Puritans did. Or the distasteful, if not entirely hypocritical, appearances of political figures, accompanied by wives and children, in the wake of sexual scandals. Does anyone really accept these meae culpae as expressions of sincere regret and honest promises of reform? In the name of loyalty, or at least of marital commitment or filial support, these wives and children are asked to sacrifice all dignity and discretion for their husband's or father's political rehabilitation—turning betrayal into cowardly perversion of a ritual of humiliation—one that deflects *his* humiliation to his (or, less frequently, her) "loved ones." What do you remember: the adulterer's set speech of regret or the downcast faces of his wife and children? Now, there is, of course, an ever more popular platform: the book that tells it all and the media events that follow. The sin becomes a commodity—to the benefit of the sinner.

Platforms can obviously be assumed and interlocutors conscripted. But however interesting the resulting confidences—the confessions—may be, they are almost by definition invasive. Whenever I come back from France, where discretion contravenes confession, I suffer a few days of emotional claustrophobia. People tell me too much, certainly more than I want to know, but I don't really know anything more about them. Their intimacies are a kind of mask—conventions really—concealing much more about them than any silence. The French have their *confidantes*, but they do not normally broadcast their *vies intimes* to strangers.

When I taught at Princeton, I commuted from New York. In the morning, traveling in the opposite direction from most commuters, my New York colleagues—there were more of us than the university liked to admit—ran little risk of being disturbed by over-talkative passengers, and we followed an unsaid rule not to talk to one another. But coming home, in the late afternoon, the trains were filled with passengers, mainly men, who seemed to have nothing better to do than talk. What surprised me was how quickly a total stranger would sit down next to one of us and "share" details of his life, ranging from his uncontrollable bouts of anger, usually toward his wife, to infidelities and fondness for kinky sex or, more often, his fantasies of kinky sex. I am quite certain that none of those men would have told their closest friends what they told me. I felt used by these monologues, though I don't think the men were aware of that or would have stopped if they had been. They needed to talk about themselves, but to talk they also needed anonymity. Once they started, they rarely asked me about myself or for my advice. They seldom told me their names or where they worked. (On the rare occasions when I ran into one of them again, he either ignored me or seemed to have forgotten me entirely.) As irritated as I was by their intrusion—I wanted to use the time to read, or grade papers, or simply sit and think—I was saddened by their loneliness and the restrictions they must have felt with their friends. But were they lonely? Did they suffer from those restrictions? Were encounters with strangers like me sufficient? What strikes me in retrospect is how many of them were extroverts. They could laugh at themselves, but there was little irony in their laughter.

I am laughing at myself—but not without irony, I hope, since I'm also assuming a platform and conscripting you, my readers, as interlocutors. It is easier to throw away a book than extract yourself from a conversation that depends on face-to-face encounters to continue. The thought is depressing. Barring narcissists such as Anaïs Nin, who can't imagine anyone not being enchanted by their story, most autobiographers and memoirists have to give their life a raison d'être that transcends it. They are looking to produce something exemplary—a moral-allegory, pedagogical, a revelation of the workings of history or society, satirical, or spiritually illuminating—in other words, something meaningful and, acknowledged or not, transformative. (Of course, there are life stories that are simply meant to be entertaining.) The autobiography is directed at someone else, the reader, whose real or imagined response will not only transform *him* but also turn back on the autobiography, giving it meaning or, I suppose, rendering it meaningless, by obliterating the "storiness" of the story, the gap between the story and the life as lived, the lived life. An autobiography strives to resurrect that life, but is destined to fail, if only because, like Narcissus, seduced by his own image, the autobiographer is seduced by his or her story. To resist that seduction is to recognize the artifice of the endeavor, its inevitable deceits and elaborations—its fictionalization.

In this respect, the autobiographical novel may actually be more honest than the autobiography, even as it tries to collapse the tension between "reality" and what the autobiographer knows and the reader suspects to be imagined or invented. Even the most naive reader will eventually ask: Did this really happen? Could this really have happened? Are we captivated by the life we read about or by our suspicions about that life as depicted? We speak of autobiographical truth when we ought, perhaps, to focus on autobiographical dubiety. Of course, we are living in an age in which fidelity has been sabotaged by the tropes of modernity and postmodernity, by irony, suspicion, playfulness, and skepticism. But they do offer us a protection, minimal as it may be, against the tyranny of prevailing literalisms.

XVII.
MEXICO

I AM seated next to the anthropologist Marvin Harris on a plane for Mexico City, where the annual meetings of the American Anthropological Association are about to start. It is 1974. Marvin is startled. He looks around to see if there are any free seats. There are none. I think, *Well, finally, I've got you cornered. You'll have to listen to me.* It's been several years since I've seen him.

Marvin Harris tyrannized Columbia's anthropology department and did his best to dominate American cultural anthropology during the fifties and sixties. At departmental meetings, you could hear him tear into any of the faculty who didn't share his views—with an angry sarcasm that even as politic an anthropologist as Margaret Mead or as gentlemanly a one as Conrad Arensberg could rarely stop. He was an ideologue, though he thought of himself as a positivist, striving to give anthropology a firm "scientific" basis without ever realizing that positivism, at least his positivism, was also an ideology. Best known publicly for his theory that Aztec cannibalism and the intertribal warfare of the Amazon's Yanomami Indians were the result of protein deficiency in their diets, he coupled an ecological determinism with a simplistic Marxism that was current in American anthropology in the middle of the last century and is not without adherents today. He dismissed as epiphenomena just about everything that did not fit into his cultural materialist paradigm. He cultivated disciples, some of whom were even more dismissive of expressive, intellectual, and spiritual culture than Harris himself. One of my classmates so identified with him that he began to speak with Harris's nasalized twang, to gesture as Harris did, and to mindlessly echo his thought. I remember Harris correcting the Harvard anthropologist Stanley Tambiah, one of the best ethnographers I have ever met, when Tambi referred to some lectures that Harris was giving in New England as a "lecture tour." "I prefer to think of them as forays," Harris snapped, and walked off. Tambi, who had never met him, looked at me in amazement. "I told you so," I said. Tambi had asked me to introduce him to Harris.

Harris had little tolerance for students who didn't agree with him. I was one of them. I found his thought simplistic. I was interested in almost everything he dismissed: the individual, subjective experience, symbolism, religion, ritual, belief, art, and—what he, like many of his colleagues, reacted to most violently—psychological and psychoanalytic approaches to human behavior and cultural expression. (By now it should be evident that I have become far more cautious about psychoanalytic interpretation than I was then.)

My advisor, Robert Murphy, told me that I'd made a mistake in choosing Columbia, since there was little interest in any of these subjects, but that as long as I did well and could work independently, the department would support me. I did, and they did, though at one point, apparently, Harris had been so infuriated by my answer to a question in the final exam of the department's introductory course that he wanted to throw me out. Instead of dismissing James Frazer, the author of *The Golden Bough*, as Harris had demanded, I wrote that despite the flaws in Frazer's approach—his fairly promiscuous assemblage of bits of ethnographic data from around the world to fit the uncritical narrative, a sort of mega-myth, he had constructed—he had, in fact, articulated many of the basic categories of anthropological description and theorizing. I knew I was provoking Harris, but

I didn't think he would go as far as he did. Murphy called me in and warned me. Over the previous summer, I had worked in the department, and one of my duties was to sort Harris's library and notes. I discovered that the main source of his discussions of philosophy in his popular book on the history of anthropology, *The Rise of Anthropological Theory*, was a cliché-ridden introductory philosophy textbook that he had underlined and annotated—one I wouldn't have assigned to a high school class. I missed Harvard. Or was it the rigor of philosophy?

None of the courses I took were theoretically challenging, or even interesting, though I found the ethnographic data fascinating. It wasn't my professors' fault. Some were excellent, others well meaning, and others, like Harris, actually believed that they possessed if not truth then a way—the only way—to find it. The fault lay in the quality of anthropological theory, at least as it was taught at Columbia then. Cultural evolution was in fashion, but little attention was given to how it reflected American triumphalism. One anthropologist associated with the department counted the cultural traits found in different societies and organized them in bar graphs, proving, I suppose, that more complex (read civilized) societies had more traits, without ever recognizing the circularity of his argument. He was, however, an excellent field researcher.

American anthropology has always had an anti-intellectual strain. I remember how shocked I was at one of the first Anthropological Association meetings I attended, to hear an anthropologist—sporting tight jeans, a trim sports shirt, and the requisite Navajo silver and turquoise belt buckle—dismiss a question about the role of symbolism in something he was analyzing, by announcing that there were anthropologists who were scientists and anthropologists who were intellectuals, and that he was proud to be one of the scientists. I suppose he meant that as a scientist, he had no need to consider symbolic culture. I would like to have asked him whether his answer met the scientific standards he was advocating, but I lacked the confidence. I was a neophyte. I should add that, though the division still exists, anthropological theory has become far more sophisticated than it was when I studied it.

Anthropology is a peculiar field. Like most academic fields, it is riven with conflict, but, unlike some (at least some of the time), its practitioners have very little self-irony. The discipline itself, at least in its American incarnation, is a kind of historical accident, in which physical, cultural, and linguistic anthropology and archeology are in uneasy tension. (Most anthropologists outside the United States do not define anthropology in terms of these four fields.) Anthropologists find themselves having straddled not just their own cultural assumptions and those of the people they study, but also other disciplines, such as sociology, psychology, economics, history, and, though reluctantly, philosophy, which have greater clout both intellectually and institutionally. This leads, as one of my professors put it, to a discipline that has a heart but no core. There are, one would think, distinct advantages to this situation: an awareness of cultural artifice, including the discipline's own artifice, an open-mindedness, a skepticism concerning social and cultural objectifications, resistance to academic sclerosis, a creative push that results from the discipline's structural contradictions, and thus in the fragility of the discipline and its research practices. In fact, these "advantages" are considered dangers, and that has encouraged a moralistic refusal to view the discipline with critical irony, to recognize the possibilities in its paradoxical nature, and to broaden the context in which it is defined. Rather, an inordinate effort is made to unify and solidify the discipline—to give it a fixed and authoritative perspective. My view that we should not even speak of anthropology (except, pragmatically, in bureaucratic settings) but of anthropologies is not shared by many of my colleagues.

Seeing that he can't escape, Marvin turns to me, combative, and launches into an attack on the anthropology program at Princeton, where I am teaching, which is centered on his anathema — symbolic anthropology. He focuses his attack on Clifford Geertz and Victor Turner, who, as he sees it, are his rivals. Neither of them is in the program. Geertz is at the Institute for Advanced Study, and Turner is visiting there. Both, however, have shaped the program intellectually and, in the case of Geertz, bureaucratically, for despite the fact that the Institute is not attached to the university, it has had an enormous influence on it. Geertz was not a man to ignore influence, provided he could exercise it backstage. I stop Marvin.

"Look, Marvin, I respect Turner, but I'm not one of Geertz's followers. I find his work shallow and conservative."

When I say "conservative," Harris suddenly appears to take an interest in what I am saying.

"I certainly believe that we should employ scientific methods when they are appropriate," I say to appease him, "but we have to seek other approaches for those areas of human life that cannot be treated scientifically; that is, as you understand science."

I could feel Harris's anger rise.

"I'm in favor of rigor — a rigorous approach to interpretation, one that recognizes its limits, just as any good science does."

I am embarrassed by my didacticism, but I still have Harris's ear.

"What I find troubling about most symbolic interpretation is its failure to consider language and a people's understanding of what language is and how it is used." He listens, but when I start to explain how phenomenologists have, in my view, failed to consider the role of language, the one they use in describing experience, Harris loses patience.

"That's what I object to. It's all unfounded speculation," he barks, and before I can answer he gets up and wanders up and down the aisle. Finally he stops to talk to an anthropologist who shares his views; at least I assume he does.

When the captain turns on the seat belt sign, Harris remains standing until a steward insists that he sit down. He does and sulks, not even attempting to read.

"Your wife wrote a book about Allen Ginsberg," he suddenly says. "I knew Allen. We were both students at Columbia together."

I wonder what possible influence Allen could have had on him.

"Did you read Jane's book?" I ask him, feigning innocence. I was quite certain he had not.

"I don't write for money," he says after a long pause, without ever answering my question and starts a diatribe against *The New Yorker*, against journalists, against the compromises you make when you are paid for what you write.

I ignore his provocation and ask him again if he has read Jane's book.

"No, I wouldn't."

"But, Marvin," I say, again feigning innocence. "You do write for money. Aren't some of your books published by Random House? That's Jane's publisher, too. And your history of anthropology? Isn't it one of the most popular anthropology textbooks in the country?"

He jumps up and starts pacing again, up and down the aisle, trying to avoid the steward who wants him to take his seat and fasten his seat belt, which he does finally and doesn't say another

word to me. When the plane lands, I ask if he wants to share a cab
to the hotel, but he doesn't have the courtesy to answer.

I meet several of my old professors, and we go to the hotel
together. They say that they've heard of a good restaurant, and
we arrange to meet for lunch. I'm staying in a different hotel.
I try to avoid conference hotels. I can't stand the professional
claustrophobia. When we arrive at the restaurant, it turns out
to be a Jewish delicatessen. Ah, New Yorkers. I wonder if we can
trust any anthropologist's fieldwork. Perhaps Harris has a point,
I think for an instant. Then I dismiss the thought.

The next day, I am invited to a reception given by a Mexican psychoanalytic society in honor of George Devereux, one
of the founders of psychoanalytic anthropology. His *Mohave
Ethnopsychiatry* was the first, and is still the most comprehen-
sive, description of an Amerindian people's understanding of
mental illness, and was complemented by his book *Reality and
Dream* — his account, session by session, of his psychoanalysis of
a Plains Indian suffering from anxiety attacks, phobias, and compulsive sleeping rituals. I am nervous. I haven't seen George since
my book on the Hamadsha came out a year earlier. He had sent
me an angry letter because I didn't cite any of his works. He is
probably right to be angry. But I'd decided not to reference any
work that I hadn't addressed directly. I did thank him profusely
in my preface, but it seems that wasn't enough. Although George
helped me enormously, I never felt particularly comfortable
with his approach to psychoanalysis and psychoanalytic anthropology. It seemed too mechanical, too reductive and, at times,
aggressive, as if he was addressing an enemy. In part, this was
true. He had been treated shabbily by American anthropology.
Though he was exceptionally intelligent, enormously erudite,
an excellent fieldworker, and a prolific writer, he never held a

permanent academic post in the United States. "Thanks to Kroeber," he told me once. Alfred Kroeber, one of the most influential of the early American anthropologists, had practiced psychoanalysis for a couple of years just after World War I and became so disillusioned with it that he felt "betrayed" (George's word) by George's research on the Mohave Indians. Apparently, he had seen to it that George was never offered a position. George practiced psychoanalysis until 1963, when he left for Paris and, thanks largely to Claude Lévi-Strauss, obtained a post at the École Pratique des Hautes Études en Sciences Sociales. By then, he had taught himself Greek, already published articles in the best classical journals, and given lectures in the classics department at Oxford. Unlike the American academics, the French appreciated his work, as clearly the Mexicans did. After his death, one of his students, Toby Nathan, founded an institute in his name.

George is sitting on a couch, holding court, delighting in the attention he's receiving. He has aged since I saw him a few years ago, but, then again, he always looked older than he was. Sometimes I had the feeling that he played on the idea of his great age. He always worried about how he would support himself in old age. He lived in a tiny apartment in a working-class suburb of Paris, surrounded by his books—those he wasn't obliged to sell before moving to Paris—file cabinets, and a grand piano, which he said he never played. Apparently he had had considerable talent as a young man but had to abandon any plans for a career as a concert pianist after an operation damaged his hand. He had also abandoned the study of physics, having concluded that he would never achieve the eminence of his cousin Edward Teller. He was living alone, though the first time I met him he was married to an American student. She was, by some accounts, his eighth wife. Rumor had it that he'd fled the United States because of the back alimony he owed, and that he was able to attend the American Anthropological Meetings this year only because they were in Mexico.

George beckons me. His expression is unreadable. "I was hoping you would come," he says. "I arranged to have you invited. We must talk." We arrange to meet the next morning. I stand there stupid. I don't know many of the guests. A Mexican woman, who, in contrast to the other women at the reception, is elegantly and expensively dressed, must have noticed my discomfort. She introduces herself. She is a museum curator and is married to a psychoanalyst. She leads me away from George and his acolytes. She is worldly, confidently so, not afraid to lampoon whatever thought-fashion is current. She is flirtatious, and, at the same time, it is flirtatiously clear that she is simply playing a part. I detect a darkness behind her play and I am not sure whether it is real or feigned. I ask myself if I am being set up for something. She seems to intuit my thought. We move farther away from the other guests, but within her husband's sight. He has been watching us.

"My husband's father was an important man, a diplomat, an ambassador to China," she tells me, catching me glancing in his direction. "I come from a simple family." Given her style, I can't imagine it was that simple. "He was dominated by his father even after his father died. When we married, he insisted that we move into his father's house. Yes, it was his house, really his father's. Everything was just as it had been when his father lived there. I had—how do you say?—no input. It was a man's house. I was a prisoner there. My husband didn't want me to work. He would leave early in the morning before I got up—I used to sleep late because I had nothing to do—and would come home late, just before dinner. He was still in training." She pauses. "You are not

American?" she asks suddenly. I say I am. "Never mind, you don't seem like an American. You will understand." She pauses again. I have the feeling, though it is only a feeling, that she has reached a moment of uncertainty. She seems compelled to say something she doesn't want to say, but I suspect that I'm not the first person to hear the confidence that is to follow. I am enchanted and enchanted by my enchantment. In that pause, she has become helpless, a lost child, bullied, reliving the moment she is about to recount, pleading for help, escape from the confines of the masculine sepulcher in which she is—is about to be—buried. I feel foolish, helpless.

In a voice that masters itself—a gift, as it were, to me—she goes on. "My father-in-law collected masks, Chinese masks, beautiful ones, rare ones. They were on every wall. At first, I pretended to like them, but in truth I hated them. I couldn't escape them. They haunted me—took possession of me. You will understand. You studied spirit possession, didn't you? I heard you had." I wonder who told her. "I am not sure they possessed me. They obsessed me. Obsession is worse than possession. You can never escape it. You can't be exorcized. I dreamt about those masks. They were nightmarish. One morning, I ordered the servants to light a fire in the fireplace. They must have thought it odd. It was summer. And then I dismissed them for the day. I took the masks, all the masks, and burned them one by one. I was transported. You will understand."

I do and don't. I am about to ask her what her husband's reaction was, but before I can, he approaches us, and, as if anticipating my question, she whispers. "He saw me for the first time as I was—a woman with feelings." Then she turns to her husband and says, "I was just telling, Vicente—it is Vicente?—how I became a museum curator." He smiles. I'm convinced he knows what she told me. "Do you practice psychoanalysis?" he asks me. "No," I say. "Ah, but you will understand. Devereux tells me you are quite brilliant."

I first met George in Paris, just before leaving for Morocco. Margaret Mead had given me his phone number, after asking his permission. "You must not give it to anyone. He is very private. You'll understand when you meet him." I began to understand when I called George to make an appointment to see him. "You are from Columbia?" he asked several times, but never gave me time to say more than yes. He insisted that we meet the next morning at eight at the café Deux Magots. When I arrived he was already there. I introduced myself.

"You are from Columbia?" he asked, as soon as I sat down. "I have not been able to sleep since your call. Do you know my wife?" When I told him I didn't—which was true—he asked me how that was possible. She was a student in the department. I said that the Columbia department was big and that, besides, I did my best to avoid it, that I preferred to work by myself, and that my social life was elsewhere. He was unconvinced by my answer but seemed to accept it. Though I resented his questioning me about his wife, I was determined to convince him that I was really indifferent to academic gossip. This was, in fact, true. I tried to stay aloof, not out of an arrogant sense of superiority, but simply because I didn't want to get involved.

Though George was suspicious of me, indeed because he was suspicious of me, he treated me as a scholar, and not a student. He seemed genuinely interested in my research. I don't remember much about our conversation except a few generalizations that he made about Arab male sexuality, which struck me as stereotypic, and a comparison with Euripides' *Bacchae* of the Hamadsha ceremonies I was about to study. We exchanged addresses, and he promised to answer any letter I wrote him—which he did with a

generosity of mind I had never experienced from any of my anthropology professors. (Margaret Mead never answered my letters,
but she would always send me a book that she thought, rightly or,
more often, wrongly, might be pertinent to my research.) George
never gave me advice, but simply let his mind wander through the
experiences I reported. It was the sort of intellectual free association that gives you a new angle on your own work.

I have used this approach with many of my students. It was
the organizing principle of my book *Imaginative Horizons*, where I
played on a montage of sharp and unexplained contrasts between
sections in order to create intellectual disturbance in my readers
and, I hoped, open new horizons in their own thinking. *Imaginative Horizons* didn't always have the effect I had hoped for, though
I was careful to explain my method. The book was mainly treated
as a collection of unconnected essays. I should have known better.

I remembered going to a lecture given by Marshall McLuhan
in New York. McLuhan began it in the middle of a sentence. At
times he spoke in the linear fashion we associate with rationality, and at times in a zigzag fashion. He ended his lecture, if I
remember correctly, in the middle of another sentence and then,
after answering a few questions from the audience with considerable respect, suddenly walked offstage in the middle of replying
to the last one. At first, I thought he was drunk, but he wasn't.
He was playing with the power of form. Given the comments I
heard as the auditorium emptied, no one had caught on to what
he had done—or why he had done it. I began to doubt my own
perception, but many years later, I described the lecture to one
of McLuhan's collaborators, Edmund Carpenter. Ted responded
with a smile that told me I was right. We both started laughing.

Ted was one of the finest anthropologists I have known, a
modest man of immense erudition and aesthetic sensibility who,

with his wife, Adelaide de Menil, supported Arctic research and published beautiful books, among them a book of photographs by Richard Harrington of the great Eskimo famine of the early fifties. Before Ted died, in his late eighties, the Musée du quai Branly, the new Paris ethnographic museum, had an exhibition devoted largely to his collection of "primitive" art. Ted curated the show. It went on to the Menil museum in Houston. The French are less embarrassed by the beauty of cultural artifacts than American anthropologists, who tend to keep their distance from art historians.

When I said goodbye to George that day at the Deux Magot, he looked me straight in the eye and asked again if I was certain I didn't know his wife. I had no idea why he was so suspicious. Did he think I was a spy? Later, I learned that the woman he referred to as his wife was the only Hungarian he had ever married. She came, Margaret Mead told me, from an aristocratic family. George came from a secular Jewish family, changed his name from György Dobó, and converted to Catholicism in 1933 for reasons that were never clear to me (since he was living in America at the time). He had always suffered, Mead told me in one of her offhand ways, from not being an aristocrat himself. His divorce was particularly ugly. "When he finally got what he wanted, he couldn't accept it," she said without elaborating.

I met George during a break in the morning session devoted to his work at the Mexican meetings. The session had begun with a talk by Hama: Utce: the Mohave woman who had translated for him and whom he had not seen since the thirties, when he did his fieldwork on the Mohave reservation. She spoke of George with great affection and humor. I was amazed at her confidence. She reminded me of some of the women I had met on the Navajo reservation. George was deeply moved. When she caricatured him

as an innocent young man who asked a lot of questions that made
no sense, he laughed. It was the first time I had ever seen him
laugh. I think Hama: Utce:'s talk had eased the strain between us.
He dismissed my apology and asked me how Jane was.

Ten minutes later, when George was back on the podium,
his mood had changed dramatically. He was drawn and clearly
angry. It was announced that he would not be speaking that
morning, because of exhaustion. It wasn't clear whether he would
speak that afternoon. He seemed pleased by the audience's disappointment. Something had happened, but I didn't know what it
was. It wasn't exhaustion.

Later I learned that he had felt displaced because a left-leaning
Mexican psychoanalytic society had managed to arrange not
only for Erich Fromm to speak—something George had known
and disapproved of—but also for Hortensia Bussi, the widow of
the recently assassinated Chilean president, Salvador Allende, to
address the association. I'm not certain whether George was upset
by Fromm's presence (in fact, he never appeared) or by Bussi's
politics—she, too, canceled at the last moment—or by a mixing of
politics with scholarship that, as he later told me, he found offen-
sive. He did speak that afternoon, after a minute of silence for
Allende. I was the only person in an audience of several hundred
who stood during that minute. It wasn't a question of politics but
of form.

Jane and I spent several months in Paris after I finished my
Moroccan fieldwork. There were a number of people I wanted
to interview there, and I was able to work in the library of
the Musée de L'Homme and at the Bibliothèque Nationale. We
saw George quite often, sometimes for lunch but usually in his
bleak apartment in Antony. We would arrive in the afternoon
when it was still light, drink tea, and talk, mostly listening

to George. His erudition, as I said, was enormous, and his memory extraordinary. He would punctuate our conversations with bursts of anger at various American anthropologists who had somehow offended him. At one point, he opened a drawer in one of his file cabinets. Inside were the notes for *From Anxiety to Method in the Behavioral Sciences*, his best book, in which he looked at the relationship between a researcher's anxiety and the defensive nature of his or her use of methodology. It turned out that he had been collecting anecdotes about anthropologists for years, particularly those who had insulted him, the bulk of them for the book. "They will recognize themselves," he said, and added with regret, "Of course, many have died before my book came out."

On our way to Paris, Jane and I had stopped in Granada to see David Hart, an anthropologist who had just moved there after living in Morocco for more than twenty years. We brought my field assistant, Youssef Hazmaoui, who had worked with Hart on many of his expeditions to Berber tribes in the Rif and High Atlas mountains but who had never before been able to leave Morocco. The government had refused to issue him a passport. Usually this required a bribe, but I was able to get him one, as my assistant. Hart, who had studied anthropology with Carleton Coon at the University of Pennsylvania, was one of those old-style anthropologists who become so fascinated with ethnographic detail, in his case kinship and tribal feuding, that they never seem to finish their research. David did manage to finish an ethnography of the Aith Waryaghar tribe of the central Rif. Coon, presumably exasperated, wrote in his blurb for the book that it "would be hard to find a more detailed account of any other people in Africa, if not the world."

Jane and I showed Youssef around Granada. He was, of course, impressed by the Alhambra, but saddened, too. "Look at

Morocco today," he told us. He was fascinated by the churches and cathedrals we visited. He had never been in a church before. It would have been awkward for him to enter a Christian church in Morocco. When the Moroccans adopted the Code Napoléon they made conversion a criminal offense. When we stopped for coffee at the end of the afternoon, Youssef expressed shock at seeing paintings that depicted God. When we told him the Christ story, he remained silent for a long time and then said, with a bitter sense of injustice I had never heard him express before, "You *nasrani*—you Christians—murdered your god. We didn't. And it is you who have power and wealth, and we don't."

While we were having dinner at the Harts' that evening, an American neighbor—just back from Portugal, where he had been buying property for the Sultan of Yemen—arrived. He was slick, in an easygoing Southern California sort of way, and, I thought, not particularly trustworthy: one of those "innocent" Americans who somehow manage to attach themselves to unworldly but immensely wealthy Third World potentates and, qualified or not, become their financial advisors. I have met several of them in Switzerland and the South of France. Hart's neighbor called himself Bruce Condé, claiming to be a descendent of the Condé princes.

When Jane happened to mention Bruce to George, he said that Bruce had to be an imposter. He certainly wasn't a Condé, because the last member of the Condé family, Louis Henri Joseph de Bourbon, died childless in 1830 and that Louis d'Orléans, Prince de Condé, who died in 1866, was the last person to hold the title. Before Jane or I could say a word, George went on, his eyes half closed, as in a memory trance, to recount in exquisite detail the history of the Condé family from Louis Bourbon, the Protestant leader of France and the uncle of Henri IV, who founded the

house in 1557, to Louis d'Orléans. His descriptions of the physiog-
nomy of each member of the family were far more eloquent than
anything I had ever heard him say. After an hour or more — by
which time we were in total darkness — George stopped. Jane
and I had been transfixed.

When Jane asked him how he had come to know the family
history in such detail, he told us that one of his aunts (at least I
think she was an aunt) had given him a beautiful leather-bound
history of the family in several volumes when he was still a boy.
He got up, turned on the lights, went into his bedroom, and
brought back the books to show us. He told us that he had read
them so many times he knew them by heart, and while he said
this, he caressed one of the volumes. "I had to sell most of my
books when I moved to France," he said, "but I could never part
with these."

I imagined a lonely little boy poring over that family history,
pretending at times that he was part of the Condé world.

After the Mexican meetings, Jane and I would see George
whenever we were in Paris, but it became more and more difficult. His bitterness had turned to spite. He spent most of the
time complaining about the people who had wronged him, and
his complaints were accompanied by increasingly sadistic erotic
fantasies. The last time we saw him, at lunch at a little restaurant near the Rue de Buci, Jane left halfway through the meal,
saying that she couldn't listen to any more — that she hoped they
were only fantasies about the unspeakable things he would do
to women. "You stay," she said to me. I did, out of respect for
George — the George I'd known — but I knew I would never see
him again. He was not in the least bit embarrassed by what had
happened.

XVIII.
ADVENTURES

I AM conducting a graduate seminar on life histories and notions of the self at the Graduate Center of the City University of New York (CUNY), where I have been teaching for over thirty years. The students in the seminar are excellent, though rather less talkative than I would like. Today they are particularly quiet. No matter what I do, I can't get them to say anything. They just sit there listening, occasionally taking notes. Suddenly they seem to lose their individuality. *What are they doing here in this windowless classroom listening to me blather? Why are they studying anthropology?* I ask myself. I ask them. They look at me blankly, avoiding my question, I suppose, by assuming that it's rhetorical. I repeat the question: "Why did you decide to study anthropology? I am serious. It's an important question." Finally one student, who has a law degree, says she has always been interested in the common law. She's studied law and now wants to study the idea of the "common," what it means. "And?" I say, thinking her answer ridiculous. She says nothing. A second student, catching her embarrassment, says that he's interested in cities and thought anthropology was the best way to study them. "And?" I say. Again, no response. A third says he is interested in South America. I'm stunned. Could these highly intelligent young men and women really have decided on such grounds? "Do you mean to tell me that you made what might well be the most important decision in your life on the grounds that you are interested in cities, South America, or the common?" They laugh but otherwise remain silent. I tell them that I can understand their reluctance to speak personally in front of the class, in front of me, that I'm not asking for a confession but for a sign of passion. As one, they look down at their notes. Have I broken a taboo? Have I shamed them, humiliated them, broken their hearts and spirits? I didn't mean to. I like them. I decide to shock them out of complacency. "Let me tell you why *I* decided to be an anthropologist. I wanted adventure — exotic, erotic adventure." Several of them look at me aghast. I have used three words that have no place in serious anthropology.

I often exaggerate or make extravagant comments to call attention to the limits of the intellectual frame in which we find ourselves. I point out the importance of iconoclasm in education, especially in college and graduate school, where unlearning what you've been taught is often as essential, and at times more, than what you have been and are being taught. This is especially true in anthropology, which I believe has a moral-pedagogic role to question the basic values and assumptions — the taken-for-granted — of the anthropologist's society and by extension other similar and not-so-similar ones.

I'm sometimes accused of cultural relativism (accused, as if relativism were a crime), but in fact I argue for a heuristic relativism — taking the part of the other, without necessarily accepting his or her position, in order to better understand the other's world and, one hopes, gain a perspective on one's own that will refine our understanding of both. It is similar to Keats's notion of negative capability: "when a man [and presumably a woman] is capable of being in uncertainties, mysteries, doubts without any irritable reaching after fact and reason." I particularly like Keats's use of "irritable" because it captures the mood of so many dogged anti-relativists. I'm opposed not to "hard facts," providing they meet the accepted standards of evidence, but to the failure to evaluate those facts from the position of the other; that is, heuristically. Anthropologists are, of course, no more immune to prevailing thought fashions than are scholars in other disciplines, but straddling their own world and the worlds of the people they study, they are constantly challenged by relativism. Anthropology can be conceived of as a stage on which the "uncertainties, mysteries, and doubts" provoked by field research challenge certainties, knowledge, and sureties in so disquieting a manner that they—the former—lose their power. The adventurer surrenders to the unadventurous, the out-of-frame to the in-frame, openness to closure, and creativity to repetition and redundancy.

"The adventure of learning" is a cliché, but do we ever talk about the adventure of teaching? I mean not only the need to adjust your teaching to your perception of your class, but also the change of perspective that comes from class discussion. I have given few lecture classes, and those that I have, I've dreaded, because they gave me little contact with the students. I never knew whom I was addressing. Often, in desperation, I would focus my attention on one or two students—monitoring in a way their responses—as if they represented the entire class. I remember some of the lecture classes I took in college and graduate school in which the professors repeated what they had said countless times, or even read the proverbial lecture notes that had already turned brown with age. They were disengaged. Engagement, face-to-face engagement, is for me a prerequisite for good education—the education that is creatively resonant. It requires vital collaboration. This is why I'm opposed to online colleges (obviously not to the use of computers in education). The immediacy of collective response is lost. Despite their claims to bringing education to all—in the spirit of democracy, they say—these colleges are in fact enforcing an ever-deepening class division between those who can afford a personalized education and those who cannot. Education may be a commodity, but it should at least be a commodity that isn't based on profit but on quality. That is possible.

I do not like to repeat myself, teaching. Even when I'm teaching the same subject, I try to change the reading list as much as I reasonably can, and, unlike most of my colleagues, I teach without notes. When I enter a classroom, I have a general idea of what I'm going to say but rarely of my first words. These are born of anxiety. They come to me as I look around the classroom, imagining how the students have read what I assigned. Recently, thanks to Google Groups, I have begun to ask each student to send me and the other students a few thoughts about the reading before class. Their thoughts serve as a guide, but only a guide, to what I say. I improvise. I think aloud, based on a careful rereading before class of the books and articles involved. It takes a lot of time and is often boring—which is one reason why I also teach comparative literature, and give classes that I think will appeal to students in both subjects. Unlike most works in the social sciences, good literature sustains countless rereadings. By the end of a class, I am drained, and if the class has been particularly exciting, exhilarated, too. I've told my students that I don't consider a class successful unless I've learned something new from it. Learning by teaching is what preserves my vitality and my interest.

Adventures have to be open-ended. They depend upon contingencies that cannot be known or even guessed at beforehand. They cannot be produced, despite adventure tourism, but we can put ourselves into potentially adventurous situations, as I did on those first trips to Mexico and Morocco—situations that are open to chance, risk, and the unexpected. But, having placed ourselves in an adventure-promising situation, do we not deny ourselves the possibility of adventure?

When I went to Morocco for the first time, on leave during my military service, I hoped for adventure. My response was unabashedly Orientalist. I was overwhelmed by the exoticism—the sensuousness—of the place, which was more powerful than I had ever imagined. I had landed in the late morning at the American naval base in Kenitra, and taken a bus to Rabat. I spent that afternoon wandering through the souk, less interested in what I saw than in the sounds I heard and the sweet smell of spices mingling with the acrid odor of the sweat-saturated, woolen *jellabas* that men wore and the heavy perfume that emanated from the veiled women who, to my surprise, pushed past me through the crowds. Later in the afternoon, I began to see. I saw the exotic: the turbaned and pantalooned men; the veiled women, their eyes, some staring at me directly, others lowered, modestly, and still others beckoning seductively. Their blue, tattooed faces—what I could see of them—that reminded me of the ink we used in school, and their heavy, lead-colored silver rings, their intricately hennaed hands, intrigued me. The poor quarters in the medina reminded me of the neighborhoods I'd seen in Mexico and would later see everywhere I traveled in Africa, Asia, and South America. I was surprised by how many French men and women appeared, late in the afternoon, in the cafés in the Ville Nouvelle. They seemed impervious to their surroundings.

There was nothing adventurous about Rabat, and Marrakech in the early sixties was already too filled with tourists to provide even the possibility of adventure. The fire eaters, the transvestite dancers (whose writhings, to my surprise, excited me), the acrobats, the bards surrounded by captive audiences who had no doubt heard their stories many times, the whining of oboes, the clanging of castanets, and the trance-inducing drumming of teams of exorcists, the smell of brochettes grilled over charcoal, and, as if they belonged, the hippies in extravagant colors, smelling of marijuana, mingling in the crowds—all this was a spectacle for the tourists. What I hadn't expected was the number of Moroccan tourists—Berbers from the Atlas Mountains and Arab peasants from the surrounding plains. The spectacles were for them, too, though they didn't have to fend off the guides, the beggars, the pimps, and the little boys who pestered me—any foreigner—to follow them through the labyrinthine passages of the enormous souk to a shop, presumably owned by a relative. One of them led me to a shop that sold steam irons!

I liked Tangiers best on that trip. Its seediness was sophisticated. The sensuous quality of life I found in other Moroccan cities was displaced there, especially in the port and old town, by blatant sensuality and eroticism. I was pursued by pimps offering every sexual enticement they could think up, from Spanish or Moroccan whores, male or female, transvestite or sadist, always thirteen years old, to themselves. I spent hours listening to old, alcoholic British colonial officers describe life among the "kafirs" in Uganda, Tanganyika, and Nyasaland, until one of them clutched my upper thigh and I fled. Among the ubiquitous tie-dyed hippies, I met an American woman their age dressed in a neat white shirtdress, who, it turned out, came from Caldwell. She worked for the Arrow shirt company and had traveled alone from Egypt to Morocco, quite oblivious to any danger she might encounter. I wasn't sure whether it was that obliviousness or her starched dresses that had protected her. I never asked her why she had made the trip. I never told her I had lived in her hometown.

I didn't think I would ever return to Morocco. I didn't like it, but somehow it insinuated itself. I remember the relief and the excitement I felt when my advisor suggested it as a field site. I had hoped to do research somewhere in Melanesia, but if I worked there, I knew I'd be caught between Margaret Mead and Andrew Vayda, an uncompromising positivist in the department who was at odds with Mead. I felt I had to go somewhere else. While I was glad to be going to Morocco, I was distressed by having landed in a department — no doubt, one of many — in which faculty bickering prevented students from working where they wanted. I swore that I would never allow this to happen to any of my students, and it never has. Sometimes you learn more from bad than from good teaching.

I am on the highway to Valencia en route to Algeciras, where I will take the ferry to Tangiers and begin my doctoral fieldwork. I've just left Barcelona. Hitchhikers, about a hundred meters apart, line the road. They are so zonked that they don't even bother to wave down passing cars. I feel as though I'm driving through a gauntlet of fallen mystics. Some appear to be meditating; others, curled like embryos, are sleeping; and at least one couple is fucking. I have a long drive ahead of me and would like company, but not any of them. Just past the gauntlet, a man who is actually standing hails me. I stop and ask where he is going. "Timbuktu," he says. I laugh and am about to drive off when he says, "Seriously, Timbuktu, but I'd like a ride as far south as you're going. I want to catch the ferry from Algeciras to Tangiers. It's cheaper than the one that leaves from Malaga." "Hop in. I'm also on my way to Tangiers," I say, and immediately regret having said it. Do I really want to drive that far with him?

Holgar is a handsome man with the angular features of a northern German. He speaks a fluent though at times hesitant English. He is in his mid-twenties, a commercial artist, and in fact on his way to Timbuktu. There is something appealing about him—an innocent, anxious maturity. I seem to have confidence in him. He wants to make the afternoon ferry the next day. It means driving all night and much of the next day nonstop. I don't mind. I'm also anxious to get to Morocco. We share the driving. He is a better driver than I am. I'm still getting used to driving a stick-shift car. Jane taught me a few weeks before I flew to Europe.

We talk all night, but are too tired to say much the next morning and doze on the crossing to Africa. There is something dreamlike about our conversation that night. I start talking about my research project on spirit possession and that triggers Holgar's long, at times confusing story of why he is traveling to Timbuktu. He tried to go a few years earlier but never made it. The desert seemed endless, he tells me, but I wonder if something happened there that frightened him. He lost confidence and is now determined to regain it by making the trip. I say I understand, but I think his trip is more than a confidence course. He is escaping. He has traveled all over Europe and once hitchhiked through Turkey and Iran to northern India, but says he did not like India and returned home after a week or two. He never tells me how he got back to Germany. It must have been by plane, since he has nothing to say about the trip.

I don't know whether he met Oyunbileg before his trip to India, only that it was before his first attempt to reach Timbuktu. She was responsible for that trip. Oyunbileg was a Mongolian woman, older than Holgar by several years, whom he met while he was studying art. I am calling her Oyunbileg, "Gift of Wisdom," since I don't remember her name, nor do I remember where in Germany Holgar was studying. I never learned what she was doing there. She was living alone. That I know because Holgar began living with her. He had fallen in love with her the first

time they met. More accurately, he had become obsessed with
her. No, that is not quite right either, since he describes himself as
in her power. It is she who obsessed him and lured him into loving her. She took full possession of him, he tells me. "I was possessed by her spirit. I was no longer the person who I had been. I
had lost myself in her. She had a wisdom I could not grasp."

As Holgar goes on talking about Oyunbileg, he sounds to
me more and more like a German romantic poet—Novalis, for
example—whose love reaches transcendent heights that are
limited only by its allegorical implications. But Oyunbileg was
no allegorical figure for Holgar. She was too down-to-earth,
too practical, and yet, he insists, otherworldly. "My world was
shrinking. I was shrinking. I wanted to escape but I couldn't.
Then late one afternoon, when I came home from work, I found
her lying unconscious on the living room floor. I thought she was
dead. She was cold to the touch. She wasn't breathing. At least,
I thought she wasn't. I don't know what got into me. Instead of
calling a doctor, I just left the apartment and walked around
for hours. Finally, I came to my senses. I rushed back. I had to
call for help. How could I have left her that way?" He found the
apartment empty. "She wasn't there. She was there. I could feel
her presence. I couldn't move. I just sat there. I must have fallen
asleep because it was quite dark when I heard someone unlock-
ing the door. It was she. She smiled. 'I must have frightened
you,' she said. 'I was away—on a voyage.' " At first Holgar didn't
understand what she meant by "voyage," then he decided that
she had been on a voyage to the spirit world. Oyunbileg told him
that sometimes she is "called" and when she is called, she must
go. She didn't elaborate, and Holgar was afraid to ask her anything. Perhaps he didn't want to know. He seemed to prefer the
mystery of not knowing.

The next morning, without telling her, Holgar left for Timbuktu. He hitched a ride with a trucker, and several days into the trip, in the middle of the Sahara, he panicked. "I heard her calling me. I was scared the way I had never been before. I was in the middle of nowhere, alone with a driver and his assistant with whom I could barely communicate. I had no bearings. I was in emptiness itself. There is something about emptiness—it needs to be filled. It was sucking me in. I wanted to get out of the truck, but the drivers wouldn't let me. Thank God. I would have died."

Holgar pauses. I remember that pause as clearly as if it were today. It lasts for hours. I can't say simply that he stopped talking. We are caught, at least I'm caught, in a suspended moment between what he's described and what he has yet to describe. Holgar may have fallen asleep, but I feel as if I am in the time, the dream-time, of his story. I keep on driving. I am very sleepy, but I know I am not going to fall asleep. The anticipation is too great. Holgar knows the sequel, and I don't. I didn't.

I can't remember what I was thinking during that pause except for a vague memory, premonitory, of what I did not know and have never known, of the dream before I went to Harvard in which the Mongolian woman was conducting a ceremony in my mother's dining room. Dreams, some manifestly, are future-oriented, prophetically toned even if we don't believe in premonitions of the future. We look to the past for meaning, but that meaning, despite its locus in the past, is always implicated in the future. Is this turning to the past for meaning a defense against the futurity of the dream—the unknown it announces? The mystery it shrouds? The anxiety it reflects? The desires it evokes? The illicit it masks? The pleasures it proposes? Whatever its affiliation with the past, the dream colors, however subtly, one's world on waking and sometimes, unpredictably, later experiences, far removed from it, as my dream of the Mongolian priestess did Holgar's narration. I'm not referring so much to the fact that a Mongolian woman endowed with mystical powers figured in both my dream and Holgar's story as I am to a mystery that conjoined them for me. Did my dream etherealize Holgar's story? Unhinged from reality, it became autonomous, as if moved by a force that could not be stopped until it stopped itself.

Holgar begins again. "I returned to Germany only to discover that Oyunbileg had gone back to Mongolia without leaving a forwarding address. I have no idea what has become of her, but I still feel her presence." Again Holgar pauses, but it doesn't have the effect on me that his last pause did. I ask him why he is going to Timbuktu now. He says simply that he has to. He cannot live with his cowardice. I don't ask him how it was possible for Oyunbileg to leave Mongolia and return just like that, given the political circumstances of the time. It would have destroyed his story—my reaction to it.

There is, I have found, a vulnerable point in any narration that fascinates us—a flaw in logic, a contradiction in plot, a loss of verisimilitude, inexplicable changes of style, figurative inconsistency, a hesitance, a gap. It undermines the narrative. It leads us to doubt its "truth," and, paradoxically, it enforces our commitment to it. This—in retrospect—I believe to have been the status of Oyunbileg. Was she who she said she was? Who Holgar said she was? Even now, reconstructing Holgar's story, knowing that I'm bound to misrepresent it, creating other vulnerabilities, I find it impossible to accept my misgivings. Holgar, as I knew him that night, Oyunbileg, as I imagined her, would then fade away, destroying the haunting intensity of my memory of that night. Words take hold as reality loosens in the darkness of the night. With dawn they surrender their hold as reality tightens its grip.

When we arrive in Tangiers, we stop for coffee at one of the cafés that line the port and exchange addresses. I drive Holgar to the road to Oran. We say goodbye. It is a sad moment. As I start to drive off, Holgar calls me back. I think he may have forgotten something, but I'm wrong. With tears in his eyes, he tells me he can't go on. It's useless. Can I drive him back to Tangiers? I refuse. I tell him, I order him really, to continue. He has no choice. I start the car again and see him waving, very alone, in my rearview mirror. I feel his terror in the pit in my stomach.

I never doubted that I'd done the right thing. It was as if I had become Holgar's alter ego and knew what was best for him. Such, I suppose, was the effect of that nocturnal collapse of identities. Many months later, I received a postcard from him from Timbuktu. It had been sent to America and forwarded to me. It read, "Thanks. I made it. I'm off to Germany and maybe to Mongolia." I wanted to write back, but I discovered that I had lost his address. I never heard from him again. It was more closure than I wanted.

The poet Paul Zweig, a friend and a colleague, argued in his book *The Adventurer* that an adventure becomes an "adventure" not in its enactment but in its telling. It requires a storyteller. How many adventures have never become "adventures" because the adventurer was not a storyteller? They are lost, and perhaps they should be. The adventure that never becomes an "adventure" retains a purity, the immediacy of action, an innocence, a nobleness perhaps. It defies the power of words—the displacement produced by words. Its loss, if it is loss, can be neither mourned nor forgotten, since it never was. It simply falls from memory—from the world, Wittgenstein might have said. Like Holgar, Paul drove into the Sahara, but unlike Holgar, he had no Timbuktu. It was, I think, the emptiness that drew him, but it was also the possibility of a story—one he wrote. I think the anticipation of a story deprived him of the adventure he sought.

There is obviously a contradiction between the way I used "adventure" when I spoke about adventures of learning and teaching and the way I am using it now. But is there? Must the adventure have a certain magnitude to be an adventure? Must it be sublime? Must it be a flight from women—from a Penelope perhaps—as Paul claimed? Or can the little excitements in everyday life, in the classroom, be adventures? We say that we are entering new or unknown territory. But to call something an adventure is not the same as recounting an adventure. It is facile. It is rhetorical. But it is also evocative of possibility.

I'M IN a hotel suite in San Francisco. Thirty or forty, perhaps more, men and women are sitting on the floor or standing against the wall. A bartender looks bereft. No one is buying drinks. It is the annual meetings of the American Anthropological Association in San Francisco, and we have all attended a session on medical anthropology. The speakers ran over their allotted time, leaving no time for me and the other discussant to comment on their papers. The organizer of the session is disappointed. As she had rented this room for the speakers to meet for drinks, I suggest that she invite anyone who wants to hear us to come up to the room. She looks dubious. She's sure no one will come. She's wrong.

I am the second discussant. I don't remember what I was going to say, but I do remember my conclusion: that in an important way that was ignored today, there is no difference between clinical and experimental medicine, since there is an experimental dimension, however slight, in the treatment of every patient.

The doctor can never be entirely sure his treatment, even if it's an aspirin for a headache, will be successful. It's one of those absurd throwaway observations that I am, alas, prone to make. I'm embarrassed, and to cover myself I say that it seems to me that medicine has lost its sense of adventure. (I didn't know at the time that there was a growing field of adventure or wilderness medicine, but, in any case, I wasn't speaking of treating people seeking adventures or in the wilderness.)

I ask if there are any questions, hoping no one will point out the foolishness of my observation. But a hand shoots up. A resident in one of the San Francisco hospitals says she agrees with me and goes on to recount her experience in treating a patient who had responded not to the standard treatment but to another one she had "concocted quite irresponsibly." It was an experiment. She remembered her fear of failure. Following her, another resident tells a similar story. It appears that there are a number of medical practitioners in the audience. The discussion goes on for nearly an hour (usually they last ten minutes) and turns into a sort of ritual of confession. One medical practitioner after another tells similar stories. Nearly all of their stories refer to taking risks. My role is simply to rephrase any one that seems to have lost track of the experimental—the adventurous—dimension of treatment. I'm left with the feeling that, with the commodification of just about everything in American life, the spirit of adventure has diminished, except perhaps in the financial markets. I am reminded of a South African businessman I sat next to on my first trip to his country. He spoke of capitalism as an adventure, which, he said, made his life exciting. It was like hunting, he told me. He often hunted in Zimbabwe and suggested I try it. "You'll experience the thrill—the risk."

XIX.

PSYCHOANALYSIS

I HAVE just reread the last chapter and realize that I didn't describe any of my own adventures. I exclude the "adventures" of learning and teaching, which are metaphors. Or are they? The closest I came to one was probably my experience of Holgar's adventure — which I'm not even sure was an adventure. Did I ever have an adventure in the sublime sense of the word? I don't think so. Some people might think of my field trips as adventures, or perhaps my confrontation with a rogue elephant in Botswana, the two of us eyeballing each other while Jane, Wicky, and the other people who were traveling with us stood frozen, horrified at a possibility I could not acknowledge, so intense was my concentration on that elephant. It was an old female who had to be shot later. I could go on: getting embroiled in a *noeud de vipères* in the Vaucluse; being caught in rain and heavy fog near the top of the Gornergrat on my first real mountain climb in Switzerland; climbing down the steps of the Rio favela at midnight; falling to the ground in midafternoon on Madison Avenue to avoid the shots of a trigger-happy New York cop chasing a black man. But none of these were real adventures. At best they are icons of adventures that never materialized.

I'm reminded of a conversation I had with a geologist in a hotel bar in Georgetown, in Guyana. He asked me if I had ever been completely alone. I said yes. "Alone, I mean, where days go by and you never see or hear or feel another human being." I had to admit I hadn't. Trekking through the jungles, he had often been totally alone. "Everything vacillates between the personalized

279

and the impersonalized. You talk to yourself. You see yourself, from afar. You find yourself talking to a tree. You hallucinate. But you have no fear, for you are other." And he quoted Rimbaud, *"Je est un autre,"* without pretension.

No, I have never had a sublime adventure. Is it a question of contingency? Is it a failure of story? Or is it because from that summer when I was seventeen and traveled alone through Europe, or perhaps earlier, when I was reading Dumas and Hugo, I began to orchestrate what I thought was my life but was only an image of my life. That summer I played the anonymous traveler, projecting, so I thought, an air of mystery. As time went by, I created a more realistic persona, one to which I aspired. I had a goal. But it always involved the projection of mystery—of a story behind whomever I was. Was there a story? Yes, but in fantasy, never clearly elaborated, as though—I'd like to say—I wanted to remain a mystery to myself, but in fact because I could never imagine how a fantasy would end. I've always had trouble remembering endings of the novels I've read. I don't know when I stopped casting myself as I would be. Maybe it was after I married Jane. But did I ever stop? I sometimes have the feeling that I am hovering between reality and fantasy, in moving immobility. As I grow older, projections of the future are truncated. An unwanted realism sets in. There is less room for fantasy, more for memory.

The first time I ever talked to a psychoanalyst was when I was about to go to college and thought seriously about becoming one. My mother arranged for me to talk to one of my father's colleagues. He was encouraging, but our meeting troubled me. At one point in our conversation, I said that I was ambiguous instead of ambivalent about becoming a doctor. He looked surprised and corrected me, in the way psychoanalysts do, if they do, by leaving you with the question of why you, in my case I, misspoke. Was I referring to myself as having misgivings or to an image of myself that had to remain ambiguous—mysterious—for me?

Childish romanticism.

Reading Freud in Vienna, I saw myself suffering from an ever-expanding series of neuroses, inadmissible perversions, and potential psychoses. I'd lie on a couch each afternoon and free-associate. I had no control. My dialogues were internal, in bad faith, since I constructed my interlocutor—my shrink—as I wanted. I was filled with insights, some of them pertinent, but many of them manufactured, affirming or disaffirming whatever neurotic trajectory I was following. I was knotted. All of this ended when I met Monika and regained, as it were, my quickened life.

It was during the first weeks of my stay in Vienna that I had an experience that instantaneously became a memory. It was one of those small events that are in themselves without significance but that remain with you for reasons you will never know. They texture your life; they are the source of much of what I have written. Some are like the symbols Freud wrote about, like climbing a staircase, that do not trigger associations. Others are richly suggestive. A few are epiphanies.

It is a gray February day. I'm lonely. I have not yet made any friends. I'm sitting at one end of a tram. I'm the only passenger. A young girl, maybe fourteen or fifteen, gets on at the next stop. She looks around and sits down at the opposite end of the tram. She is pretty, dressed in a red tartan skirt—a sign at the time that she comes from the upper classes. She glances at me, a bit embarrassed, I think, because she is lonely, like me. I wish I could talk to her. I wish she were a bit older, because I'd like to become her friend. We sit ignoring each other and yet fully conscious of each other. A few stops later, still with no one else in the tram, she gets off, glancing at me one last time, not quite smiling. I watch her walk away as the tram departs. I wish I could say that she turned around and took one last glimpse of me, but she didn't.

When I thought about writing this book, I was reminded of the girl in the red tartan. Or perhaps, reminded of her, I thought about writing this book. It is an embarrassingly romantic image. I decided not to include it. It was to be the secret source of the book, but its exclusion troubled me. It can't be its secret source. How would I know? The secret must remain a secret. It simply indicates the presence of a secret—the presence of an absence. It would be an aspersion, a derogation of the memory, a defamation of the girl in the red tartan.

I HAVE always thought of psychoanalysis as a legacy of romanticism, conceived by a man who couldn't live with his. In practice, not in theory, it is a voyage inward, not without its risks, for, as it is constructed, its revelations have to be understood as potentially dangerous, shattering in possibility—an adventure turned in on itself. I am saddened by the loss of that interior voyage in today's pragmatic, psychotropic pill–popping psychiatry. For me, the choice of therapy (if indeed we have to decide between the two) is not about efficacy. It is existential—the perpetuation of a dimension of life that is devalued by robotic images of humankind. Of course, Freud's reductionist explanations are in spirit the avatars of psychotropic psychiatry. They could never fully contain human potential. Drugs are more efficient, devastatingly so, in this respect.

Within weeks of beginning to teach at Princeton, I began to suffer a claustrophobia that I escaped only when I returned home to New York, and even there it would wake me up at night. (Since Princeton couldn't provide us with satisfactory housing, we decided, to our relief, to remain in New York.) I liked my students but I couldn't stand the pretense—the self-importance—of the university, its hierarchical structure, the pettiness that lay behind its veneer of politeness, the smugness of the lesser professors, which sometimes infected the brilliant ones who had no need of that protection, and the lack of anonymity, the anonymity that affords truly creative space. Everyone seemed to be watching everybody else, sometimes competitively, sometimes out of curiosity, a gossip's curiosity, and occasionally out of genuine interest. It was no Harvard. It was much smaller, its teaching more personal, cloyingly responsible, its education more seamless and therefore intellectually less troubling than Harvard's, which left irresponsible gaps in your education, producing intellectual neuroses in serious students who struggled for years to fill them. Princeton was a suburban university.

I was at a meeting of faculty members who wanted to protest Nixon and Kissinger's intensification of bombing in North Vietnam. They discussed the ways in which they could use Princeton's clout—they didn't use that word—to stop the bombings and at the same time enhance the university's reputation. There were times when I wasn't sure which was more important to some of them. Finally, in disgust, I suggested that one way Princeton could accomplish its two goals was to call meetings with the pro-war unions in Newark. I would like to say that my suggestion was ignored, but it disappeared before it could be ignored. It was the first and last time I ever spoke in a meeting like that.

By my third year, I thought seriously of giving up teaching and becoming a psychoanalyst. I had seen a psychotherapist when I was discharged from the army. Many of my friends were in one form of psychotherapy or another. Some talked about it openly; others tried to manipulate you so that you became a substitute shrink for them. I had several students who tried to turn me into their therapist. (The line between teaching and therapy is never clear.) I refused.

I remember Yvonne—that's not her real name—who used to come to my office in tight sweaters and brown corduroy jeans, ostensibly to talk about class. She wore a wide black belt, which she opened and closed alluringly as she talked about her relations with her father. I told her to stop fussing with her belt, that I was married, and not a shrink. She left my office sobbing but came back the following week to apologize. This time she was wearing a thin belt and kept twisting its buckle. I accepted her apology and dismissed her rather abruptly. Twenty years later, I met her in a box in the opera. She told me that she had become a psychotherapist. She was a Freudian, unlike many of my students, who preferred Jung. There was a popular Jungian therapist in town.

I discussed my plans with Devereux. He recommended that I train in London. I had told him that I didn't want to do a research analysis in which I promised not to practice clinically, as was required by the two Freudian institutes in New York if you didn't have a medical degree or an acceptable one in psychology. Aside from the fact that I wanted to practice, I thought that such a promise would put my analysis on a wrong footing. George agreed and put me in contact with the British psychoanalytic association. He was against my training in France. "It is always better to train in your mother tongue," he told me. It was odd for a man who had trained in English, practiced, if surreptitiously, in French, and was a native speaker of Hungarian. I knew he was adamantly opposed to Lacan.

I did apply to the British psychoanalytic society, and, after surviving a series of bureaucratic obstacles, I was admitted. Jane accepted my decision, though I was quite sure she didn't think it a good idea. We spent a summer in London, during which I met my training analyst and had a few preliminary sessions. I was to begin the following spring, to take advantage of the sabbatical Princeton owed me. Needless to say, my analyst lived in Hampstead. I don't remember much of what we talked about, but I do remember the damp, lumpy chair in which I had to sit; he said that he didn't want me to lie on his couch until we could meet regularly. As the summer progressed and I found myself spending a lot of time trying to figure out where we could afford to live, I became disillusioned with my plans. It seemed ridiculous to study in London when neither Jane nor I was sure we wanted to live there. Did I really want to spend my life sitting in a chair, listening to patients talk? After all, one of the reasons I had chosen anthropology was the freedom it gave me. But perhaps more than anything, I didn't want to live what I saw as a vicarious life. I knew the temptation.

I assumed—after I had finally made the decision not to become an analyst—that my frantic search for the right place to live in London was a working-out of that decision. What I didn't know then was that it was the beginning of an obsessive hunt for the perfect house in Europe. It went on for years, spoiling our summer vacations there, as Jane reminds me whenever she is angry at me, until we finally bought our Italian house. I suppose I wasn't really looking for the perfect house but a house that reflected the image of myself I wanted—not the one I had. I am reminded, as I write this, of the house plans I drew after my father died and we moved to the house we hated. I was searching for a nest—not the roots my mother sought but a home that sheltered me from the imposition of place while giving me a place to live.

When I returned to New York, I began to see Kurt Adler, Alfred Adler's son. He was an eclectic analyst with a weakness for old-fashioned Marxism. We arranged a program that was at once therapeutic and didactic. He thought it would be ridiculous for me to attend an institute, since I was probably a better reader than any of the usual candidates, but said that if I decided to practice, he would arrange for me to have the necessary clinical experience. He was a practical man, and I learned a lot from him. He freed me from the need to protect myself with rigid theory rather than follow my own inclinations. In fact — and this came as a surprise, but not quite — I was already doing this and had been doing it for most of my life. I couldn't bear the constraints any theoretical position put on me. I had to undermine it and thereby master it.

Can we think of psychoanalytic sessions as narratives, as some theorists have done? In an extended sense, I suppose we can, but when we reflect on what has occurred, we construct a secondary narrative, which by turning those sessions into a story, gives them meaning, or the possibility of meaning. In psychoanalysis, a secondary narrative is always in tension with a tertiary one — a theoretical one, like the Oedipal, that has overriding but reductive authority.

My friend Moulay Abedsalem, an ancient, illiterate Moroccan shroud maker and pallbearer, a man of great wisdom, who knew nothing about psychoanalysis, understood dreams this way. It is the mind (*'aqel*) that distorts the dream by putting it in words, he once told me, with a cynicism that edged on disgust. He had little trust in words, other than those in the Koran, which we can never fully understand.

I went to Morocco, as I have said, with a psychoanalytic orientation, and, thanks to people such as Moulay Abedsalem, I came back a skeptic. Once, I tried to explain to Moulay Abedsalem the psychoanalytic theory of projection. He understood what I meant—that is, until I explained that psychoanalysts understand spirits and even God as a projection of the soul. He was appalled. We had got it backward. God and the spirits are not projections but—I don't remember exactly how he put it—introjections. The spirits can enter us; God makes his presence known to us. He was equally mystified by the belief that events you experienced as an infant could affect your thoughts when you were an old man. I was referring to those psychoanalytic theories, popular at the time in psychological anthropology, that gave singular importance to weaning practices, sleeping arrangements, and early initiations, such as circumcision, in the formation of (national) character. Had Moulay Abedsalem the vocabulary, I'm sure he would have accused us of primitive thinking. I ended the Abram Kardiner Lecture I delivered in the eighties to psychoanalysts in New York with Moulay Abedsalem's critique. The analysts clapped but were otherwise embarrassedly silent. As questions were not permitted, I have no idea, though I can imagine, what they thought. I suspect it had less to do with Moulay Abedsalem than with me.

I justified the discrepancy between the way in which psychoanalysts, and more generally Western culture, understood psychic reality and the way Moroccans did by arguing that while we shared an understanding of intention and motivation, we placed their origin in different spaces—the unconscious or the daemonic.

Do I still believe this?

During the summer before I started to teach at Princeton, I prepared a graduate course on structuralism. I had initially planned to concentrate on Lévi-Strauss and structural theories of language, but after spending several weeks in Paris and the rest of the summer in Bonnieux, I decided to rethink the course. I realized that structuralist thinking, or, more accurately, thinking that claimed to be structuralist, had spread wildly in France—from myths and kinship studies to art, music, literature, history, Marxism, and psychoanalysis. I read Michel Foucault and included *The Order of Things* in my syllabus as well as Lacan, whose writings I found intriguingly impenetrable so long as I tried to systematize them but exquisitely insightful when I read them aphoristically. His focusing on mirroring, on the other, on the singular importance of language in psychoanalysis, on the disjunction between signifier and signified and the plays of signification it permitted, on the complexities of interlocution, its role in the formation of the unconscious, and his disdain for those theories of psychoanalysis that attempted to turn it into a positivist endeavor opened me to a new way of thinking about psychoanalysis and the practice of anthropology.

While I found Lacan's division of modes of apprehending into the imaginary, the symbolic, and the real too schematic, I was intrigued by the way he distinguished reality from the real (*réel*)—that which remained outside imaginal possibility and symbolic articulation. Wholly outside, it could on occasion—as by chance, traumatically—intrude into our imaginary and symbolic constructs of experience. This outside seemed to me to be of particular relevance to my ethnographic experience: that which was outside my understanding—my framing of the world—was not necessarily outside the understanding of the others with whom I worked, and vice versa.

Our experience is bounded by an ungraspable outside that troubles the "inside" in which we find ourselves. It is not so much cultural differences taken concretely, as beliefs and practices, that unsettle field researchers as it is intimations of an unreachable outside, an unknowable known, a present absence, a hovering, uncanny surround that is differently shared and unshared with those with whom you work. Its acknowledgment can be, like feelings of the sublime, at once liberating and terrifying—a boundlessness, something like the uncentered emptiness that the Japanese refer to as *sūnyatā*. The closest I have ever come to experiencing anything like that is when I lie alone, or with Jane, in a field looking up at the Milky Way and imagining what lies beyond it.

I realized, thinking about the *réel*, how Lacan must have struggled between theorizing (his commitment to Freud) and the evocation of experiences that resisted that theorizing, any theorizing. His language turned on itself, often simultaneously illustrating whatever he was asserting. It led to a Mallarméan style that, like the poet's, always edged on the unsayable—the *néant*, nothingness, pure absence. It was this style that led the first English-speaking psychoanalysts who tried to read Lacan to declare him a schizophrenic. I came to realize that his public antics, his bald narcissism, and his self-dramatization, coupled with a seriousness of thought and, despite rumors to the contrary, his practice, paralleled a literary style that was punctuated by puns, obscurantist wordplay, and figurative elaborations that seemed to lead nowhere and were suddenly followed, as if by magic, by moments of penetrating clarity. He was a show-off.

I decided to write about him. Given that I had no personal contact with him or anyone near him, I had to depend on his publisher. They were not particularly encouraging, but they did give me the names of several people who might *possibly* introduce me to him. I tried reaching several of them with no success, but just as I was about to give up, I reached Maud and Octave Mannoni. Maud was a psychoanalyst and a friend of Lacan's. Octave had written on colonialism. They invited me to their home. We talked generally about Lacan but circled around the subject of my meeting him. "He has been burned by an American scholar," they told me. Fortunately I knew the story. Anthony Wilden—or his publisher—had failed to include Lacan's name on the cover of Wilden's translation of and commentary on Lacan's Rome discourse, the lectures he gave after being thrown out of the International Psychoanalytical Association for his irresponsible approach, in the Association's eyes, to training analysts. Lacan, who was never adverse to publicity, was, quite rightfully, furious. (Later editions of the book included his name in the title and on the cover.) When I told Maud and Octave that I thought this an insult to Lacan, and added that I had problems with Wilden's commentary, Maud's eyes lit up. "Would you like to meet *le maître*?" she asked me, as if it had never occurred to her that was why I had come to see her and her husband. She went into another room to call Lacan, and though I could hear only part of her conversation, it was clear that Lacan knew all about our meeting and was expecting a call from her. A meeting was arranged for the next afternoon.

Lacan's secretary led me into his waiting room and asked me to fill out a card, which was clearly for patients. I told her I was not a patient, but she insisted that I fill it out "for the doctor's records." The room was furnished with chairs and a couch upholstered in mauve velvet with gold fringe. There was a copy of the art magazine *L'oeil* on the coffee table. There were no other magazines or books. Lacan's office door was open a crack. I suddenly realized that he was watching me from behind. Five or ten minutes later, he came out. I stood up. He extended his left hand, but before I could introduce myself, he beckoned me to sit down. I did dutifully. He crossed the room, entered his secretary's office, and came back reading the card I had filled out, reminding me of Hamlet reading as Polonius watches him. He returned to his office, this time leaving the door wide open so I was sure to see him observing me. Finally, he waved me in. I introduced myself. He still hadn't said a word. He was waiting for me to ask a question, and when I did, at last he spoke. *"Et puis?"* ("And then?") I asked another question. Another *"Et puis."* I hadn't prepared a list of questions, and soon found myself free-associating them. Finally, he stopped me. "The questions you ask are very difficult. I am an old man..." Before he could finish, I started to leave, furious, but he called me back and said, "As you are leaving Paris tomorrow, come back in two hours, and I will try to answer your questions." I had never told him when I was leaving. Maud Mannoni must have told him. I left, went to the nearest café, and ordered a cognac.

Two hours later, Lacan opened the door himself and led me back to his office. I started to take notes but soon realized that he was repeating, word for word, what he had written or said countless times. I stopped taking notes, and this seemed to disconcert him. I saw at our first meeting that he wasn't looking directly at me but past me, over my shoulder, as if he was in conversation with another—the Other. I knew what he was doing—disorienting me, producing cognitive vertigo, preparing me to cling uncritically to his words. It was an old shaman's trick. I had seen several Moroccan curers use it. I began to look over Lacan's shoulder. Finally, he grew silent. I didn't say a word. I just sat there waiting, looking over his shoulder, past him, as he was looking over mine. Finally, I asked if he had ever thought about the echo. He seemed surprised, but said, "Of course." He waited for me to explain. I told him that my daughter, who was at the age he called the mirror phase, was fascinated by her echo—in a cave, in churches we visited, and in the bathroom while she was being bathed.

Almost immediately our relationship changed. He began to confide in me, personally, intimately, as though I were *his* analyst. I took no notes. It would have been hugely inappropriate. He told me that he was old and worried that his truths—*"mes vérités"*—would be lost. Referring to Wilden, without mentioning his name, he said that he had not been understood. "He—there are many of them—look for influences. They don't realize that when I refer to Nietzsche, Heidegger, or Saussure I am using their words metaphorically, as a way to convey my truths." "And Freud?" I asked. "Do you use his words metaphorically?" "Ah," he said, and we both laughed. He went on to say that while he had met many people who were intelligent, brilliant even, he had *never* felt understood. "There is one, a *normalien*, who has an understanding, but he is ambitious and that ambition..." He stopped himself. He was referring, I believe, to his son-in-law, Jacques-Alain Miller, the sole editor of his *Seminars*, who has since become Lacan's posthumous publicist.

I was deeply moved. I was listening to an old man who, all pretense aside, was worried about his legacy. I had no idea why he was confiding in me. What had the echo inspired? What did he want from me, if anything? He fell silent. We had been talking for several hours. It was time to stop. He walked me to the door, and, opening it, he started to invite me back, but interrupted himself and asked me my daughter's name. "Aleksandra," I said, and in a gesture of self-restoration, he repeated her name three times, each time deepening and extending its middle syllables dramatically. "When Aleksandra reaches the age of reason, tell her that the French psychoanalyst Jacques Lacan thought her a very intelligent little girl." We shook hands. This time he extended his right hand, and we looked each other in the eye for the first time.

A few months ago, I saw a short film of a lecture Lacan gave, in Louvain, a year or so after I had met him. He had aged enormously, and his usual antics seemed stale. I could see flashes of brilliance muted by the recognition that he was no longer able to sustain the drama and tension of his earlier performances, for performing he always was.

What surprises me as I think back to our meeting—and, earlier, to the excitement I'd felt in first reading Lacan—is that I had sought training in the most orthodox schools of psychoanalysis. Adhesions, I suppose, to a past that had ended but whose ending I hadn't really recognized before. Fortunately, the gods saved me. I became neither an analyst, though I did turn again to psychoanalysis, this time on the couch, nor a devotee of Lacan, as many of his followers had. I was able to work myself through Lacan, in part thanks to Moulay Abedsalem, in part thanks to Lacan himself. But, perhaps most important of all, thanks to an incidental remark made at a cocktail party by a sculptor who, I am sure, will not remember it, or me for that matter. She told me that she had ended years of psychoanalysis when she realized that personality was an illusion.

XX.
THE
WORKINGS
OF
NOSTALGIA

I HAVE been writing from our house in Italy. Wicky, her husband, John, and Garrick arrived yesterday from Paris. They had been staying in the apartment on the Rue du Cherche-Midi that we had rented from our friends André Newburg and his wife, Elsie, for more than sixteen years. Andy and Elsie, understanding her attachment, lent it to them. During those years, Jane was working out of Paris, and I had spent as much time as I could there—summers, Christmas and Easter holidays, sabbaticals, and whenever I was teaching in Paris, or there on a research grant. Wicky went to school there for several years.

Wicky, like everyone I know who has lived in Paris, is filled with nostalgia for the city. She has written about it and won awards for those enchanting pieces. When she arrived yesterday, she told us she cried leaving the apartment. It was so filled with memories for her. For us all. It was a beautiful apartment, with a large, shady garden, hidden behind two apartment buildings with courtyards between them. It was once the first two stories of an eighteenth-century house; the roof was removed in the nineteenth century and three stories were added to it for apartments. It is said that Georges Sand lived there and described the *parquet de Versailles* in one of her novels. Andy had been able to buy the apartment from his law school roommate, who had inherited it from an uncle. The roommate, after taking part in the liberation of a Nazi death camp, had sworn never to set foot in Europe again and had wanted to get rid of the apartment as fast as possible.

Listening to Wicky talk about her memories of the apartment and the neighborhood, I was startled by how different they were from mine. I usually assume that people who have shared the same experiences share the same memories, but it is not true. Wicky showed me pictures of the places where our dog, Romeo, had slept, a closet where her *National Geographic*s are still stored, and the marble tops of the kitchen cabinets, which had been changed since our leaving the apartment sixteen years ago. The shops in the neighborhood have changed, Wicky tells me, but the neighborhood remains very much the same. I have tried to avoid it whenever I'm in Paris.

Sometimes, when I'm in New York and leave our building on Central Park, I remember a postcard I had as a child of a stag standing frozen in a forest clearing. It is more than a memory but not quite a vision. I loved that painting, and whenever its image passes through my mind, I am reminded of Paris, not really Paris, but the unalterability of Paris—my memories of Paris. I suppose that my recollection, inevitably abstracted on such occasions, doubles on itself like the stag frozen in the clearing and now frozen in my memory. I can think of no other reason why Paris and a picture of a stag are linked.

Perhaps the unchanging character of Paris, or rather the illusion that Paris is unchanging, despite the dramatic changes that have occurred there in my lifetime, is what produces the nostalgia I feel. But, of course, this argument is circular, since the nostalgia produces the unchanging character of Paris just as Paris's unchanging character produces the nostalgia. We say that nostalgia is built on loss or the idealization of a past moment, on time stopping as that idealized moment is sought, if not in fact—say, some lovers' sentimental return to the place where they first fell in love—than in a revivified memory. But is this necessarily the case? Is nostalgia not built on the desire for loss, the sadness and the pain it brings, the irreality that it relies on, the luxuriance of that irreality, pain, and sadness—indeed, on the failure, the ontological failure of regaining time past? Is nostalgia not then founded on disappointment—a *Heimatlosigkeit*, a loss of home, sensations of the uncanny that is sought, as though it can be sought. Nostalgia, like the uncanny, like my sudden memories of the stag in the clearing, depends on happenstance. It cannot be produced, despite the vast industries that attempt to do so—music, tourism, and, in its way, psychoanalysis.

I know of no other city like Paris, certainly no other city where I have lived. Vienna comes closest, but my memories of it are mediated by my mother's and grandmother's descriptions of it. They both visited the city many times and always talked about how it had changed. I remember the first time I went there. I was sixteen. My mother, sister, and I drove there during Easter vacation. It was gray, filled, at least in my imagination, with all the intrigue in *The Third Man*. It evoked memories in my mother, which she attempted to share with us. I pretended to appreciate them, so as not to disappoint her. They were not so much recollections as silent responses. A moment of distraction as we passed the Albertina, a glancing back at the Burgtheater, as if to restore the magic of a play she may have seen or failed to see there, a slight panic as she lost her way to Demel, where my sister and I were looking forward to the pastries, a pervading sense of her not being there, not elsewhere but simply not quite there: it turned Vienna into a place of irredeemable personal loss. Of course, my mother's memories were affected by the war, which in 1956 was still very much in evidence in the bombed-out areas and scarred facades of buildings At Demel, where she pronounced the pastry too sweet, she told my sister and me how disappointed she'd been the first time she had visited Vienna. "I felt I had come too late," she said. I wanted to say I felt the same way but didn't. Belatedness is an essential dimension of nostalgia.

I didn't like Vienna. There was something unresolved about the place—a failure, I now know, to acknowledge its past. But how would I have known that then? How could I have felt it? I am probably projecting backward feelings from five years later, when I was studying there. Then, the city felt moribund. It wasn't the palaces, the museums, the Prater, and the Danube—which wasn't blue but a muddy gray—that I remember best but going to a restaurant that was reputedly the oldest restaurant in the city still owned by its original family. It was now housed in a modern building. The owner talked to my mother several times during the course of dinner. Our waiter—a very old man with a bushy white mustache, reminding me of the emperor Franz Joseph, only without the beard—was excited by the attention my mother was getting. He told us that it was the first time he had ever seen the owner pay as much attention to any guest, even those he had known forever. He added that the owner was the last surviving member of the family and, unhappily, was unmarried. The restaurant would fall into other hands or close. As we were leaving, he told us to come back soon. We promised we would but never did.

The French have so imaged Paris, in art, literature, music, photography, and movies, that, I suspect, most people visiting for the first time are nostalgic before they arrive. But of course that nostalgia is manufactured. The Parisians are proud of their city, though their pride doesn't prevent the destruction of much of what they value. I think of La Défense, one of the coldest projects

I know of, the subsidized housing that surrounds the city, the ugly sculptures by third-rate artists that decorate squares and parks and that are always unveiled with a lot of fanfare, and, worst of all, the razing of Les Halles, the central market opened in the twelfth century and the heart of Parisian life until 1971, when it was replaced by a market in Rungis, on the outskirts of Paris. This was a rational decision, I suppose, justified by traffic congestion but, in fact, confirming the transformation of the personalized commodity into the impersonal one — with all the traces of provenance and production slipping away, creating, perversely, a new nostalgia. What was left was a hole, le trou des Halles, that was finally filled eight years later by an underground mall, the disastrous Forum, a failure from the start and, since then, in every redesign. It is sleazy, moribund, without a trace of the energy of the old food markets, the restaurants where expats, writers such as Hemingway and Fitzgerald, and countless artists banally went for soupe à l'oignon in the small hours of the morning, and the prostitutes who just as famously satisfied the truckers and more than one teenage boy.

I'm wandering around Les Halles one night in the late fifties. I have to return to Harvard the next day. I've always wanted to see what Zola called le ventre de Paris — Paris's belly filled with, as I expected, stocky, red-faced truckers with skinny adolescent assistants, unloading crate after crate of vegetables, fruit, fish of all sorts, sides of beef, oysters, cursing as they slip on squashed tomatoes, fish scales, and onion peels, joking, flirting with slit-skirted women, promising to buy them a Calva before une pipe pour célébrer — to celebrate what I don't know. It's just a façon de parler. The blow job is self-celebratory. Words, curses, shouts, the noise of crates falling on the ground, the scraping sounds as they are pulled into market stalls...the smells of fruits, greens, freshly baked rounds of peasant bread, overripe cheeses, fish rotting on the pavement, Galloises, cheap perfume, sweat, sex, pastis, cognac, beer, throw-up...mangy dogs barking, eczematous cats carrying mice or rats in their mouths, raucous laughter, chansons, Patachou, Brel, Barbara, Brassens, out-of-date dance hall music, the kind I heard in Marcel Carné's movies, and provocative songs that I remember from striptease scenes in the films noirs that my school friends and I would sneak into in the seediest streets in Geneva's Old Town, to get a look at a naked breast being squeezed by a gangster with huge paws...* It is earthy, loud, vulgar, habitual, excited and exciting, friendly, sensuous but never really seedy — healthy in its way.

I push my way out of the crowded bar where I had stopped to sample the ruckus, overwhelmed, carried away, joyous...I was the only stranger there, or so I thought, since no one paid much attention to me except a couple of worn prostitutes who didn't really take me seriously. They had seen the likes of me before.

I trip, and am caught by a beefy-faced man who is pushing a rather attractive hooker, younger than any I've seen, who smiles at me sympathetically and then shrugs as she goes off with her man. There is no embarrassment, none of the shame, the loneliness I've seen in the faces of the men on the Place Pigalle or the Rue Saint Denis, or the sordid quarters near the opera. Sex is sex here, physiological, a need requiring release...friendly and irresponsible. I find it troublingly simple.

I know France well enough to know that I don't know it. Perhaps the acknowledgment of not knowing what one knows is the mark of the good ethnographer. It is the acceptance of a final

---

* You had to be eighteen to go to the movies in Geneva at that time. It was actually easier for us to get into a strip joint.

alienation from the other—another, any other—a disturbance
in perception, an awkwardness felt in the gut that preserves the
distance necessary for knowing (as we understand knowing) that
other and, at the same time, includes a desire not to know, not
really. We do not easily cede the presumption of—and the fascination with—self-knowledge. The voyeur is driven to discover
elsewhere what he or she (though I know of no women *voyeuses*)
refuses to know, what he already knows in himself. Is it illicit
desire? Or is it an inner emptiness? Or simply the pleasures of the
disquieting?

Why am I so attached to Paris? Why do I feel such an intense
nostalgia for it—for my past there? Jane says she does not feel any
nostalgia for Paris. There are times she misses the ease, the pleasures of daily life, the early-morning walks through the neighborhood with her market basket and the stop at the corner café that
followed, but with time she became bored living in Paris. It lacks
"energy," she says, as the Parisians sink into their self-important
complacency. (I have sometimes felt this, too.) Unlike Wicky, she
did not live there as a child. She did not live there during the post-
war years that extended into the sixties, before the vibrant style
of existentialism gave way to the techno-mechanics of structuralism. She did not experience firsthand the years of Marxist tur-
moil, the anti-Americanism, the divisiveness, the pain, and the
blemished pride that followed the loss of Indochina, Algeria, and
other colonies. France was energized then. It was the Paris I identified with, though I was never really part of it. I was too young.

There is another dimension to nostalgia—displacement.
When I think of Paris, I think of my removal from Parisian life:
feelings of being out of it, inevitably, disconnected, off-key…I
don't want to identify this sense of alienation with that of the
exile, the refugee, or the immigrant—with people who do not

have the luxurious possibility of departure. Living in Paris is for me an indulgence. My friend Edgar de Bresson was once particularly outraged by a wealthy American friend who moved to Paris after living in London for years and then moved to Cyprus. He argued that she used countries capriciously for her own pleasures. I know I may not be doing justice to Edgar's argument. I did not agree with him, but I took his words as an admonition, though I certainly don't feel that I lived in Paris in those years—or anywhere else—simply for my own pleasures. Aside from the obvious fact that neither Jane nor I have the wealth to live anywhere just for pleasure, neither of us can live anywhere without engagement. It is one of the reasons why neither of us is a good tourist, as Jane has written, though she thinks I am an inveterate sightseer. We feel "nowhere" when, on rare occasions, we stay anywhere resembling a resort, though Jane loves the relief of being "nowhere." She stayed on the beach at Mill Reef, where we were staying with friends, the day I went to Saint John's, Antigua's capital. The town was ravished by the invasion of day-tourists from the gigantic cruise ships that towered over it in the harbor. I was sorry to have gone, but that sorrow gave me a sense of place.

I sometimes wonder whether I need to feel disappointed or alienated in order to know where I am. To know where you are, you have to be where you are not—at a remove.

It is late afternoon. I am sitting in a café on the Rue du Figuier, just around the corner from the little hotel where I am staying. My aunt recommended it. She is always looking for little hotels—"off the beaten track," she says—on her trips to Paris. She likes to replay her student days there, when she was studying art and scandalizing her parents with her pointedly bohemian life. I have just arrived from London after my fight with Mariam. The café is full except for a few tables near the street, where the sun is blinding. A very drunk clochard weaves his way between those empty tables, mumbling, begging for a handout, ordering people at the nearby tables to buy him a drink, cursing them because they ignore him, apologizing for disturbing them, haranguing them, telling them that they should get their big, fat bourgeois asses off their seats and work the way he does...Some people laugh; others, mainly the students there, chide him; the majority ignore him, turning away or concentrating on the newspapers or books they're reading. At first, the waiter ignores him, too, but when the clochard becomes more belligerent, he tells him to scram. This leads to an even louder harangue. The waiter turns away, and the tramp calms down—or so it seems at first. Then he begins to spin around dizzily, clutching at his heart, and falls to the ground, hitting his head on the edge of one of the empty tables. He is bleeding slightly from a scratch. Everyone ignores him, relieved that they won't be disturbed any-more. No one, not even the waiter, takes a step to help him. I'm shocked, but I don't move either. I notice blood is trickling from his mouth. I mention this to the two elderly women sitting at the table on my right. At first they ignore me, and then they say indif-ferently that he's probably cracked a tooth. This is seconded by the old man on my left. I see that the drunk's breath is becoming more and more irregular and that even his red wino cheeks have lost their color. I cannot believe that he is still ignored. Finally I call the waiter over and ask him to do something. He says that the man is an old drunk who comes around at about this time every day. Forget about it. But I insist. I say that I think he's had a heart attack. Several people scoff at me. Finally, the waiter walks over, lifts the clochard's head, and is doused with blood that is now gushing from his mouth. The waiter drops the clochard's head—I hear the thump—and wipes his hands, irritated, on his apron. The *patron* of the café has emerged, notices what's happening, and calls for an ambulance. No one pays any more attention to the drunk, even when the ambulance arrives and carries him off. I feel very alone.

Where am I? Do I really know?

I am teaching a course at the University of Paris at Nanterre. They have invited me, but when I arrive in September, they tell me there is a problem. The department and the faculty forum had unanimously approved my appointment, but it was denied at the last moment by the Ministry of Education, along with every other appointment Nanterre made that year. It's a question of politics, they say. François Mitterrand and the Socialists are now in power, and they have rejected all these recommendations because they came through Annie Kriegel, Nanterre's liaison with the Ministry. Kriegel is considered a turncoat by the French Left. She had been a Communist until the Soviets invaded Hungary in 1956, after which she quit the Party and, in neocon fashion, began writing for the conservative daily *Le Figaro*. No one made any attempt to apologize to me. They simply shrugged their shoulders, attempting, as the French frequently do, to save face with a cynical attitude. Fortunately, through contacts — *tuyaux*, as the French say — and the good graces of the anthropologist Maurice Godelier, who was directing the Centre National de la Recherche Scientifique (CNRS), I was awarded a research position but expected to teach.

Academic politics are universal, but their style is different in different countries. I was once asked to present my candidature for a professorship in Berlin and was about to agree when I noticed that, while the letter to me was dated in early May, the envelope was postmarked in late September, and that was when I got it. I wrote a letter of query, which was never answered. Since

then I have met the German Arabist who invited me several
times. He offered no explanation; he simply said how sorry he
was that I'd had "personal problems" with the invitation. Later, I
learned from a friend that the position had been filled in July but
that the committee needed to show that they had made an international search to justify their choice.

It may sound odd, but shocked as I was by the degree to which
national politics at their most petty level penetrated French university life, I was more troubled by finding myself treated as a
bureaucrat, a *fonctionnaire*. I felt, for the first time, that I had a
job, like everyone else. At the University of Cape Town, where
I once agreed to teach a course—I needed a visa to continue my
research in South Africa—I had felt constrained by the demands
made on the faculty. Midmornings and afternoons, we were
expected to leave our offices for the faculty lounge for tea and
conversation. We sat on hard chairs lined up against the walls,
circling an empty space that I soon identified with the emptiness
of those conversations. They were, in fact, a way to guarantee
that everyone in the department had showed up for a full day's
work. The chairman was definitely my boss. I have never felt
that I was an employee, a bureaucrat, or a worker—a man with
a boss—at any of the American universities where I have taught.
Is this because we are treated here as professionals with greater
independence? Or does the professional veneer simply mask our
real status? Does it matter?

There were no obligatory teas at Nanterre or any of the other
programs in anthropology in Paris. Professors arrived, taught
their classes, and left. They were alienated, at times peevish, and
felt exploited, as they were. There was little contact with under-
graduates. I taught a graduate course on life histories that fall.
The students were friendly, talented, and serious. It took some

time for them to adjust to my way of teaching—which was far less formal than they expected—but when they did catch on, I felt that their understanding of anthropology deepened. I came to admire the organization of their class presentations.

Teaching at the École Pratique des Hautes Études en Sciences Sociales was different from teaching at Nanterre. I would come as a visiting professor, for short terms, a month or two, to give one or two lectures in seminars conducted by Pierre Bourdieu or Marc Augé and on occasion to be an external examiner at a doctoral defense. It seemed to me that the relationship between the graduate students, certainly the senior ones, and the faculty was closer than at Nanterre. I was reminded of the cosmopolitanism of the Graduate Center.

Bourdieu's seminars were pragmatically focused almost exclusively on his own research projects. Augé's were more open, serious but not without lighthearted moments. Marc was genuinely liked. By the time I came to know him, Pierre worked with a team of researchers—disciples, really—who carried out most of his field research. He would then fold their findings into one of his theoretical paradigms. Over the next years, and especially after his election to the Collège de France, he became more and more of a celebrity, even to himself. His stories of his modest background became more rhetorical than the source of social and critical self-reflection that had once enriched his work. They began to sound more and more like the conventional French parable of the poor provincial boy who makes good in Paris, but misconstrues the Parisian world to which he aspires. (I have heard sniffy Parisians claim that he never nailed the French class structure in *Distinction*, his book on taste as a class marker.) He risked becoming a type—a stock character, as Walter Benjamin understood the slippage from individuality to anonymity as a product of modernity—despite his spreading fame. Unlike Balzac's Lucien de Rubempré, Pierre kept a critical eye on his own trajectory, supported, as it were, by his sociology, which may well have been a source of his misapperception (*méconnaissance*). His sociology, like all sociologies that implicitly or explicitly classify individuals in terms of status and role, encouraged the typification it was meant to describe, and in a way echoed modernity's delimitation of the individual's creative and transgressive possibility.

Pierre suffered a terrifying writer's block when he began to prepare his initial lecture (*leçon*) for the assembled notables of the Collège de France to which he had just been elected. It was only when he retreated to the Béarn, where he was born, that he was able to finish it. On the day he delivered it, he was so drenched in sweat that when Jane went to congratulate him, he apologized, thinking his embrace might stain her blouse. He knew, of course, what he had been through. Though we didn't agree on many theoretical issues—on creativity and my regard for Derrida—he was a loyal friend. I remember a small dinner we had in Chicago, during which he claimed that Derrida's entire career was based on elaborating the anecdotes that students at the prestigious École Normale Supérieure (where they both studied) used to decorate their exams or distract the examiners from their hedged or slippery answers. He was referring specifically to the double meaning in ancient Greek of the constellation of terms surrounding *pharmakeia* (pharmaceuticals) as both remedy and poison.

Before retiring from the presidency of the École des Hautes Études, Marc Augé asked me if I wanted to teach there on a permanent basis. I had thought about this over the years, but rejected the idea because the salary discrepancy was too great. I could commute between Paris and New York monthly and still have more money at my disposal than I would have in Paris. By the time Marc asked me directly, I was too close to the École's required retirement age (sixty-five). I like to teach and had no intention of retiring at that age. Nor did I want to run through the gauntlet of professors whom I would have to please, especially as the first go-around was known to be a ritual of humiliation. I wasn't about to put myself through it.

In some ways the moments of alienation I have just described (and there are many more) have challenged my sense of where I am or rather where I would like to be. Our sense of identity — however interiorized and seemingly independent of others — is never as independent as we assume it to be. "Being somewhere" is always more than being somewhere on a map. Being-in-the-world is, as Heidegger put it, being-with-others in a caring, concerned mode. It is encrusted with an ever-shifting past and a future that is caught in the play between realism, desire, and hope. Most of the time we understand why we — or others — do what we do in terms of the situation in which we find ourselves.

I put on sunblock because I am in the sun and don't want to get sunburned. This explanation is, under most circumstances, sufficient. Sufficient or not, it resonates emotionally, in intensity, with past experiences. I remember, for example, the times I was badly sunburned, the articles that I have read relating the effect of sunrays to the ever-decreasing ozone layer, Wicky's slathering thick layers of creamy block on poor Garrick — she's doing it as I write — my arguments with climate change deniers, or the sensuous strokes of Jane spreading lotion on my back.

The pragmatics of the occasion — not getting sunburned — usually override these memories, but during crises, during reflections on the past, or in dreams, the encrustations of memory surface capriciously. It is presumptuous to dismiss them, their possibility, when we attribute motivation to others and indeed to ourselves; this is why rational-choice theorists, who focus on the rational dimension of decision-making, are so often bewildered by the choices people actually make. A case in point is the frequent failure of economic predictions of those economists who base their models on rational choice. Obviously, predictions of group behavior are mediated by probability. But what about the individual? I think of an acquaintance who, against all "rational" advice, refused to sell the stocks he'd inherited from his father because his father had worked so hard to own them.

How does nostalgia figure in our present-day understanding and our sense of the future? In what we actually do?

Before I began working with the Harkis, I was often asked if I had ever considered doing field research in France. Although my answer was always the same—that to preserve my sanity I needed a place of abode that was free from my anthropology—it was not quite accurate, on two counts. The first was that it is impossible to bracket one's "anthropological perspective." The second is that I had thought of many possible French projects but in the end rejected them. In one instance the project proved impossible. I had just finished writing about South Africa and was thinking about working with mercenaries, starting with the French Foreign Legion. I discovered that there was a retirement colony for the Legionnaires in the South of France, but to work there I needed permission from the Ministry of Defense. I was refused, even though a retired general who had served with the Legion as a young officer wanted to accompany me. "They're old men," I was told. "They'd have nothing to say of interest." So I had to abandon the project, though not without a certain relief—which I attributed to the exhaustion I'd felt after months of having to listen to racists in South Africa. I thought, too, of writing about the Beurs—the children of North African immigrants—but I could not find an "angle" that caught my imagination.

I am a strong believer in the role of inspiration in choosing and sustaining a research project. Without it, as I've seen with some of my students and colleagues, fieldwork remains flat. I remember talking to a student at the University of Stockholm who had spent more than a year in a small German village. She was bored, disliked the villagers (who were not particularly welcoming to her), and felt claustrophobic—feelings she had had in the Swedish village where she had grown up. "Nothing ever happened there," she told me. Her dissertation was competent—just competent. I am certain that as closed and closed-minded as the village was, there were things of interest that had escaped her attention simply because her ethnographic imagination was muted. Margaret Mead used to tell her students that there is always something of ethnographic interest happening in even the most boring research sites. You just have to know yourself well enough to find it. She meant that you have to know yourself well enough to know the blinkers imposed on your perception by your personal style and history. True, so long as you recognize that boredom itself—yours and your informants'—is of "ethnographic interest." It is among the most pervasive of social phenomena—and the least studied.

XXI.
STORIES
THAT
CANNOT
BE TOLD

E VERY anthropologist I know has had experiences that, while illuminating, cannot be related, not only because they would harm or expose the individuals involved, stipulated by the ethics of the profession, but also out of personal discretion, respect for and sensitivity to those individuals, and sadly but inevitably the ideological assumptions that mark membership in the anthropological community and advancement in that community.

As time passes, the significance of our encounters changes for us and the people we study. We know little about how they are reevaluated by our informants. Our contact falters and loses its immediacy, and undeniably so does the moral pressure that immediacy imposes. Events that seemed of critical importance when they took place fade, freeing us, rightly or wrongly, to describe what at the time we felt compelled to keep to ourselves. We see them—remember them—differently, their implication shifts, the urgency diminishes, and they become stories that seem to have an independence of their own.

The anthropologist Victor Turner referred to certain constellations of significant and at times transformative events—events that disrupt the normal flow of social life—as social dramas. They reflect the inner workings, the structural tensions, in the society in which they occur and the external pressures on it.

Turner was interested in both minor dramas, such as the breakup of lineages and clans, that do little more than readjust a society to changing circumstances (increases in population, for example) and major ones, such as revolutions that transform the society.

When I was doing fieldwork in South Africa at the beginning of the eighties, one such "drama" occurred in a nearby village, revealing a crack in the rigid separation of peoples of different races and origins imposed by apartheid. I couldn't write about it at the time. It had been in the news, and any mention of it would have revealed the location of the village where I was working and the identity of many of my informants. I had promised them confidentiality and anonymity. My worries were unwarranted. As I was the only American anthropologist in the country doing research on its white population, it was easy to discover my whereabouts, despite all my attempts to disguise them. A second reason for not writing about what had happened was that it was still sub judice.

A twelve-year-old girl, whom I'll call Emma, is awakened by strange noises in the middle of the night at her uncle's house, where she and her younger sister like to spend their weekends. It is next to their parents' home. Emma goes to see what is happening and intrudes on two "colored" (that is, in apartheid understanding, part white, part black) thieves who have just murdered her uncle because he refused to give them money. In fact, he had no money to give them, since he kept no money in the house for fear of being robbed. The thieves threaten Emma, telling her that they will be waiting outside and will kill her if she screams or leaves the house. In the morning, the girls' nanny, who has come to take them home, finds Emma frozen in terror at the entrance to her uncle's bedroom, where she has stood guard to prevent her younger sister from seeing what happened.

The girls' parents are wealthy English farmers who, as I was often told, treat their workers harshly, "like animals," and are hated in the adjacent colored community. In contrast, the girls' uncle, a retired sea captain, is much loved in that community, for he spent a lot of time with the children, supplementing what little education they received in the "for colored only" school and organizing soccer matches and other sports events. His brother disapproves, warning him that his behavior is dangerous and will make those children — and their parents — uppity.

The police are called in and find the murderers in a couple of hours. They had worked for the farmer until he had them arrested for, if I remember correctly, drunken fighting. They are released the day of the murder. Always terrified at the least change in the status quo, the white community goes into panicked mourning. Emma's uncle was liked. Her father and mother do not appear to have changed their attitudes toward their workers. The colored community goes into shamefaced mourning, especially when it is discovered that Emma's uncle has left them money to build a proper soccer field. The funeral presents a problem, since the local Anglican church, the only non-segregated church in the area, is too small to seat so many mourners. Much to everyone's surprise, the *dominee* (the minister) of the local Dutch Reformed church, which is strictly segregated, agrees — or maybe simply offers — to open his church to colored mourners, providing they remain in the back of the room. (Even in the anti-apartheid Anglican church, whites were able to sip from the Communion chalice before the colored congregants, who were seated in the back.) It is also the first time many of the English-speaking whites have ever entered the dominee's church. I wish I could say that the dominee's gesture changed relations between whites and coloreds (there were few blacks in the area) or between English- and Afrikaans-speaking whites, but it didn't. And yet—I must believe this—a seemingly small gesture, the lending of a church for a funeral, leaves its trace. It becomes a reference point for the villagers, though they did not take it to be a harbinger of change.

Whenever I think of my experiences in South Africa, Emma's story comes to mind. It dramatizes the tensions in the apartheid state in its last punishing decade. To be sure, I witnessed more violent dramas—peaceful protesters in front of the Houses of Parliament in Cape Town surrounded by soldiers with no name-tags who threatened them with angry dogs baring their teeth, or riots clearly instigated by the government to put fear in both the peoples of color and, perhaps more significant, in the whites, to fortify its position—but by the time I was living there, protests and riots were so frequent that their real (if they ever had any) and symbolic power was dissipated.

Regardless of privilege, everyone was trapped within the cruelties of apartheid. Some prospered from it, and others, the majority of South Africans, including some whites—those in prison for protesting it—suffered unspeakable degradation. The threat of violence simmered beneath the surface of daily life, often erupting in unpredictable ways. Fear was always in the air. It was the one thing everybody—black, white, Asian, or colored—shared. At some point in every interview I had with whites they expressed the fear of an eventual bloodbath, the inevitable reaction of a tiny dominant class confronting the oppressed majority, which they failed utterly to acknowledge or understand. I had hundreds of interviews and conversations with those whites and rarely heard any of them, even the most liberal, engage with—or even imagine—what nonwhites were thinking or feeling. I see them in the dominee's church, whites and coloreds, English speakers and Afrikaners, sitting and standing in their own groups, with little sense of or even interest in what the other groups are feeling. Their isolation from one another was chilling. But the fact that they did not, and probably could not, acknowledge the loneliness that separation produced in them was truly terrifying. A corpse had brought them together, but it could do no more.

Writing about the people I knew who have died—my father and mother, Rudolph, Mariam, my roommate Bill, Jim Bucciarelli, Tuhami, Moulay Abedsalem, Margaret Mead, George Devereux, or Pierre Bourdieu—is mediated both by my respect for the dead and by the license that their death has given me, the transgressive possibilities as well as the decorum it affords, their interplay, and the interpretive space—the reading between the lines—that I imagine it offers my readers. I know that they will read what I say about the dead very differently from what I say about the living. The etiquette that surrounds the death—mourning, grieving, remembrance, memorialization, and forgetting—is culturally bound and affects the way we understand responses to the dead in other cultures.

The Navajo do not talk about the dead or even mention their names. Anthropologists, based on what the Navajo have told them, attribute this silence to the fear of ghosts. Most seem satisfied with this explanation. I am not questioning that, but I have to ask if it does justice to the Navajo's attitude toward death. Does it impede the anthropologist's "deeper" responses to death—the Navajo's and his or her own? Does it ignore the Navajo's sense of human dignity? Their sense of the word, of talk? Their stoicism? Their bravery? Their emotional economy? I don't know, but surely these questions are worth asking. I'm not even sure their silence is exceptional. I remember the discomfort I felt when one of my professors mentioned, almost as an aside, the fact that many Amazon Indians would simply walk away from old men and women who were too weak to continue trekking, leaving them to die alone in the jungle. Did those Indians talk about the dead?

Despite Wittgenstein's famous adage — "Of that which we cannot speak, we must remain silent" — we do speak of death, the dying, and the dead continually. It is part of our mourning ritual. It figures in our therapies, in our memoirs, and, in excess, in this book. It figures as fact and metaphor. Think of memorial services, where people who have known the deceased "remember" them. The speakers construct their biographies, their values, their legacy, their goodness, if you will, with the appropriate sensitivity, sadness, and, at times, loving humor. They create a revival image of the corpse, which, as the French literary philosopher Maurice Blanchot would say, begins to resemble itself. I'm not questioning the speaker's sincerity. Their praise is heartfelt. The goodness they attribute to the deceased may, in fact, be true. There are, after all, good, likeable people who die. The speakers are actors, however, performing before an audience, and, as in all performances, they are never wholly the parts they play. That inevitable remove creates a space in which feelings, such as sincerity, grief, sadness, and sensitivity, are less than secure. Think of Brutus's words said over the man he has just helped slay: "So are we Caesar's friends, that have abridg'd / His time of fearing death" (act 3, scene 1, ll. 104–105). Or Mark Antony's funeral oration: "I come to bury Caesar, not to praise him..." (act 3, scene 2, l. 80). Or his final words over Brutus's corpse: "He was the noblest Roman of them all..." (act 5, scene 5, l. 68). Think of the negations and counter-negations. It is the space of irony, rhetorical play, dubiety — of bad faith, or, as we like to put it, having it both ways. Negation exists in even the most ordinary circumstances, but in those cases, it is usually masked by convention, habit, and conscience—the blinkers of conscience, anyway. "I don't want to sound blasphemous" is a phrase so ingrained in us—in me, at least—that I feel it now, writing this page. Am I vilifying this everyman or woman—the memorializer—with insinuations of insincerity? Am I being too cruelly cynical about situations in which cynicism and skepticism are inappropriate?

And yet, has anyone ever attended a memorial service without recognizing the idealization of the deceased? Has anyone never been offended by the praise heaped on the deceased by a speaker known to have disparaged him or her? What do we ourselves feel, reflecting on the deceased at that memorialization? And later, after the intensification of grief diminishes? Please understand me: I am not saying that all mourners are hypocrites, that images of the deceased are idealized, or that even those memorializers—a colleague, say, an editor, a boss, or a distant relative who may have even disliked the deceased cannot be so carried away by their performance that they sincerely believe themselves. Ritual is not without efficacy.

I have spoken at only two memorial services, one a small family service and the other a public ceremony for my friend and colleague Paul Zweig. I had little to say in Paul's case, or rather little that wasn't inadequate to my sense of the living Paul. I felt as though I was deceasing him anew. My words seemed sententious and peremptory. Fortunately, the other mourners took my abrupt conclusion as a sign of grief. At least, I hope they did. I had to leave early. I couldn't stand the encomiums. The Paul I knew and liked was disappearing—disappeared.

Last week, our gardener Oriano's mother died. His father had died a few months earlier—both after prolonged suffering. I went to the funeral. I had never been to a funeral in the Umbrian countryside. I didn't even know how to dress for the occasion. Finally I decided to wear a blue blazer and gray trousers. Not a tie. It is midsummer and, even for Italy, exceptionally hot. When I arrived, the church was full to overflowing. I was overdressed. No one wore black. None of the men wore suits or jackets. Most of the women wore their everyday clothes. I was surprised. I stood out, of course, but I would have anyway, as the only foreigner. I stood near the church entrance and could barely hear the priest, who was reciting, I believe, some all-purpose funeral mass with no mention of Oriano's mother except for her name. It seemed routine, and the mourners, those I could see, took it as such. Some were even talking among themselves; their attention was elsewhere. And yet, as the priest went on talking about salvation, I felt relief in the impersonality of his words. Oriano's mother, whom I had never met, was cast, or more accurately recast, in a transcendent drama, inevitable in its generality, destined in its particularity. Prayers were said, some repeated by the mourners, but, at least during the service, they did not fashion or refashion her biography. They relocated her or, one could say, confirmed her relocation—her death and salvation. When I saw Oriano a few days later, I said how surprised I'd been by the informality. After a long pause, he said it was more human that way.

I remember Baudelaire's comments in his *Salon, de 1846* on wearing black at funerals.

> Take notice that black suits and frockcoats not only have their political beauty, which is an expression of universal equality, but also their poetic beauty, which is an expression of the soul—a long procession of undertakers, political undertakers,

amorous undertakers, bourgeois undertakers. We all celebrate some burial or another.*

A uniform livery of desolation attests to equality; and, as for the eccentrics, revealed by clear and violent colors, they are satisfied today with subtleties in design and cut, more than in color. Do these twisted folds, playing like snakes around mortified flesh, have a mysterious grace?†

Yes, Oriano was right.

There are, of course, countless stories about me, and the people I know and see, that I would like to recount but cannot out of discretion, embarrassment, and even fear of litigation. I don't want to steal anyone's story. I don't want to hurt anyone. Or do I? It is so tempting to avenge oneself in a memoir. Or to flatter in one's own interest, or, more generously, to raise somebody's self-esteem, or simply make him feel good. The line between these intentions is sometimes difficult to maintain.

I think, for example, of an anthropologist who died in 2006. He had become my nemesis, for reasons I have never been able to determine. I was by no means unique. Clifford Geertz was

---

* Remarquez bien que l'habit noir et la redingcote ont non-seulement leur beauté politique, qui est l'expression de l'égalité universelle, mais encore leur beauté poétique, qui est l'expression de l'âme—une immense défilade de croque-morts, croque-morts politiques, croque-morts amoureux, croque-morts bourgeois. Nous célébrons tous quelque enterrement.

† Une livrée uniforme de désolation témoigne de l'égalité; et quant aux excentriques que les couleurs tranchées et violentes dénonçaient facilement aux yeux, ils se contentment aujourd'hui des nuances des dessins , dans la coupe, plus encore que dans la couleur. Ces plis grimaçants, et jouant comme des serpents autour d'une chair mortifiée, n'ont-ils pas leur grâce mystérieuse? [134, salons 1846]

working in Morocco when I was a student. I wrote to him for advice. He wrote back immediately, suggesting that I work in a shrine community that had already been studied years before by a very distinguished French scholar of North Africa and the Middle East—a man who, even I knew this, was famously prickly. I knew better than to do my research in the same community he had. Hadn't Geertz recognized this? I didn't take his advice.

A year or so later, when Jane and I were settled in Morocco, we received an invitation to have lunch with the Geertzes in Sefrou, the town—formerly a summer resort for French colonists—where he and his wife, Hilly, were doing fieldwork. They were very friendly, but our meeting was surreal. Geertz's Morocco, a place he was to characterize as "a wild west sort of place," had little to do with the Morocco that Jane and I knew—one that was saturated with beliefs in spirits, possession, and ecstatic states. Geertz dismissed my research as completely marginal to Moroccan culture. Whatever did he mean by that? Indeed, he said he saw no reason why I was doing the research there when I could have done it anywhere. Jane and I woke in the middle of the night wondering where we were, and whether everything we had observed was delusional—knowing of course that it wasn't. I wrote a polite letter to Geertz, explaining, among other things, why my research was intimately related to Moroccan "culture." He didn't answer my letter but remained friendly. Several years later, I learned that one of his principal informants was a leading member of one of the ecstatic brotherhoods, similar to the one I was studying, whose importance he had dismissed. Apparently, his informant had never bothered to tell him. Still, I cannot imagine this was the source of his hostility.

After I began teaching at Princeton, Geertz moved from the University of Chicago to the Institute for Advanced Study in Princeton, where he started a social science program. In turn Hilly received an appointment in the university's anthropology department. I saw Geertz from time to time, sometimes at dinner, when Hilly invited me to meet one of the visiting anthropologists — Louis Dumont, Pierre Bourdieu, Victor Turner, or Raymond Firth. Geertz would sulk when the conversation became cosmopolitan, which is to say foreign. I always felt that he was something of a xenophobe, but he wasn't unique in this respect. I have known several anthropologists far more xenophobic than he was. Anthropology for them and, perhaps for him, was a way of conquering otherness, just as psychoanalysis for Freud was a way of conquering the irrational.

As time went on Geertz became ludicrously self-important. He had little if any self-irony and was socially quite inept. I remember his referring to an interview he had just had with Gian Carlo Menotti, who was composing an opera, *Tamu-Tamu*, that took place in Indonesia, where Geertz had done most of his fieldwork. Geertz said he was surprised by how culturally sensitive Menotti was, as though cultural sensitivity were the sole province of the ethnographer.

When Geertz first arrived at the Institute, he bragged to me about having demolished a grant proposal for an archeological dig on the Navajo reservation. He knew I had written about the Navajo but had no idea what my relations with the archeologist were. Aside from the breach of confidence, I wondered why he had been chosen to review a project that had absolutely nothing to do with his expertise. Why hadn't he refused? He was not, in my experience, a particularly generous man. I once attended a weekend conference on ethnomusicology in which he refused to say a word during the sessions and only rarely at meals, even when he was addressed. In time, Geertz became so hostile that it was clear I shouldn't stay at Princeton, which, as I have said, I hadn't planned to do. My departure was controversial. I soon discovered that he had blackballed several prestigious grants and job offers for which I had been nominated. He always did so without leaving a paper trace. Once, when he was in Naples to give a lecture, he was seated for dinner next to a friend, a Haitian poet married to a historian, who would translate for him if necessary. They had, she told me, a lively conversation until she happened to mention me, whereupon he turned his back on her and remained silent for the rest of the dinner. The disappointment was enormous, since, unlike the French, the Italians admired his work, and not without reason.

I was not the only young anthropologist whose career Geertz tried to destroy. At least one of them was forced out of academia entirely. Geertz didn't like his "left-wing" politics. In a profile of Geertz in *The New York Times Magazine*, when he was asked about me, he answered, "I don't like him. There's a story behind all that, but I am not going to tell it." The author of the article felt he was jealous of the younger generation.

Am I being indiscreet in writing this? Am I avenging myself? He who lives longer has the final word—well, not quite. What may remain of us all are crumbling brown pages in the back stacks of university libraries, or Internet links that threaten to disappear with an accidental or purposeful click. So much for delusions of permanence. Delusions are more friable than browning paper and more susceptible to psychic intoxication than to digital accident.

By now, you have seen how I have attempted to reframe my discussion in order to commit an indiscretion without committing one. In the end, all I can do is laugh, but laughter demands some acknowledgment of the disappointments I felt and the futility of anger. It is telling.

Thinking about Clifford Geertz reminds me of Julie Martin—an admittedly odd pairing. I have begun to ask people I know about nemeses and have been surprised by how many of them have had one—or its opposite. Most of their nemeses are in the workplace. They are held responsible for losing a job, failing to receive a promotion, or even being unable to take a planned holiday. Their effect is cumulative, both serious and trivial, but trivialities accrue and can even become more important than serious interferences. It could be argued that nemeses are a characteristic of modernity. Didn't Salvador Dalí suggest that capitalism demands a paranoid attitude? Perhaps. So does depression, and depression may be conceived of, I suppose, as paranoia inwardly turned. The anthropologist Emily Martin has focused on the affinity between mania and manic depression and contemporary American values. Paranoia, depression, mania—what is of interest is not the particular malady but the fact that we choose psychopathological metaphors to describe culturally conditioned and condoned styles of personality and behavior. Baudelaire began his reflections on black as a color of mourning by asking, "Is the required costume of our suffering age, borne on thin, black shoulders, the symbol of perpetual mourning?" ("*N'est-il pas l'habit nécessaire de notre époque souffrante et portant jusque sur ses épaules noires et maigres le symbole d'un deuil perpetuel?*") Perhaps the clothing metaphor, even one that refers to mourning, is less constraining than the pathological ones, if only because it opens the way to irony, however grotesque, and humor, too.

Still, to limit nemeses to modern societies would be to dismiss their importance in less-than-modern societies, where people find themselves and think of themselves not only as victims of their communities but of a surfeit of spirits, ghosts, ancestors, sorcerers, witches, and abstract but personally directed powers, such as the evil eye and punitive destinies. What they share with modern nemeses is a failure of irony — an inability to laugh at their nemeses. Of course, they see danger where we deny fear.

XXII.

BETRAYAL

ANTHROPOLOGY, like the other human sciences and, indeed, like everyday social life, is edged with the possibility—the reality—of betrayal and the twisted revelations that inevitably arise out of the omitted, the secretive if not the secret, and quite simply the silent, as every gossip knows. Of course, consideration of the role of betrayal in social and professional life requires, among other things, an acknowledgment, less of sincerity as a state of mind than of the rhetoric of sincerity—which is to say that skepticism, if not cynicism, is required. It could be argued that skepticism is demanded by modernity. It is certainly what I would argue; our mistake is to render modernity exceptional. The more interesting question is how skepticism (as well as betrayal, sincerity, and the constellation of associated sentiments and evaluations) is framed in a particular culture and under what circumstances.

Living, as I do, in the Italian countryside each summer, I'm constantly aware of the way in which betrayal figures in the lives of Italians. I'm not speaking of the caricatures—say, of the southern Italian *nonna* who warns her granddaughter never to trust a man. She may be right. Rather, I'm speaking of an assumption that trust is fragile, and that giving one's word is a convention that has to be met with skepticism and yet believed—with skeptical belief. The looping is exquisite.

One frequent maneuver in negotiations that bolsters trust in the professed word is the accompanying discussion, peppered with innumerable examples offered by all parties to the exchange,

325

of how untrustworthy Italians are, meaning everybody but one-self. Sometimes the stories of being cheated or betrayed are true, sometimes not, but the response to them—a shrug of the shoulders or a knowing smile—is almost invariably the same. Once, Jane discovered a painter, who had just painted our pump house, walking away with an empty can of cheap, commercial paint instead of the hand-mixed natural paint we had paid for. His response was that ubiquitous shrug followed, with not a trace of embarrassment, by *"Ah, signora, è l'Italia,"* after which he bowed and went his way. Yesterday, I was told another *è l'Italia* story. The mayor of a nearby city had built a swimming pool without permission. The court ruled that, as he was mayor of the town, it was up to him to decide whether he should be fined and, if so, by how much.

In Umbria, we live in a *commune* with almost no foreigners (that is, citizens of other countries, with a smattering of Romans and Florentines who are, in some respects, considered more foreign than we are). It is not just us—we are known collectively as the *stranieri*—but also the villagers who have stories of being cheated and betrayed. They are both the source and the fuel of lifelong animosities, to which the *stranieri* are not immune. Unless their cause is exceptionally egregious, these animosities are set aside for weddings, festivals, and funerals. As paradoxical as it may seem, they also create a sense of community, one not of victims but of an intricate web of we've-got-to-believe-it-but-would-be-fools-to-believe-it-but-do-believe-it-knowing-we-are-fools-but-aren't-really-fools-since-we-know-we-are-fools. What binds this Goldoni-like community is the phrase *"ci penso io"* ("I'll take care of it"), which is believed when the speaker is a relative or a friend, is apt to gain something for himself in taking care of it, wants something in return, or is simply a scoundrel who hopes to improve his reputation by making a *bella figura*—a restorative flourish. *"Ci penso io"* cannot be reduced to a simple exchange.

I remember talking to a local builder—a devotee of Berlusconi, as it turned out—who said it was necessary to distinguish between corruption and accommodating oneself to reality. He was, in fact, so corrupt himself that we had to sue him, along with the architect, who had used him to restore our house. We went to court and actually won, mirabile dictu, after years of litigation. No one thought a foreigner *could* win against a "local." The decision was, in my view, appropriate, but the architect hired a Roman lawyer to appeal on trumped-up grounds, and managed to halve the amount they had to pay. He claimed in the aftermath, so I was told, that it was he who had sued us.

Restoring a house in Italy is never simple, and the problems are by no means restricted to foreigners. The difference is that, unlike the Italians, the foreigners—at least some of the Americans among them—sentimentalize their relationship to Italy. In our *commune*, few of them speak Italian well enough to have a serious or amusing conversation with a native. They rarely have an Italian to dinner (unless of course the Italian speaks English and, better still, has a title). They do love Italy, but they live, for the most part, at a remove, in an Italy that has been sanitized, idealized, and estheticized. They are true expats. They rarely ask how the "locals" view them. I will never forget the bemusement of two maids who were serving dinner at a *castello* when the American owner asked his guests to join hands at the table while he said grace. Obviously the relations between *stranieri* and locals are collusive, not simply because of the salaries that the locals depend on but because of an ambiguous reverence for class. It should be remembered that Italy did not have a revolution, as the French did, that sharecropping (*mezzadria*) ended in our area only in 1982, and that the *jus primae noctis*—the right of the first night—was practiced, I have been told, by a count there until after the Second World War. (It was outlawed in Italy in 1924.) But, beyond material gain and class considerations, there is also a pride in service.

I hope you realize that, in some ways, I am repeating, even parodying, prevailing stereotypes of Italians in general, villagers in particular, and (American) *stranieri*—that is, those who do not earn their living in Italy. There are foreigners who are deeply engaged with the country and its people. I'm thinking of friends, many of them artists, writers, and actors, who also live around us, but also others working in cities or at universities and research institutes. There are, of course, innumerable Italians who remain defiantly upright—often under exceptionally difficult circumstances. They possess reserves of dignity and finesse that cannot be explained away by reference to honor and shame—the timeworn response of many social scientists to Mediterranean manners. The existential is not a code. Italians themselves often employ words such as "honor" and "shame," but for them, these words tend to have a rhetorically justificatory function, with little or nothing to do with self-understanding.

Stereotypes aside, my parody is in one way serious, for there is a parodic dimension, a light and at times gentle, at times trenchant, humor, to both American, more generally Euro-American, and Italian characterizations of the Italian, Italian society, and Italian manners and mannerisms. It is an asymmetrically shared imaginary that has to be reckoned with, because it bears not only on Italian relations with foreigners but also (if differently) on relations among Italians themselves. It figures in the way in which responsibility is assumed and evaded, as in the painter's *"Ah, signora, è l'Italia"* or the builder's differentiation of accommodation and bribery, or in a comment made to Jane by one of Berlusconi's defense lawyers, who was also head of the judiciary committee of the Italian senate at the time, when she asked him, in good American fashion, if he wasn't troubled by such a blatant conflict of interest. "What conflict of interest?" he answered, not as flippantly as it may sound to foreign ears. "In the morning I wear one hat, and in the afternoon another." He meant it. In fact, that he could make such a comment to a serious journalist who was writing a profile of his patron for *The New Yorker* is indicative of what I am tempted to call the earnestness of parodic self-understanding.

Parodic self-understanding is obviously a risky business, at least if you are not sheltered under a billionaire prime minister's umbrella.

Is it possible to imagine a society that functions on mistrust rather than trust? I doubt it, but posing the question is instructive—a way of refiguring social and personal relations, and especially the importance we place on trust in raising children. It calls attention to the way children learn not only to trust their parents, siblings, and teachers but also to respond to breaches of trust, the shock and disappointment they feel. Betrayal can produce complicit bonds of guilt and shame—as I saw working with the Harkis—which play themselves out as long as the relationship itself continues and, later, in dream and memory.

The instillation of mistrust varies from culture to culture and from family to family. It is subject to different moral evaluations. In some societies, it is given conventional, indeed ritual form, as, for example, the Moroccan circumcision ceremony I described or the denouement in some tribal initiations, particularly puberty ceremonies, in which the initiates learn that the grotesquely masked spirits who have terrified and tortured them over long nights are in fact their fathers, or, less painfully, a child's discovery that Santa Claus doesn't exist. The initiates are destined to reenact the drama when they reach the appropriate age.

What role do secrets play in the creation and maintenance of trust? What preserves the (shared) secret other than trust? Must there be some implicit threat of betrayal in order to maintain that trust? An if-you-tell-I-tell understanding? We usually associate trust with personal and social alliances. Are such alliances constituted on a potential breach — a violation — of trust? My friend and fellow anthropologist Michael Silverstein once said that in the past lawyers tried to write contracts that could not be broken, but today they write them to ensure minimum damage when they are broken.

After the Army Language School, I was sent to Germany, where I was trained in the transcription of intercepted messages, largely about Warsaw Pact maneuvers. It was tedious work, and, according to the career soldiers who had been transcribing for years, it would damage your hearing. Fortunately, I was made an instructor, which meant that I only had to listen to "sensitive" recordings — the ones that presented problems.

My orders ranged from the absurd — having to stamp an article in *Pravda* top secret because it accurately described the location of where I worked and the work we did there — to the alarming. One highly coded message sent directly to the president reached us by accident. It concerned the American provocations that led to the Gulf of Tonkin incident, in which the destroyer *Maddox* attacked North Vietnamese torpedo boats, and to our escalation of the Vietnam War. My colleagues and I were sickened by what we'd learned. We already knew that America was far more involved in Vietnam than the White House admitted. But now we felt that Americans had been betrayed. Had

Richard Rovere not—as he put it—"raised some serious questions about the sequence of events in the Gulf of Tonkin" in the
August 13, 1965 issue of *The New Yorker*, I think one of us might
have leaked the message. (Rovere understood Tonkin in the context of Barry Goldwater's recent nomination for the presidency
by the Republicans.) Of course, Americans were superpower
smug in those pre–Vietnam War years. Once I was discharged, I
could not bring myself to participate in any antiwar demonstra-
tions. It seemed so futile. I was wrong. They did put pressure on
the government to end the war. Still, I miss that passion that is so
lacking in the punching bag complacency of so many Americans
today.

The army spent a fortune training its soldiers to learn "vital
languages"—Russian, Chinese, Polish, Turkish, Vietnamese—
for intelligence purposes rather than using native speakers,
many of whom were probably far more patriotic, or at least less
alienated, than the American soldiers. Reenlistment among the
graduates of the Army Language School was very low. In part,
this was because they weren't commissioned. I trained, not without protocol difficulties, Canadian lieutenants and even a British
major who could not understand our peculiar status.

Once, I was escorted, hush-hush, by the sergeant running
our unit—a man who knew little Russian and was resentful of
what he called "those college kids"—to an equivalent air force
unit to listen to a conversation intercepted and recorded somewhere in Eastern Europe. It was in several languages, and, as I
had the reputation of knowing a lot of languages, I was asked to
decipher it, if I could. This was considered so urgent that the air
force colonel in charge had decided to bypass the usual clearance
formalities. The sergeant, impressed by but seething over the fact
that I'd been sent directly to a colonel, hovered over me until the

colonel dismissed him. The intercept was, in fact, of very little consequence. It was in Russian, an Eastern European dialect of German, and Bulgarian—of which I had some understanding. The colonel asked how I knew so many languages, and why I wasn't an officer. I told him that I did not qualify. He was surprised. It turned out that we had both gone to Harvard. He told me—just as the sergeant reentered the room—that if I wanted to make a career in the air force, he could arrange for my immediate transfer to that branch as an officer. When I declined, he said he was disappointed but understood. The sergeant took it out on me until I was discharged.

The sergeant's resentment reached serious proportions when word came from one of the listening outposts that a Soviet invasion of France was imminent. The tape was flown by helicopter to our office, where the sergeant insisted on listening to it first and then confirmed the imminent invasion. By this time, we were told that the U.S. Strategic Air Command was on high alert. The colonel in charge of our unit, who knew no Russian, asked me to listen to the tape. What I heard was laughable, dangerously so. Two Russian radiomen were gossiping on their radios; one was in Warsaw, where they both had been stationed until a few days earlier, and the other now in Berlin. Warsaw told Berlin that he had been fucking the girl Berlin left behind. Furious, Berlin retaliated by telling Warsaw that Berlin girls were better than any Warsaw whore. The sparring continued, getting more and more intense, until one of them—I don't remember which one—finally said, probably to ease the tension, "I hear the girls in Paris are the best fuckers of all," or something to this effect. His friend answered, "I'll see you in Paris tomorrow!" I can't take credit for this. Anyone with a half-decent knowledge of Russian would have understood the exchange. America's absurd obsession with monolingualism can be matched only by its absurd (and provincial) association of patriotism with that obsession.

My reputation for knowing languages was both true and false. Yes, I knew French, Italian, German, and Russian and could read some Spanish and get the gist of Bulgarian, which resembles Russian. But I was listed as knowing far more languages than I did. It happened at the beginning of my military service, when the army tested our knowledge of the foreign language we claimed to know. I took the tests in French, German, and Italian, and realized they asked the same questions in the same order and corrected the answers with one stencil. By then I had memorized the questions. I asked to take the test in Dutch, Swedish, Spanish, Portuguese, etcetera. (I actually don't remember how many and which ones.) The sergeant who monitored the tests was getting irritated, but since I was getting perfect scores, he couldn't stop me — that is, until I said "Chinese." He shouted, "Enough is enough, trooper. No one can know all those languages," and sent me off to get my head shaved.

Betrayal is a harsh center around which a constellation of acts orbits: treason, treachery, perfidy, sedition, subversion, double-dealing, infidelity, unfaithfulness, disloyalty, duplicity, deceitfulness, mendaciousness, swindling, cheating, breach of promises, lying, and many others. The number is surprising and indicative of the prevalence of betrayal in social life. It is also interesting that while some of the terms refer to political relations and others to personal ones, they often refer to both.

WHEN I was working with the Harkis — who, as I've said, felt betrayed and abandoned (a term I should have added to the above constellation), I asked myself how our social and political, indeed our psychological, understanding might change were we to give primacy to betrayal rather than loyalty, mistrust rather than trust, and infidelity rather than faithfulness. Once I overcame my own uneasy response, I began to realize how moralized our understanding was. I thought of the government, probably because of its unabashed surrender to private interest and ambitions. Suppose we stressed betrayal rather than representation? What would our congresses or parliaments look like? I'm not just thinking of congressional double-dealing, so nakedly displayed in the television series *House of Cards*, but also of the structure of representative government. Representatives, as well as presidents and even justices of the Supreme Court, especially a court as blatantly politicized as today's, will have to betray — given the diversity of desires and values in any nation-state — some, perhaps all of the people they are said to represent at some point in their career. I mentioned this view to an outstanding member of the House of Lords, but before he could respond, his wife, a woman I admire immensely, said, "Vincent, how cynical can you be!" Calling me cynical protected her, and perhaps me, too, from a shift in perspective that might expose social processes that are evaded, if not effaced, by our personal and collective moralisms.

I'm not a political philosopher. The last time I tried to explain my ideas about political expectations, I was silenced. This happened on a radio interview about my book on literalism in American life. The interviewer wasn't interested in what I had to say about constitutional literalism, only about Christian Fundamentalism. Speaking broadly about literalism, I had said that we had to differentiate between creative democracy and its frozen variants, but before I could explain what I meant and why I considered it important, he interrupted me and changed the subject. I think he was from Colorado, perhaps from Colorado

Springs, the center of conservative evangelicalism. I still believe in the distinction and think we're lost in sclerotic democracy—an expression I would not have dared to use on that program. But think about the way in which we blind ourselves to the part that betrayal plays in our society and how it affects our psychological understanding.

I remember the shock, and indeed the ridicule, that followed Jimmy Carter's remark—in *Playboy!*—that lustful thoughts were as sinful as were lustful acts. Sin aside, the former president's words deserve consideration before dismissing them. They raise the question of infidelity and betrayal, which are not identical in meaning and implication. Unless they happen to believe in open marriage, Americans—and much of the world—are obsessed with marital infidelity. Why not? How marital infidelity, faithlessness, and betrayal are conceptualized and evaluated, under what circumstances and by whom, varies widely. I think of the ease and humor with which some Italians could accept my father's affair with his friend's wife but not his remaining in the United States because of Fascism. I think, too, of the adulterous affairs some of our English friends often have with the husband or wife of someone they are close to. From the outside, it's impossible to avoid the question of whether the thrill of betrayal and secret attachment does not figure in the intensity of these affairs. I could also mention the observation of a Venezuelan friend that marital affairs are an art form in Caracas or a Brazilian student who once told me half-seriously that she couldn't wait to be married so she could commit adultery. And there are, of course, countless other societies where fidelity is by no means a requirement for marriage—even a happy marriage.

What interests me here isn't the obsession but the literalism—the punctuation—that lies behind our notions of fidelity. It sometimes seems as though all that matters is a single act — the penetration of the vagina (or other bodily orifices) by the penis. I don't want to deny the importance of that singular event, nor its symbolic or legal significance, nor even the way it can be used in all sorts of psychological and interpersonal ways, ranging from guilt and remorse, vengeance, sexual titillation and disappointment to challenging, enhancing, or ending a commitment to someone. These psychological and relational factors, their range and variants, have been the principle theme of our literature, much of our gossip, and, indeed, our talking therapies and confessions.

Although sexual infidelity involves at least three, more often four, people, its horizon (probably an inappropriate word) also involves a real or fantasized audience, most likely both, whose own values, if and when they are known, figure in the relationship in both passive and, at times, active ways. I think of those Christian Fundamentalists who assume that any bodily contact between a man and a woman will lead inevitably to intercourse. It is a purely mechanical view of sexuality, but it extends to those few Americans who will hesitate to invite one member of a couple to a dinner party when the other is away. Do they think they would be setting the stage for adultery?

What would the French make of those Americans? The Italians? Or the Angelinos, who never hesitated to include me when I was living alone on a fellowship at Caltech? I often have students, obviously among them female students, come to my house for advice or tutorials. Benny, one of our old doormen, was convinced that I was having trysts and once even hinted this to Jane, who laughed. Was Benny disapproving or admiring or, as I imagine, both? An "audience's" perception is never pure. But its punctuation of that perception is definitive. Or is it? Doesn't it turn the erotic into simply the sexual, when in fact the erotic can never be reduced to a single act? I would define it as the creation of desire that can only edge on fulfillment if it is to continue. By "fulfillment" I don't mean sexual satisfaction or, if that is the goal, dissatisfaction. There is a sense, as the troubadours knew, in which the erotic plays on the impossibility of sex.

Is erotic betrayal the same as sexual betrayal? The allure is different. Can we relate them to political betrayal? There is enough gossip to warrant asking the question.

JANE AND I are in Prague, our first stop on our trip to the Soviet Union for the Chicago Center. We have just returned to our hotel from the theater—an adaptation of Pushkin's short story "The Queen of Spades." We go into the bar. It is gloomy—neon-lit. The bar forms a square in the middle of the room. Four or five hookers are sitting to one side, gossiping with one another as they try to catch the attention of an equal number of men sitting opposite them, two or three stools apart. The men don't talk to each other. One of the hookers is wearing a pink tutu. The tutu is pathetic and absurd. It is midwinter. Jane feels sorry for her, and I find something desperate in her attempt to look sexy. All the men are middle-aged, clearly married, probably salesmen from the West—Holland, I think, Hamburg—who are hoping to take advantage of the opening of the Eastern Bloc. But are they all from abroad? There is something *malsain* about them. They look at the hookers clinically, without desire, almost out of a sense of obligation. None wants to make the first move. Perhaps they are hampered by one another's presence, not by shame (nor guilt, I imagine) but by being watched by one another. Prostitution is illegal in Czechoslovakia, and that is probably why the hookers don't solicit them directly, but men have certainly been less cautious in other countries they frequent. These are caught in the pervasive mistrust, the surveillance, the threat of blackmail, the possibility of arrest…Am I exaggerating? I'm exhausted, jet-lagged; Jane is leaning on my shoulder, asleep. We left the theater early. Without Czech, the acting was not strong enough to hold our attention.

XXIII.
ULIE

AUGUST 22, 2013

We learned yesterday that Ulie has incurable stomach cancer. She is almost nine. She has refused food for over a week and is by now on daily intravenous sessions. She has maintained her spirits. Jane and I will take her to Dr. Cicero in Deruta, who will "put her down." What a horrible expression! Is this a betrayal? Is the gift of death a betrayal? Unknowing, she spent the early afternoon watching Oriano and his friend Tomasso dig her grave.

XXIV.
THE
ECHOING
WORLD

W ITH ULIE'S death, the world has lost another kind of punctuation. It isn't so much the sense of absence, or the memories that rush in unexpectedly, reminding Jane and me of her—her absence. I hear the bark she gave each morning in Italy when we let her out, announcing, for us at least, the day, for her, I imagine, greeting the world with her presence. I see her sitting on the lawn in front of the porch while we are having dinner, listening to the sounds that disappear and the new ones that come with nightfall. I am filled with sadness, especially when I remember calling out to her "inspection time" and the two of us walking around the house before I lock up for the night. It is difficult to talk about dogs after their death without sentimentalizing them, even when—as was the case with Ulie and the other Bouviers des Flandres we have had—they dislike surfeits of attention. There is really little one can say about dogs; their relations with humans are wordless. We speak of the unquestioning trust they have in us; that is, if we do not mistreat them. It is real, but there is something more that attracts us: their being, their being-with, simply being. It is the loss of that "simply being" that causes the world to slide away. The world may still be there—in its facticity—but it doesn't echo.

A FEW days ago, Jane and I attended a concert given by Walter Branchi, an electronic music composer. It was given at twilight, on the terrace of the Castello di Sismano. The composer asked us to remain silent for a few minutes before he began to play. We listened to the swoop of pigeons, bird songs, a tractor in the distance, leaves blowing, at first as a simple sound and then fracturing into a myriad of sounds, and of course the breathing and shifting of the audience. Then Branchi played his composition. I suppose you could say that he alerted us to the echoing of the world, always changing. He didn't want us to applaud when the concert ended. The silence broke when he himself started speaking. We asked questions, he gave answers. It was as if we were fleeing those echoes by reasserting the worded world.

But the worded world has its own echoes. At some level they are the stuff of poetry, the triumph of poetry. Poets are heralds, and what they herald resists — as it has to — articulation. It can be repeated, but each repetition transforms it. However more deeply we think that we understand it, it is never finished. It floats in its own context.

I know very little about Japanese esthetics, but I've always been fascinated by them. I remember a temple garden that Jane and I saw in Kyoto. It was on a slope, under trees, not quite a woods, certainly not a forest, halfway up the incline, circumscribing the garden without delimiting it, for the tops of the trees formed an undulating line that mirrored and was mirrored by the moss-covered slope, not only in line but also in color. At first I didn't see the reflection. I was simply embraced by the peacefulness that the garden produced in me and — I knew — in Jane and the few other visitors. We were not viewing the garden but contemplating it, experiencing a transcendence that could not be divorced from its materiality: rocks, moss, bushes, and sound—the composed, syncopated rippling of water flowing from rock to pool, pool to rock, of a tiny waterway, a series of miniature waterfalls, which echoed in sound the lines of the trees and the moss. Sight and sound, the tactile and the earthy smell—the taste almost—of the moss, formed a whole. We were in its midst—in a resonant space—the space-time of the interval, between and among objects that the Japanese refer to as *ma*.

It is the ungraspable that lures me. In what little of their esthetic theory (no doubt the wrong word) I have read, I find that the definitions of these moods culminate in an image or series of images that evoke, rather than state, what is being defined. *Aware,* usually translated as a sadness of things, their perishing, will be imaged by a falling flower or an unwept tear; today its popular meaning is "wretched." I wish I could equate my mood with *aware*, but it relates to feelings that arise from beauty, and it is precisely that experience that is overwhelmed by Ulie's death. Behind that death there is nothing, no mystery, not yet, no depth, absolute, unquestioned, unquestionable contingency. Ulie's cancer was sudden, entirely unexpected, and precipitate. She simply stopped eating. I have not yet had time to return her body to her—the dog she was. I simply see a furry paw that jutted out from under the blanket we had wrapped her in to bury her. In its lifelessness, it signals, perhaps but only perhaps, her return to the dog she was, now in memory, in story—the final death that comes with revivifying memory and story. The paradox is insurmountable.

And what of the words I have been writing? And you have just read?

I had planned to write a chapter called "The Echoing World" before Ulie got sick. I am not superstitious, but somehow I relate that decision to her death. Jung would call it synchronicity, but that would grace the coincident with a protective covering—a transcendental dimension it does not have. Reality is too much for us to handle. Freud and T. S. Eliot understood this. Perhaps it is also why Lacan saw the source of trauma in the real—the *réel*, which lies outside of symbolic and imaginative possibility, and which, without warning, intrudes into our expectations like a trickster, the cruel Tyche, whom even the Greeks had at times to recast as Eutychia, good fortune, so devastating was her whimsy.

Why is Tyche, why is Fortuna, female?

With the violent collapse of Heian society in the twelfth century and the years of bitter warfare that ensued, *yūgen*, another near-untranslatable word, came to pervade Japanese esthetics. It refers to a redolent dimension of objects and events that, defying verbal precision, evokes a vague, allusive sense of mystery, remote quietude, and depth. The fifteenth-century poet Shōtetsu wrote that *yūgen* could be suggested by "a thin cloud veiling the moon or by autumn mist swathing the scarlet leaves of the mountainside." It cannot be located. One "who does not understand this truth is likely to prefer the sight of a perfectly clear, cloudless sky." It evokes a dimension of the material that challenges our puritan epistemologies and ontologies. This dimension, even its possibility, is missing, as far as I know, from discussions of material culture that have recently become de rigueur in anthropological circles. There is apparently a limit to our presumptive cross-cultural sensitivities. But never mind.

I am neither a poet nor a mystic. I have argued that our flat-footed empiricisms, as productive as they are, cling to a determinable sense of reality. In our attempts to understand human behavior and intention, we ignore (if we recognize them at all) the wondrous overlays of whatever reality we construct and act upon. They are part, perhaps the most important part, of that reality. They may not, except at some subjective level, be known, purely or fully, but they — their existence — have to be acknowledged in any sophisticated empiricism. I have called them scenes.

That night, after we buried Ulie, Jane and I opened a bottle of our best wine and sat on the porch, silently mourning, a tearful haze over our perception of the darkening landscape. It was a night of the full moon and, as if projected by Shōtetsu, dark cirrus clouds blew across the moon, striating it in light and darkness. It was beautiful; it was mysterious; it was remote. I knew that, but only that. Cognition without affect. Perception without resonance. My focus, and no doubt Jane's, was inwardly turned, irretrievably for the time. Fading away.

Yesterday, there was a lightning storm. They are frequent on our hill in the summer. (Once, when we were out, lightning struck our heating unit and soldered its parts together.) Whenever it thundered, Ulie would rush into the house and lie down next to one of us, seeking our protection. That memory broke, at least I think it broke, the deadened images of her, in the blanket, paw extended, I was having, and she began to become the dog I knew.

I am embarrassed by this moonlit image. It verges on the sentimental, the romantic, the absoluteness of death, but this isn't what I mean to convey. It is simply the break from the self-absorption that follows upon the death of a being close to you. Our first response to death — its immediacy — was selfish, not in the demeaning sense, but in the need for emulative solitude. When our first three dogs died, I didn't want another dog. But this time, I do. It is a terrifying desire, for given my age, given Jane's, I am not at all sure we would outlive it. Our mortality, our eventual debilitation, the forces of entropy cannot be denied. Would another dog be a ruse?

My first sense of my own mortality came thirty-five years ago, lying on a stretcher on the floor of the departure lounge of Málaga Airport, where Jane and I were waiting for a medical flight to Zurich. We had been left in the charge of a drunken porter by the two ambulance drivers who had driven us from a clinic in Jerez, where we had been sent two weeks earlier after a head-on collision on the road to Seville. In minutes the porter had vanished. It was the first of August. Hundreds of tourists were milling about, some nearly tripping on the stretcher, a few irritably stepping over me. But what I remember most vividly is a group of American women gaping over me, one saying, "He looks half-dead," and then another, "Yeah, and so young." I tried to tell them to go to hell but couldn't say it. My throat had contracted; my tongue had thickened; my lips were parched and wouldn't move. No words came out, not even a grunt or a raspy sound. I was absolutely alone, defenseless, as I was waiting for Jane, who was somewhere across that vast lounge, searching for someone who could help me. It was that inability to speak, that uncontrollable silence, and with it a sudden drop in energy, my eyes blurred by the sweat dripping into them, substituting for tears I couldn't have produced anyway. It was the helplessness I felt, not my awareness of death that frightened me. It was that I was alive, on some goalless, exhausting, depleting, but, paradoxically, endless trajectory that undid me. I slipped out of consciousness and awoke with a start when someone, Jane, not yet figured as Jane, touched me.

I cannot go into all the sordid details surrounding our accident, though I would if I could. The German travel magazine *GEO*, which was starting an English-language edition, had asked Jane and me to write a story from the Kenyan coast. We decided to take Wicky and one of her cousins with us. Wicky was seven, and her cousin eleven. When Lara heard about it, she asked us to spend our last week in Europe at her family home in Andalucía. We accepted, and on the night of the accident we were on our way back from Seville, where we had spent the day with Lara. Wicky and her cousin were at home with Lara's children, looked after by her servants.

The Spanish were doing roadwork, leaving essentially a narrow two-way stretch of road. They had not bothered to put up warning signs: the result was two cars coming toward each other to avoid a huge pile of rubble down the middle of the road. I was badly injured, Jane less so, and Lara, in the backseat, had a broken nose. The driver of the other car had not been injured. His wife, who was pregnant, had a broken leg but didn't lose her baby. They came to see us in the hospital, and we apologized to each other, knowing that neither of us had been responsible. They told us that ours was the third or fourth bad accident since the roadwork had begun there.

The clinic where we were sent on the advice of one of Lara's friends was, in fact, a primitive Catholic hospital where the nuns carried a portable x-ray machine, the only one they had, to my room and took x-rays without any protection for themselves or me. I could see radiation burns on their arms. It was there, and not at the public hospital where we were first taken, that I regained consciousness. It was in the middle of the night. An older man, one of Lara's friends, was watching over me. After asking in beautiful English how I felt, he told me that he had arranged to have us transferred from the public hospital. "All my children were born here," he said, "and all my family and friends die here. You will receive more attention here." I was still too dazed and drugged to appreciate the ominous implication of his words. The next day I remembered them and dismissed them as symptoms of the proverbial Spanish obsession with death. They didn't really register.

Our doctor, an orthopedist, was excellent. He discharged Lara after repairing her nose, and arranged for Jane and me to be transferred to the maternity ward, where we could share a room. (Pregnant women often came to the clinic with a servant.) Dr. Abado told us how lucky we'd been, and a few days later he brought an American colleague to see us, a reserve officer and pilot who had served in Vietnam and had arranged to fly to Cádiz every couple of months as part of his reserve duty. Unlike kindly Dr. Abado, he treated me arrogantly, as though I were an ignorant soldier just back from the front lines. He did make me get up, stumble around, and sit in a wheelchair despite the pain I felt, in order to prevent blood clots. It probably saved my life.

A week or two after the accident—I have no sense of how much time I spent there or in Zurich—Dr. Abado advised us to leave Spain as quickly as possible. He said that very powerful people had taken an interest in our accident. Lara had meanwhile put Wicky and her cousin in a hotel near the clinic, claiming that despite her cook and other servants, it was too much work for her to feed them. She sent our things to the hospital and promptly visited us with an ambitious young lawyer, who probably saw the accident as a chance to improve his standing with her family. (I should add that I was fully insured and had already asked to pay any expenses that Lara herself incurred.) The lawyer started making frequent visits, suggesting that he might take legal action on Lara's behalf. He said I had broken "the royal nose of Spain." We felt trapped.

It was almost impossible to make a phone call from the clinic, especially an international one. Jane did manage to get to William Shawn, the editor of *The New Yorker*, who called daily, sometimes more often, and helped us arrange for Wicky and her cousin to go to Lisbon. Our friend Julietta Rodrigues, who lived there, sent a young Austrian couple who, hearing about two small girls alone in a hotel, had volunteered to drive them to Julietta's. (We learned later that she had only just met them and had no idea where they went after leaving the girls with her. Later, she heard rumors that they were involved with the Baader-Meinhof gang.) Mr. Shawn contacted Paul Parin in Zurich for us. Paul was an old friend, a psychoanalyst who had done anthropological research in Africa. He conferred with Dr. Abado and arranged for our arrival in Zurich. Dr. Abado told the clinic that he was transferring us by ambulance to a hospital in Madrid. The morning we left, he drove behind the ambulance for a few blocks, and as soon as it was out of sight of the clinic, he hailed it to stop and ordered the drivers to take us to Málaga Airport instead.

Our flight was called; the porter had not returned; the Swissair desk was closed, and we were panicked. Jane was finally able to find a porter who understood our desperation. He ran for a wheelchair, lifted me into it, and pushed it onto the runway in front of our plane, which was about to depart. The hoist that was supposed to lift me up to the plane door had already been dismantled, so the porter and a steward bounced me—I was still in the wheelchair—up the steps to the plane. Once the plane took off, I took a sip of champagne and lost consciousness for a while. Jane thought I was sleeping.

It was probably then that I suffered massive pulmonary embolisms in both lungs. I was not in pain—I was told later that the pain comes when the oxygen-starved tissue starts to rot, which it did the next day at the Hirslanden Clinic, where Paul had sent me. It didn't have the trauma facilities it has today. I was rushed to the intensive care unit in the Kantonsspital, where I remained

for well over a month. I was weak, highly sedated, and surrounded by unconscious patients, most of them motorcycle accident victims suffering road burns, suspended in liquid, but I had
no idea of how anxious Jane was each morning as she waited for
a call from Dr. Glinz, the head of ICU, who rarely said anything
more than that I had survived the night. Jane called him Gloomy
Glinz, but he was careful to improve my morale. After hearing
how Lara's "ambitious" lawyer had suggested that I had broken a
royal nose, Dr. Glinz would appear each morning wearing a bul-
bous red carnival nose. More important, he arranged for Wicky,
whom Julietta had brought to Zurich, to visit me in the ICU. "For
her sake," he told me, "and for yours." It must have been scary for
her, but we were so happy to see each other that I think it made
up for her fright. I hope so.

Paul would visit me as often as he could get away, and when
I was finally released from the ICU, he or one of his psychoanalytic trainees would spend an hour or so with me every day,
encouraging me to express my fears, to talk about death as well
as life—in fact, about anything. It was a delicate form of sup-
portive therapy, which I'm certain kept me from sinking into a
debilitating moroseness. I never felt the world slip away while
I was at the hospital or, later, in Gstaad, where Jane had rented
a chalet so I would—we would—be living in mountain air and
have the best possible physical therapy. It was August 1978, and
in America most physical therapy was for athletes. The ski areas
of Switzerland were more advanced. It was there, at a concert
given by Yehudi Menuhin and his string quartet in the church in
nearby Saanen, that I began to return to the world I had lived in
before the accident.

But I was overenthusiastic. When I was back in New York, and
well on my way to full recovery, I was suddenly overwhelmed

by a sense of debt to Lara—because, despite her betrayal of our friendship, I had caused her harm—and, obviously, by a debt of enormous gratitude to Jane, whom I had also harmed, and to Wicky, for the terror of abandonment that she must have felt. At the time, I was rereading *The Magic Mountain*, one of my favorite books. It saved me. I saw that I had been sinking into a lifelessness not unlike the deadening institutional involution of the sanatorium on Hans Castorp's mountain. I got up, determined to go to the pool at the YMCA and swim myself out of all self-pity. I was still walking with a cane, and when I hailed a taxi, the driver, seeing my cane, started to drive away. Enraged, I smashed it on the trunk of the cab. He screeched to a halt, jumped out, and started to attack me. Then he saw the jagged end of the cane I was still holding, cursed me, and drove off. Without thinking, I walked back home without my cane and didn't use it again. I was ashamed of what I had done, but not all that ashamed. I felt alive again. I had acted.

Still there was something—I didn't know what—that held me back. A few days later I had a call from Roger Kennedy. Roger was then a vice president at the Ford Foundation; he had just heard of my accident and wanted to talk to me about it. He said he had nearly died in an accident a year or two earlier and was determined to help anyone he knew who had had the same experience. I had met Roger only a couple of times before, but I agreed to have lunch with him the next day. I was surprised, though, that he insisted on our meeting at his office, since he didn't really know how mobile I was. But at lunch I realized why he had. He said that he wanted to share with me those small daily fears that doctors never mention. One, he said, was the fear of moving. I was too ashamed to tell him about the taxi. Then he asked me if I liked to sing. I told him that I had a terrible voice. By way of replying, he said he had joined a choir after his own accident, and, before I could say anything, he asked me if I could remember the sound of the crash. I had never thought of that, but realized that I couldn't. That was the empty moment that was haunting me. I heard a slight buzzing, a pulsating in my head, as he continued to talk, but I have never been able to recall that sound. It remains a lunchtime buzzing. But I still remember the sound of my cane crashing on the cab.

XXV.
THE
ECHOING
WORLD
ECHOED

I CAN date the moment when I decided to write about the echoing world. It was in late July, three weeks before Ulie stopped eating. Jane was in Modena, working, and I had been skimming through Nicholas Fox Weber's biography of Balthus in the middle of every night. I rarely sleep through the night. I get up and read, trying never to read anything having to do with work. I have little enough time to read for pleasure. Sometimes I'm transported by a novel — almost the way I used to be as a child, by Alexandre Dumas, the Horatio Hornblower stories, or, earlier, the Boxcar Children. That total absorption of childhood has, for the most part, given way to a kind of critical exercise in which I am simultaneously reading and reflecting on what I'm reading. It is a form of double consciousness.

I found Weber's book in a bookcase devoted to biography but filled with the children's books left by Garrick whenever he visits us in Italy. I didn't know that we had it. A guest may have left it or an editor may have sent it to Jane. I was, I must admit, less interested in what Weber had to say about Balthus's art than about his life, which is largely his own invention. I've come to know his son Stash, who sports a long pigtail, marking his rock days, and insists that his father's elaborate title is legitimate, despite the fact that most people consider it a fabrication. Balthus called himself

Count de Rola, traced his origins back to the tenth century, and claimed that Rola had inspired a Merlin-like figure in Polish folklore. Stash is in fact a gentle, charming man, who bonded with me on discovering that we had both studied English literature with Mme Briquet at Ecolint. He is interested in alchemy—has written two fascinating books on the subject—and one afternoon showed us the alchemic symbols in the early friezes and frescoes at Monte Cavello, his father's castle in the Lazio, where he and his brother Thadée still spend part of every summer.

Looking at the reproductions in Weber's book, I became intrigued by the disjunction between Balthus's settings and what seemed to be happening in the minds of the figures in them. (They reminded me of some of the images in the Thematic Apperception Test I tried using, with little success, in my Moroccan research. They were too anxiety provoking.) This is especially true of Balthus's less erotic works, such as *The Children*, in which a schoolboy leans across an empty table gazing at something we know we will never know; or *The Three Sisters*, one seated on a chair looking at a magazine, the second sprawled on a couch in a loose red dress looking outward, and the third, the youngest, on the floor, cuddled against the couch, looking across the room. They are utterly disengaged, one from the other. What are they seeing? What are they thinking? There is no clue.

I was reminded of Edward Hopper's *Morning Sun* and other paintings in which a woman is gazing out of a window. It is not a suggestion of influence. Balthus claimed not to know Hopper's work. But the pairing of the two painters, of several of their paintings, brought me from thoughts of alienation, loneliness, and solipsism to the certainty that while their settings may have echoed their own thoughts, there was no way that I could "know" those echoes. It was the absent echoing that echoed for me. Hopper's figures were much starker than Balthus's. There was a warmth in Balthus's paintings, whatever their subject, that was absent in Hopper's.

I must have slept, because I awoke with a start and the words "I have lost the echo." I'm not sure if they referred to what I was writing or to my life—most probably, both. There are moments when I can't distinguish between them. I could see how Balthus came to believe the myths he fashioned about himself and his family, if he believed them. Didn't Nietzsche say "The hypocrite who always plays one and the same part ceases at last to be a hypocrite"? (*Human, All Too Human*, para. 51) Self-invention is always tempting, and, lacking irony, it can easily become reality. Even irony can waver, though it usually alights on one of the ironist's two stances, or is presumed to by whoever is listening to the ironist.

I have often wondered—and am now, with a certain anxiety—how autobiographers view their past after the autobiography ends. Do they accept themselves as written? Does their inevitable fictionalizing become their past? Are they obsessed with correcting it, elaborating it, or rewriting it? Some do by continuing it, as Rousseau did, thereby subtly—in Rousseau's case, not so subtly—modifying what they'd first written. Texts freeze. Memory flows. Self-fashioning, especially textually, invades the privacy of our past and our sense of self-continuance. How will I live with what I have written? Will my intimacy with my past, its comforting co-presence, happy or sad, be lost? Will my past lose all connection with my present or future? Will it even be mine?

Last night, I described what I was writing to Bill Pepper, a journalist and author, now in his mid-nineties. He and his wife, Beverly, the sculptor, live near us. I had begun talking to him about it a week ago, and he wanted to know more. Despite his age, he has an extraordinary memory and the curiosity of a boy's initial puzzlement, which is the source of his reflections. Friends joke about our interminable discussions of theology. His humanity is often a corrective to my cynicism. I don't know why, but I told him about Mariam. He was moved and then, much to my surprise, referred to it as a story—the emotions, the pain I felt. He had a distance I could never have, and this terrified me, thinking of how I would be read. Perhaps as a reaction to my terror, I went on to tell him painful details about my family, my relations with my mother and sister. I couldn't stop myself. It wasn't a confession. There was nothing to confess. It was rather an appeal, a way to regain the person I felt I had lost with Bill's well-meaning suggestion. He is an irrepressible journalist, always sniffing for a story, always calling Jane with new ideas. Yet his stories, nowadays mainly about the people he interviewed decades ago, are humane, at times saccharine, but always respectful of the moral and spiritual dilemmas people experience. I wanted to remind him of *my* feelings. Fortunately, it was late, and Bill, at ninety-six, was tired. Where would I have gone?

But today, reflecting on what happened, I see that I was able to tell Bill what I still can't bring myself to write. I have justified my silence as "discretion," but while "discretion" constrains me, it also protects me—from pain, anger, betrayal, exclusion, and above all the violation of family ties so elemental that even as I try to deny them, they return with the force of sanctity. I could go on with these abstractions, but to what end? They are beginning to sound like something out of *The Castle of Otranto*—a curse that haunts what I write. But there was no curse.

"And then he cursed me again and died." I'll call him Rodney. He was an interior decorator: Australian, gay, working in New York, hugely successful, with an unrivaled sense of color;

a gentle man, slight, gray eyes, thin lips, easily seducible, I thought, charmingly innocent. He spoke well, with a slightly Americanized British accent that had clearly been cultivated, masking an even slighter Australian twang that emerged when he said, in a constricted voice, "Cursed me again." He was not, however, given to the mannered speech affected by other decorators I have met.

Jane and I met Rodney on Fishers Island, where we were staying with our friends Gillian Walker and Al Maysles. It was a beautiful autumn morning, and we were walking through the woods on a path toward the sea. The leaves hadn't yet changed color. Rodney was talkative. He had regaled us with hilarious stories about his clients at dinner the night before. But that morning, there was something serious, almost compulsive, about his talk, as though he knew it was leading to some revelation that he would make, even though he didn't want to make it.

Jane had asked Rodney how he came to New York. "I didn't have a choice, not really," he said with unexpected bitterness. His father had been a farmer, with a large station somewhere in the outback. He was apparently a rugged, strong-willed man. "Uncouth, with a terrible temper, which my mother suffered until she died," Rodney said. "He came to despise me. I was his only son. I was meant to take over the station. Me!" Rodney laughed. "When I told him I wanted to be an artist, he lost his temper. 'No son of mine will be one of those namby-pamby artists. They're all a…'" Rodney stopped himself. It wasn't clear whether he didn't want to finish his father's sentence or whether his father had stopped, suddenly, realizing his son was gay. Rodney stood up to his father. No one had ever done this before. "I think he secretly admired my willfulness," Rodney said rather lamely, "and that must have infuriated him even more. He cut me off completely, without a penny, and cursed me. I can't even repeat his words." Rodney was near tears. Jane expressed her sympathy. "It must have been awful." "It was." Rodney nodded. If I remember correctly, he also said that he'd inherited enough money from his mother to make his way to England, where he studied at one of the art institutes and soon realized that his talent was in decoration, not painting. He decided to move to New York, where there were more opportunities for him.

We walked on in silence, embarrassed by that silence. There wasn't much we could say. Finally, Jane—I think it was Jane—asked Rodney if he ever saw his father again. "Yes, one last time," he answered. There was again a long silence, but this time we all knew it was up to Rodney to break it, and he did, with a cracked voice that was at once wounded and aggressive. I could not look him in the eye, and focused on his sweater. It was a pale gray cashmere; he had worn a pale green one at dinner. "Yes, once more. My sister called me this summer to say that my father was dying and that I should hurry back. He wanted to tell me something before he died." Rodney took the first flight he could to Australia. He didn't say a word about how he felt, but now his silence was more eloquent than any words. All I could do, and I'm sure the rest of us could do, was to imagine his feelings—his hope of forgiveness, the lifting of the curse. I imagined his father extending a callused but weakened hand from beneath the blanket, squeezing Rodney's, restoring thus some primal bond between father and son. His expectation must have been exquisite. "I arrived," he said, "and knew right away...the anger, the furor, in his eyes...'So you've come back. I knew you would. You could never resist...the money...'" "No, the money means nothing," Rodney started to say, but before he could finish, his father interrupted him. "I'm glad you did...before I die...I wanted to tell you. I don't want you ever to forget the curse. You are no son of mine and never were." "And he cursed me again and died," Rodney said with a fierce determination to end the story, and then rushed past us. Neither of us tried to catch up. Infinite privacy.

There is very little we can say about violence, despite the innumerable theories that have attempted to explain it. It's ubiquitous. The circumstances in which it occurs can never fully account for its occurrence—its solidity. It is excessive even when it seems appropriate. In nature, it edges on the sublime, but that can't be said about human violence, however elegant some of its descriptions; say, Nietzsche's descriptions of the beauty of warfare, or Karlheinz Stockhausen on September 11 being "the greatest work of art that ever existed in the cosmos." Think of Goya's *Disasters of War* or Otto Dix's painting of trenches filled with gasmasked men (pertinent at the time I am writing), dead, dying, fighting.

Violence is a violation—an act of violating someone, something, a community, for example, a value, a law, a border, a state of affairs, a government attempting to preserve peace, a mood, a moment of intimacy, as in so many of Balthus's paintings, someone meditating, sleeping, trying to stay awake, indeed violating...Its verb form—"to violate"—is more immediate and more prone to question, interpretation, analysis, reflection, and judgment than its nominal form: "violation." Then it is objectified or at least objectifiable. Violence would then be an objectification of an objectification. The act of violation is twice distanced. "Violate," "violation," and "violence," as well, incidentally, as "vehement," are derived from the same Indo-European root, *wei, meaning force, or to force. My point is simple: that the remove produced by naming and objectifying the act—to violate—eases us into our prevailing prêt-à-porter moralities and the rhetoric, casuistry, justifications, and judgments that follow in consequence.

I am less interested in the philosophical merit of my suggestion than in its grounding a thought experiment, one that I have often used. Namely, before using "violence" or even "violation," translate whatever you are calling "violence" or "violation" into its verbal form — "to violate" — and you will find that it exposes a lot of moralistic chicanery and theoretical obfuscation. The raw act of violation echoes heartlessly.

Perhaps the Navajo's desire to preserve the harmony of a universe that is constantly under threat, by even the most ordinary act, has had a greater effect on my thinking than I ever imagined. When I returned from the reservation, I found a ringing telephone a near-intolerable intrusion. What I didn't realize at the time was that even more disharmonious than the ringing was my own irritation. And my irritation? You can follow the stages of disharmony, I suppose, to the cosmos itself. The Navajo, like everyone else, have never been able to live up to their ideals, but their ideals infuse their attitude toward life. When I was on the reservation, many Navajo had a recurrent dream of the chaos, the destruction of the world that would follow man's landing on the moon.

Walter Blanchi's asking his audience to remain silent for a few minutes before starting his concert and then violating his own request — that no one applaud, that they be silent when it ended — by speaking himself has led me to a disturbing observation: the first note or chord of any piece of music, whether a boisterous Rachmaninoff concerto or the most subtle strumming of a guitar, is a violation. Even in a concert hall, where the audience anticipates the performance, that first note or chord violates the individual or collective mood. It is why we are there, but at that moment it forces us into another world—not ours but the world of the performance. We are swept into this new world and are suddenly sensitive to other violating sounds—a subway rumbling under Carnegie Hall, a cough, a whisper, a cell phone ringing—sounds that in another context we might never notice. Then there are the sounds at the end of the concert: the surge of clapping, the bravos and bravissimos, the stamping of feet in rhythm, converting appreciation into command for the musicians to reappear, to play an encore. They are ugly sounds, brutal, finally, to the beauty of the music. Why do we show our enthusiasm for what we have heard this way, annihilating the silence of its echoes and re-echoes? Is beauty too much for us to bear?

The silence of an audience can be extraordinarily powerful. I remember my school friend Anna Bozza telling me about a piano concert at her grandmother's house in Venice. Her grandmother was something of a grande dame of taste. Her guests would always wait for her opinion before venturing theirs. On this particular night, she did not applaud after the performance, and as a result none of the guests did either. But their hesitation was too apparent. The pianist, still lost in his music, stood up and bowed several times before realizing that no one was clapping for him. He fled. Anna's story has haunted me. Did the pianist ever play again? Did he lose his confidence? His soul? I imagine him as an old beggar, still dressed in his morning coat—now wrinkled, torn, and dirty—stretching out a trembling hand, no longer capable of even a single note, at tourists who ignore him. Anna's story has become an allegory of humiliation, and not just of the tyranny of taste. Poor Anna died before she was old enough to appreciate the formidable implications of her story.

When the Soviet Union invaded Hungary, in 1956, the Budapest String Quartet gave concerts throughout Europe to help the tens of thousands of refugees who had fled to neighboring countries. Two Hungarian flags, with their centers ripped out, hung above them. I went to one in Geneva. It was the first time I had ever attended a charitable event on my own. The audience didn't clap after a piece was played, but stood up, silently, and bowed. I can still hear the echoing of those last notes. It seemed, for that instant, that the music would go on forever, as would Soviet domination. It was impossible to separate the beauty of that music from sadness, grief, bloodshed, and violence. I left the concert hall trying to hold back my tears.

Rarely, though, applause will create its own silence. In 2009, a few days after the choreographer Pina Bausch died, her dancers performed her last work in Spoleto. The performance was superb—weighed by the dancers' sadness. When it ended the dancers disappeared. They did not reappear, but the audience applauded for more than ten minutes at an empty stage. It was a way of acknowledging their loss—theirs and that of the hundreds of people who stood clapping—honoring Bausch as they mourned her. It reminded me of the silence at the Hungarian concert. For once, silence and applause were echoing the same grief.

Echoing isn't necessarily a repetition, like a yodel. Repetition is staccato. A definable sound sounds again. Echoing can also be a continuation—a reverberation, a resonance, and even a regeneration—and not a projection in the psychoanalytic sense, if only because it is indescribable, only evoked. "Footfalls echo in memory," Eliot writes in the beginning of the *Four Quartets*,

> Down the passage which we did not take
> Toward the door we never opened
> Into the rose-garden. My words echo
> Thus, in your mind.

"But to what purpose?" Eliot asks, not knowing the answer. They simply disturb "the dust on a bowl of rose leaves," he observes, echoing the redemptive melancholy of the *Quartets*.

Echoing is an anticipation of the return of what has been projected. It calls to mind the suspense buried in even the most mundane perceptions: the recall from the elsewhere of what has been perceptually projected; the change of perspective, the sleights of hand inherent in all perceptions, which have to be ignored if we are to live with what we have "perceived." It is easier to grasp our referents when they are people (or animals), for they respond, than it is when we refer to the echoing of an inanimate surround. But we speak easily of a place as having "bad vibes." You could say that "vibes" is a metaphor, and I would ask for what. I'm not arguing for animism; in fact, echoing may be the source of animistic thought. I am simply calling attention to a mode of response — to one's environment, to others, and, in a way, to oneself, which, as we have cast it out of our gated rationality into the "mystical" or "nonsensical," we are free to ignore rather than acknowledge. Whether such echoing exists or not, it serves as a metaphor for a whole range of experience that defies our constituted mode of understanding. How we configure it shapes the experience itself.

Sensitivity to resonance is, of course, cultivated in many societies—societies we have all too quickly called primitive. Freud's discussion of the uncanny (but not his explanation for it) may come as close as we have to such experiences in the human sciences. No one seems to doubt the experience of the uncanny. But surely there are similar experiences that cannot be reduced to the "uncanny." They merit consideration—rhetorically, but also epistemologically— as marking the boundaries of our conceptual thought.

We are in the Okavango Delta in Botswana. The dugout lands on an island our guide has never seen. Landmasses often shift in the swampland. As we walk across our little island, passing the gray-white baldness at its center—an accumulation of salt—we feel as if we have entered a primordial landscape where no human has yet set foot. It is just a feeling, but it evokes certainty. We spot a lone lechwe—a reddish-brown antelope with a white belly, about a meter high, that can leap through swamp waters with extraordinary speed and grace. This one is a baby, probably a female, since it does not have antlers. It watches us with no apparent fear. Wicky, at fourteen, is enchanted and, without saying a word, moves slowly toward it. The lechwe watches her approach. When she is no more than ten or fifteen feet from it, it leaps into the reeds and disappears. It is a beautiful moment, this meeting of innocents, caught in mutual attraction and inevitable distance.

I watch Garrick reading. He is caught. I envy his absorption: the vividness of what he reads. If I interrupt him, he tells me, irritably, to leave him alone. Is Garrick lonely? Are we lonely when we read? It is an odd question, but worth reflection. Even in rooms filled with people, we are alone, reading. I think of the times I have spent doing research in the New York Public Library or, for that matter, any other research libraries. I am caught in what I'm reading, but I often look up—to reflect, to rest my eyes, but also to confirm the existence of other readers, indeed of the peopled world I normally inhabit. Or is it my own existence in that world? I move from one "province of meaning"—to use the sociologist Alfred Schütz's term—to another. It's an abrupt transition, a gentle violation. I catch sight of another reader—a good-looking woman, a man whose mouth twitches while he reads, the person across the table from me. I avoid eye contact (though I didn't when I was a student staring at a Cliffy, hoping to get her attention). I wonder what that person is reading? I speculate or try to steal a glance at the book's title. I'm pulled in many ways, by the book I must finish, by the ordinary world, by my speculations, fantasies really, about who that reader is. Am I lonely? Do the people in what I'm reading, particularly if it's a novel, become companions — shadowy others who are at once the author's creation and my own? This is certainly true when I write. The people I write about are both themselves, recalled and limited by that recall, and my reconstruction that tempts me to transgress its limits.

There is no doubt that the scholarly world is lonely. Walter notwithstanding, Faust was lonely until he met Mephistopheles. So are writers. Fortunately, I teach. I like teaching and dread stopping. The days will be too long. When I was younger, I used to dream of being a full-time writer, but then I had a different sense of time. I couldn't imagine empty time. Now I see it among friends who retire. They age rapidly. They do puzzles or play chess with themselves; they take cooking classes, prowl farmers' markets, join wine-tasting groups; they watch old movies on television or spend hours on the Internet. Mainly, they arrange and rearrange piles of papers on their desks — which they describe as doing business. Their world, I imagine, has lost its resonance. Or has it? Some of them volunteer. Others have hobbies, garden, become desperately attached to golf, or spend too much time with their grandchildren (at least as their grandchildren see it). Those who can afford it travel, but they come back talking about the restaurants they ate at, the hotels they stayed in, the airports in which they had to wait. They tell me about some of the sights they have seen, but rarely about *their* experience of those sights. Am I mean-spirited? Have I no empathy? Oh, I forgot, they talk about health, their own and their friends'.

I'm surprised. I see a nasty streak in what I have written. I don't think of myself as vindictive, though I do have a terrible temper, and worse, once it subsides, I usually forget it—and even its cause. I've learned that this can be more painful to the person, usually Jane, who's upset me than the anger itself. Jane never forgets my blowups. She looks at me, infuriated, in disbelief when I don't remember a fight we have just had or how much I have wounded her. Is my forgetting defensive? Is it a repeated aggression? Or does my fury obliterate itself? I find it nearly impossible to apologize. I am always embarrassed when someone apologizes to me.

I often wonder what goes on in the heads of the passengers I see on long plane trips, sitting there, neither dozing, nor reading, nor watching a movie. At least the proverbial pensioner who spends his days looking out of a window at the street below has something to watch. Empty time needs study. But is theirs empty? Or is it rich in thought—in fantasy? Perhaps those people on planes don't need the crutch of the novel— don't need other people's fantasies. Perhaps literature is our compensation for loss of fantasy, its deflection, in the rationalist regime of modernity.

I have been reading T. S. Eliot over and over. Has my imagination been stolen by Prufrock, measuring his life with coffee spoons, never daring, never presuming, imagining an old age with the bottoms of his trousers rolled up? Am I using Eliot—or is it Prufrock?—as a crutch?

Do I dare? Does the loss of daring—daring to do, daring to think, daring to feel, daring to be happy—signal old age?

Those early poems of Eliot have a tawdry loneliness. They are terrifying, especially when you remember how young he was when he wrote them. But they resonate. They did when I read them first in college, and they do now. The paradox—even the echoless echoes.

XXVI.
I SHALL
NEVER KNOW
THE ENDING

TODAY, no, actually more than a month ago, before I flew home to New York from Italy, I decided to write my last chapter. It was, and is now, an utterly arbitrary decision. There is so much more to say, but I am depleted by what I've written and by its unwritten—unwritable—surround. I did not anticipate this. I expected the deadening effect of the written on the lived and on the recalled but not on that surround—that aura of liveliness, of desire and undesire, of the possible and the impossible, of the familiar and the unfamiliar, of the discoverable and the undiscoverable, of hope and the illusion of hope, of longing for and dreading the presence of the other, of the inseparable entanglement of love and its opposite, which is not hatred but a kind of neutering.

There is only one absolute ending, and that ending we can never know, for, as Wittgenstein says, "death is not an event of life." It is not lived through. *Den Tod erlebt man nicht.* We cannot describe our ending. We focus on the moment of death—of anyone's death. We may be horrified by another's death, but we cannot escape the curiosity that accompanies our horror. Perhaps that is in our self-interest, since we know that we can never know. We are at our own limit, confronting another's—the unknowableness. Your death, my death, a stranger's death are, despite their singularity, the same. In the end, it's so powerful—not the unknown but the unknowable—that we shield ourselves from

367

it. And yet, quite reasonably, we insist on the difference between another's death, your death, my death. We are soothed by those differing perspectives, and act according to the temporalities they presuppose.

But you will remember, at least I hope you remember, but never mind, I remember, that moment when the three of us, the sacrificer, the sheep, and I, were as one, united by the fear of dying—so I described it—in that tacky Moroccan sacrifice choreographed for strangers.

But was it the fear that united us?

Or the immediacy of death?

How can I answer? How do I know what the man with the knife felt, caught in the enactment of a transcendental drama (as the scholars of religion put it, though on what evidence I do not know), or the sheep, to whom we deny the knowledge of death (again on what evidence), or indeed myself, as that moment fades into a past that is no longer mine, however much I cling to it?

Yes, let's refer to the fear. It's easier that way. Social life demands that we be bad epistemologists. We are destined to live not in illusion, not in reality, but in oscillation between them—in what we declare illusion and reality to be, without recognizing that that distinction is made from within the oscillation itself. We do not have the requisite distance to make distinctions. We have no firm reference points. At best, we are caught in an intolerable sway. We confuse dying and death: one is the entryway to the other, which is its full stop. Death is the culmination of dying. It is dying's release, an easing we prefer not to consider…The corpse embodies that release, that easing, the liberation that arises from its unquestionable facticity, that nothing-more-to-be-said that demands a saying, not to document but to resurrect the person who has died.

It is noon. I am alone, upstairs in the hematology section of the laboratory where I am working, the summer between my first and second years of college. The lab is in a rundown building, next to a barely used railroad siding, on the grounds of the hospital where my father worked. Since I was eleven, I have spent my Saturday mornings there—at first doing the washing up, but later doing urine analyses and blood differentials. (It was quite illegal, but I was watched carefully and instructed.) The histology section is on the ground floor, next to the autopsy room and the morgue. The smell of death emanates from the scarred gray-black soapstone table. It leaches into the histology lab in the summer heat. It was there that I saw my first autopsy when I was twelve. But never mind. Ruth, the histologist, is working as usual through lunch hour. She is old and frail and will retire at the end of the year.

Ruth screams and then calls me. I rush downstairs and find her in the pathologist's office. Dr. Englander is lying on his stomach. An electric wire extends from under his chest. I'm sure he's dead. I think he has been electrocuted and follow the cord to unplug it. But, to my surprise, it leads to a Dictaphone. Dr. Englander was dictating autopsy notes. He has died of a heart attack. I am asked to listen for a last message on his Dictaphone. I do. No one else wanted to. There is no last message, just descriptions of the cadavers he has been dissecting. They are suddenly interrupted by a choking sound, a thud as Dr. Englander hits the floor, the microphone recording his death—his irregular and then fading and final heartbeats, the rasping rattle, and the silence that follows, interrupted two or three times by a kind of wheezing—the expiration of what little air remains in his lungs. The recording is so steely that for an instant I forget that what I am listening to is a man dying. And then the reality sets in—the

sounds I heard begin their echo in me. Mr. Seachrist asks me if
there is a message. I shake my head. No, there is no message, but
yes, there is. It isn't so much the pain of the attack but the pain of
his struggle to survive it. Had Dr. Englander clutched the mike to
record his death? I don't think so, though I'd like to believe that.
It would have validated his death—his science.

The corpse was. That is all I can say. It was empty, less of life
than of story. That came later, a week later, to be precise, when
Mr. Seachrist called me down to Dr. Englander's office, ostensibly to express my condolences to Mrs. Englander, whom I had
never met. She was uninterested in what I had to say. She had no
idea who I was, no idea that her husband used to take me for rides
in his long black Cadillac and tell me about his research, or that
he dictated his findings to me as he was performing an autopsy.
She just wanted to know if I had seen her husband's sapphire cuff
links. They were missing. She was sure he had been wearing
them that day. Before I could answer, Mr. Seachrist led me out of
the room, patted me on the back, and then turned to Mrs. Englander and told her who I was. She didn't apologize. It was then
that Dr. Englander died for me—that he ceased being a corpse
and became a person again, married to a woman I didn't like.

We are spending Thanksgiving weekend with Wicky, John,
and Garrick in the country house they bought last year. When we
arrived Garrick and his dog, Griffin, jumped out of the car and ran
around the garden, circling, charging each other, with indomita-
ble energy until they both collapsed on the lawn, exhausted. Now,
after dinner, Wicky asks me how my book is going. A writer herself, married to a novelist, both parents writers, she hesitates to
ask me about work. I say I'm writing the last chapter and describe
the depletion I feel. "What a bleak vision!" she cries. I'm jolted.
Clearly, I have surrendered to one of the moods I have recently

had while writing. It was not my mood when I began the book. Then I had been setting out on a narrative adventure. I knew the terrain—an archipelago of memory—but I had never mapped it. As I proceeded, island by island, I was carried by strong currents, some expected, others not, to dark coves and occasional bright, sandy beaches, which, to my regret, soon clouded over.

The reality behind the romantic melancholia I feigned—to protect myself from that reality—soon dominated my writing mood. I discovered I was telling a story of loss—less of disappearance than, to my surprise, of exclusion. The pleasurable moments in my life became obscure—in my written, though not necessarily in my lived, life. Death figured in what I wrote but was removed from the life I was leading—that is, until Ulie's death, when the two lives collapsed—for a time—into each other. Death ceased to have the allegorical possibility it might once have had. Then it could have figured the ending of my book, but now it was too close. I never felt anything like it when I finished my other books. I was either elated or disappointed. Is it that this may be my last book? I have had a fantasy that I would die just after finishing it—less a loss of spirit than of my ambient world. Am I mourning myself? Am I writing a confession, despite myself?

I am sickened by this indulgence, physically so. I think of the people living in refugee camps, hiding in cellars in war zones, tortured in rendition centers, or fighting meaningless battles who have survived—or been devastated by—the omnipresence of death. Yet, as I saw two years ago when I visited Cambodia for the first time, they go on living, some bearing the scars of torture, others limbless but still managing to play for tourists in little orchestras by ruined temples in the hope of a few coins. I was puzzled. Were they haunted by the hundreds of thousands of nameless dead, thrown without ceremony into enormous burial pits? I knew so little about Cambodia and its people. They seemed to survive in stubborn silence, but I had no idea whether this was really the case. I felt a pervasive but cautious fear similar to that I had felt in the countries of other repressive regimes. Were they afraid—at least those who had lived under the Khmer Rouge—that genocide was still a possibility? "Terror haunts the constantly shifting ground upon which the inexplicable and the unspeakable dwell side by side," one observer wrote of the country in the nineties, but that was more than a decade ago.

It was only our guide, Poeu (meaning the youngest one), who expressed bitterness as we passed children playing in front of a school on our way to temple ruins in the farther reaches of Angkor Wat. He told us how he had hidden under a bed, teaching himself English, whenever the Khmer Rouge were rounding up villagers in his neighborhood. He did not tell us what they did to those villagers. Was it too painful? Was it that he didn't know us that well? Or was the horror of those years too commonplace to consider? He simply said, "Kids don't know the meaning of education today. They don't know." He prided himself on his knowledge of American slang.

Poeu talked about his life only when we were driving. It reminded me of the anthropologist Clyde Kluckhohn's observation—and my own—that the Navajo talked about witchcraft only when they were traveling. Then, even the most laconic would begin talking about the places we passed, about something that had happened to them there or to someone they knew: having a flat tire, or catching sight of an antelope paralyzed by their headlights and wishing that they'd brought a rifle. Or they would refer to mythic figures—the hero-twins, who had stopped there in their search for their father, the sun. Movement through a storied landscape generated *their* stories.

I think of the peripatetic philosophers who conversed walking the colonnaded arcades in the Athenian Lyceum and the monks who meditated circling their monastery's cloister. I remember, at sixteen, walking around and around an arcade in one of Rome's national museums, filling time. I was bored at first, but then, walking, I suddenly began to think, not about myself the way I usually did, but abstractly, impersonally, losing all sense of time. I have no idea how many times I walked around that arcade.

What is the relation between movement — walking — and story or thought? Is it a way of enacting the story or the argument, its creation? Or is it a way to move beyond the punctuation of story and thought, to seek a dénouement, an unknotting of a story, resolution, in that of thought? I haven't walked in a disciplined way, though I have often paced, since I began this book. Now that I'm finishing it, I feel an urge to move, a pressure behind my knees. We sometimes forget that writing is movement. It resists cessation, but it tires. I'm more sensitive to its movement when I write in longhand than when I type.

The physical act of writing is a movement forward. It is in tension with the movement of its narration — which may move toward the future or the past. But whatever is being narrated or thought about is already past by the time we have written it. Montaigne said this. Was he right? The narrated detaches itself from us, and we want it back. It is we — not our sentences — who are aware of the commitment and the responsibility that the sentences demand. They figure in our editing and our self-censuring. There is always more to be said, and said better, and what remains unsaid hides somewhere between the unacknowledged and the secret. Literary and social conventions shield us from unacknowledged demands and deny what the secret flouts.

There is so much more I want to write. Maybe. Maybe I feel as though I need what I have not written in order to preserve my self, much as a secret does. I am suddenly overwhelmed with memories of pleasurable events—driving through France, when Wicky was three, desperately looking for a zoo (or circus) where there was an elephant. We had told her we were going to the land of Babar. Finally, we found a couple of miserable-looking elephants in the Marseille zoo. I can still hear her hesitant voice. "Bonjour, Babar." Or Jane and I laughing, embarrassed, as we took Polaroids of each other, naked, on the rocks behind the Duells' house in Bermuda, where we were staying. Or the peace we felt a couple of winters ago in Luang Prabang in Laos. The concerts, the dinners, the mountain walks…There are so many, but I must keep them to myself, selfishly.

My sense of who I am lies less with *me* than with those around me. Does this make sense? Obviously, I can't escape the *I*, but I can disengage myself from its objectification—the *me*. I can think about the *me*, attempt to describe it, to change it, to reject it, but I can't describe, change, or accept or reject the *I* without its becoming a *me*. The *I* is at once my center and nowhere. It always changes. I am becoming dizzy, thinking about it now. Linguists say that the *I* only indexes the speaker—the thinker, I would add—as the *you* indexes the interlocutor. For Sartre, the *I* equivalent—the *pour-soi*, the for-itself—is empty, a *néant*, nothing, forever in quest of what it cannot be, the *en-soi*, the in-itself, the amalgamation. The for-itself discovers itself in the gaze of the other.

But I'm not thinking in dialectical terms—or in linguistic ones—when I say that my sense of self arises from those around me, those I have encountered. They are there, they look at me, they objectify me. I become for myself a thing. But the people

I have encountered, those I remember, and, I suppose, those I expect or wish to meet have an ambient existence for me. They are not always looking at me, turning me into an object. They are simply there in their warmth, their coldness, their closeness, or their distance. They are a presence, in fact, in memory, or in expectation. Their presence is reassuring. That is why we miss them when they are absent (though, of course, we may be relieved by that); we grieve for them when they die. Memory becomes restorative. It protects us from accentuated loss.

As I come to the end of this book, I recognize that I've learned what I suppose was obvious — that is, once it *was* recognized. Autobiographies, memoirs, and other narratives of the self are centered on the autobiographer at the expense of those who have peopled his or her life. Some are mentioned, others not, but we assume their existence. It is they who lead us away from ourselves, giving us a sense of engagement and the responsibility that comes with it. Whether we like them or not, we feel, at least I feel, indebted, ontologically, to them in their singularity and as a group — not quite a community, familial but not connected by kinship or any other social institution — determined by chance or sad or serendipitous association. A sociologist might call them an ego-centered group, but that would miss my point by stressing a center, a central figure, rather than the shifting, cloud-like formations that endure, if they do, through memory rather than by structure or repetition. Ego is — I am — in their midst.

I AM troubled by a gap in what I've written — a gap that covers most of my adult life. I have said so little about the people I love, those I have known and lost track of, many of them students, and all those I still see, friends and colleagues, and enemies, too.

There are so many of them. Have they lost meaning for me? Have I no affection for them? On the contrary, they are shielded by intimacy — the responsibility it brings, the discretion, the sensitivities that cannot be ignored, the respect that must be maintained, the animosities that must be denied (or recognized), the confidentiality that cannot be masked, if only because the unmasked will recognize themselves, be hurt, embarrassed, or elated.

Still, I cannot dismiss the thought that intimacy may be my cover. Of what? What in fact have I written? It is what it is — that's simple. But what is not so simple is the effect writing has had on me. In recall, in resurrecting memories, some of which are shadowy, others ghostly, voices echoing in the present — my writing present, if it can be separated from my living present. Through recapitulation have I not also expelled those memories? No. Exorcisms are rarely successful, since they confirm the existence of the demon as they ban it. They can only repeat. Is this — and I would like to say it is but know that it isn't fully — the reason why I have sheltered those closest to me? To shelter others in order to shelter your self offers those others — and you — no shelter at all. They can, of course, live without me, but I can't without them.

Have you ever been lost in a crowd? You are conscious of yourself but cannot find a point from which to see the crowd — to center your self. Shifting from this spatial orientation to a temporal one, you find yourself in the same dilemma with respect to the appearance, disappearance, and reappearance in fact and in memory of all the people you have met throughout your life. You order your meetings chronologically or map them in some sort of personal geography, arresting the flow, distorting your experience of that flow — the vertigo it can produce.

I am on the outskirts of the old town in Meknes, where I am attending the *musem* — the annual pilgrimage to the shrine of

Sidi ben Aïssa, the founder of a brotherhood similar to, though much larger than, the Hamadsha. By some estimates, there are as many as a hundred thousand pilgrims crushed together. Some, in trance, were floundering about in search of those musicians whose whining music would please the *jinn* that possessed them, releasing them to dance and thus ensuring the *jinn*'s future support through the power, the *baraka*, of the founding saint.

I was advised not to go to the *musem* by the *pieds-noirs*, the former colonists, who own the bookstore where I bought—should I admit this?—a Skira book on early Flemish paintings because I missed the colors, the texture that I couldn't find in Morocco. Remembering the violence, decades earlier, after the French tried to ban the pilgrimage, they said it was too dangerous for a European to attend. I dismissed their warning as typical of those colonists who had stayed in Morocco after independence, simply because they had nowhere else to go or didn't have the will to start afresh.

I'm alone. I see no other Europeans. I feel that violence in the crowd. It isn't directed at me or at anyone else. I am in fact ignored. I don't feel in any danger, but suddenly I'm overcome with fear. I feel the crowd pushing me. I don't know where I am. I begin to lose my sense of me, merged with a people I really don't know. When I first arrived, I saw a few familiar faces, but now I don't see anyone I know. Did I ever? What does it mean to know someone?

And then, as in a dream, I'm a little boy, but like a big boy. I've just come out of the men's room in a large department store, perhaps Bamberger's, in Newark. It's Christmastime. I hear jingling bells and Santa's loud "ho, ho, ho." It is the first time that I've been allowed to go to the men's room by myself, and now I can't find my mother. I want my mommy. She is supposed to be here, in front of the door, waiting for me. She isn't. She's nowhere. I'm nowhere. Everyone seems very tall. They don't see me. They don't look down. I don't want to — I *won't* — ask for help. That would be babyish. "I'm a big boy," I keep repeating, stanching the tears flooding my eyes. Where am I? In Meknes? In Bamberger's? They blur, but now I'm not teary-eyed. I'm not crying. I've been pushed into a circle of men who surround a group of musicians playing trance music for the dancers — men who are jumping up and down, their faces gleaming with sweat. Some of them are roaring like lions, sounding *like* lions. I have heard them and their music before. They are known for mimicking — in their terms, becoming — if not lions, then lion-like, in their trances. But I'm not listening. I don't have the distance to listen. I am within, somewhere in the hearing. I am and am not.

I don't know how long I've been standing there, engrossed, absorbed in that music, that frenzy around me. But moments later, I am pushed out of the circle, into the milling crowd. I leave. I have "experienced" the *musem*.

I remember finding my mother. She is standing next to the line of children. (I wasn't allowed to say "kids." "Children aren't goats," she would say, and my father would laugh.) She's waiting for me. She tells me she knew I would find my way to Santa, but I don't believe in Santa anymore.

I'm no mystic, no visionary, no Aschenbach carried away by Dionysian frenzy. I have not come to my end. I am not seeking it in a plague-bearing miasma in Venice or anywhere else. Was Aschenbach that different from my roommate Bill? Bill had no Tadzio, I'm quite sure. He was absolutely alone.

One day, in a taxi, on my way back from a Center meeting in Chicago, late for a Seder — the second one I've ever attended — the driver, a man in his forties, handsome, dressed in black, soft-spoken, articulate, clearly educated, but ashen in color, blemished in soul, I couldn't help thinking, tells me — having heard that I'm an anthropologist — that he, too, wanted to teach. He had nearly finished his doctoral dissertation when a blackness — "absolute, paralytic blackness" — enveloped him. "My world was gone," he tells me without emotion. "I can't say that I tried to commit suicide. There was no trying. There was no decision. Just absolute blackness. They told me later that when they found me, they didn't think I'd make it. It wasn't that I had so overdosed on the pills I had swallowed — I don't know what they were or where I found them — that they couldn't bring me back. It was that there was no one to bring back." He pauses. I can say nothing. "Here I am. It's eight years now that I've been driving a taxi. No real stress, just enough to remind me that I am." When we arrive at my friend David Fromkin's, the driver says he's sorry to have burdened me with his story. "You probably won't believe me. You're the first passenger I've ever told." I want to believe him, but though he sounds sincere, I can't quite. Getting out, I feel I'm abandoning him. "I just felt you should know," he says out of the cab window. "I guess you can say I crossed over." He laughs. "But I don't know who my Moses was." I laugh with him.

Had Mariam been forced into that blackness? She died with full clarity. How else could she have? Had Jim? I doubt it. He had his faith.

Had Bill sunk into the same blackness? I don't think so. He was too much of a coward. He had simply isolated himself and, perhaps to his surprise, lost the sentient presence of all the people in his world. Mann's Aschenbach was led to surcease by inadmissible love, Bill by a paranoia focused on the most banal of clichés: the CIA.

Why do I come back to Bill? Is it because he reminds me of what happens when you lose the presence of those you have known—loved, hated, or simply met?

Mariam never did. She had no choice.

So. There are many people I would like to have mentioned but don't dare to—not from discretion or lack of interest or fear, but to keep alive the shrouded possibilities of those inner motions we call fantasy that liven our souls. They, the undersong, perpetuate our storied lives just as they distance us, in acts of sublime perversity, from the intimacy of loving and hating, desiring and dreading, the host of emotions, that comes with living…

And so, ellipses but no full stops, intimating shadowy possibilities that fall out of the frame in which we are destined to live as we imagine, still within those limits, what is unreachably outside—the gardens where I was not allowed to play. Were there any? I don't remember. I don't want to remember them.

ACKNOWLEDGMENTS

THERE ARE so many people I would like to thank, if thanks are indeed even appropriate. Foremost are those to whom I refer in *Recapitulations*, and the many more who remain in its silent surround. There are others whose incidental remarks unwittingly triggered memories as I was writing. Patricia Williams was the first to suggest that I write an autobiography. I had played with the idea over the years and rejected it as a narcissistic indulgence. But that suggestion, coming from Patricia, an editor whom I admired and always associated with the most serious university presses, made me reconsider it. I knew that I wanted whatever I wrote to be about more than myself. All lives, even the most superficially uneventful, are potentially interesting—something that depends less on the details of a given life than on the way they are fashioned and given significance.

I didn't act on Patricia's suggestion until I met Judith Gurewich, the editor and publisher of Other Press, at a book party for Anka Muhlstein. Judith, having read my book *Tuhami*, wanted me to write a book that would renew interest in the complexities of human behavior that are ignored, if not denied, by the social, psychological, and cognitive sciences that have adopted an impoverished—a robotic—image of the human. I shared Judith's concern, and though I didn't want to write the book she would have liked, her suggestion did serve as a catalyst for *Recapitulations*. I realized that I could use events in my life as a way to think philosophically about what it means to live in a world, that, as it grows more complex, is diminished in our understanding.

What I wanted to write was the kind of memoir that demanded critical reflection—my own and hopefully the reader's. I did not want to write a conventional autobiography, certainly not a confession, nor what anthropologists have come to call an auto-ethnography—which, to my mind, means little more than a reduction of the particularity of any individual's life to a set of symptoms of the anthropologist's understanding of his or her contemporary social and cultural world. Judith encouraged me from the start with her characteristic enthusiasm and the sounding board of a keen, critical intelligence. I would like to thank her and her staff at Other Press. I am particularly grateful to Keenan McCracken and Yvonne E. Cárdenas.

I would also like to thank Louis Begley, Noelia Diaz, Steven Foster, Larry Hirschfield, Jonathan House, Susana Maia, William and Paula Merwin, Caroline Moorehead, Anka Muhlstein, Beverly Pepper, the late Curtis Bill Pepper, whose respectful humanity always served to temper my cynicism and pessimism, Jane Schmidt, Ahmed Sherif Ibrahim, Ann Stoler, Katherine Verdery, and Gary Wilder, and the students at the CUNY Graduate Center who attended the seminars on life histories and existentialism and phenomenology in which I rehearsed many ideas that have been incorporated into this book. I am particularly beholden to my daughter, Aleksandra, who read an early draft of *Recapitulations* with an attention to detail that could only come from one's own child; to my son-in-law, John Burnham Schwartz, who has been consistently encouraging; and to my grandson, Garrick, whose curiosity about my life quickened an innocence of response that had lain dormant in me for so many years. Above all, I want to thank my wife, Jane, who not only encouraged me but edited my work with her extraordinary sense of style and, I have to admit, grammar. Finally, I must acknowledge Ulie, our wise and much loved Bouvier, whose presence and sudden death accompanied my writing, giving it, as only a dog can, a sense of life and time that tempered some of my memoirist's inevitable self-presumption.

REFERENCES

For the sake of readability, I have restricted references to only those works I refer to directly. I apologize to all those writers whose influence I have failed to acknowledge. There are so many.

CHAPTER TWO

Augustine. 1959. *The Confessions of Saint Augustine.* New York: Sheed and Ward, Book 10, chapter 8.

Lacan, Jacques. 1977. *Ecrits: A Selection.* New York: Norton, pp. 1–7.

CHAPTER THREE

Crapanzano, Vincent. 1972. *The Fifth World of Forster Bennett: Portrait of a Navajo.* New York: Viking.

———. 1973. *The Hamadsha: A Study in Moroccan Ethnopsychiatry.* Berkeley: University of California Press.

Jeanmaire, Henri. 1951. *Dionysios: histoire du culte de Bacchus.* Paris: Payot, p. 121.

CHAPTER FOUR

Foucault, Michel. 1977. *Discipline and Punish: The Birth of the Prison.* New York: Pantheon.

Rilke, Rainer Maria. 2006. *The Notebooks of Malte Laurids Brigge.* New York: Penguin.

CHAPTER FIVE

Crapanzano, Vincent. 1980. *Tuhami: Portrait of a Moroccan.* Chicago: University of Chicago Press, p. 60.

————. 2011. *The Harkis: The Wound that Never Heals*. Chicago: University of Chicago Press.

Freud, Sigmund. 1959. "The Uncanny." Pp. 368–407 of *Collected Papers*, vol. 4. New York: Basic Books.

CHAPTER SIX

Hegel, G.W.F. 1949. *The Phenomenology of Mind,* 2nd Edition. London: George Allen and Unwin, pp. 231–240.

Kittay, Jeffrey, and Wlad Godzich. 1987. *The Emergence of Prose: An Essay in Prosaics*. Minneapolis: University of Minnesota Press, pp. xii–xiv.

Kojève, Alexandre. 1980. *Introduction to the Reading of Hegel*. Ithaca: Cornell University Press.

Lacan, Jacques. 1977. *Ecrits: A Selection*. New York: Norton, pp. 1–7.

Sartre, Jean-Paul. 1956. *Being and Nothingness: An Essay on Phenomenological Ontology*. New York: Philosophical Library, pp. 47–73.

CHAPTER SEVEN

Barthes, Roland. 2000. *Camera Lucida: Reflections on Photography*. London: Vintage.

Evans-Pritchard, E. E. 1937. *Witchcraft, Oracles, and Magic among the Azande*. Oxford: Clarendon Press.

Nietzsche, Friedrich. 1937 "The Genealogy of Morals." Pp. 617–807 of *The Philosophy of Nietzsche*. New York: The Modern Library, p. 673.

CHAPTER EIGHT

Butor, Michel. 1960. *Degrés*. Paris: Gallimard.

Crapanzano, Vincent. 1992. "Rites of Return." Pp. 260–280 of *Hermes' Dilemma and Hamlet's Desire*. Cambridge: Harvard University Press.

Otto, Rudolph. 1958. *The Idea of the Holy: An Inquiry into the non-rational factor in the idea of the divine and its relation to the rational.* New York: Oxford University Press.

CHAPTER ELEVEN

Aristotle. 2011. *The Nicomachean Ethics,* translated by Robert C. Bartlett and Susan D. Collins. Chicago: University of Chicago Press, Book, 4.6; 8 and 9.

Baudelaire, Charles. 1954. "Le Gouffre." P. 244 of *Oeuvres complètes.* Paris: Editions de la Pléaide.

Blanchot, Maurice. 1982. "Two Versions of the Imaginary." Pp. 254–263 of *The Space of Literature.* Lincoln: University of Nebraska Press.

Freud, Sigmund. 1964. *The Interpretation of Dreams.* London: George, Allen, and Unwin, p. III, fn 1.

Lacan, Jacques. 1977. *Ecrits: A Selection.* New York: Norton, p. 263.

Montaigne, Michel de. 1958. "On Friendship." Pp. 135–144 of *The Complete Essays of Montaigne,* translated by Donald Frame. Stanford: Stanford University Press.

Russell, Bertrand. 1969. *Autobiography: The Middle Years, 1914–1944.* New York: Bantam.

Whorf, Benjamin Lee. 1956. *Language, Thought, and Reality.* Cambridge: MIT Press.

CHAPTER TWELVE

Begley, Louis. 2013. *Memories of a Marriage.* New York: Nan A. Talese/Doubleday.

Crapanzano, Vincent. 2000. *Serving the Word: Literalism in America from the Pulpit to the Bench.* New York: New Press.

Falls, Susan. 2013. *Clarity, Cut, and Culture: The Many Meanings of Diamonds.* New York: New York University Press.

Laing, Ronald. 1969. *Self and Others*. Harmondsworth: Penguin.

Machiavelli, Niccolò. 1981. *The Prince*. New York: Bantam, pp. 62–63.

CHAPTER THIRTEEN

Austen, Jane. 1976. *Mansfield Park*. Pp. 569–919 of *The Complete Novels of Jane Austen*, Vol. 1. New York: Vintage. See Chapter 13 and following.

Hawthorne, Nathaniel. 1937. *The Complete Novels and Selected Tales*. New York: Modern Library, pp. 746–747.

CHAPTER FOURTEEN

Kramer, Jane. 1969. *Allen Ginsberg in America*. New York: Random House, p. 13.

CHAPTER FIFTEEN

Crapanzano, Vincent. 2000. *Serving the Word: Literalism in America from the Pulpit to the Bench*. New York: New Press.

CHAPTER SIXTEEN

Gide, André. 1958. *Romans, Récits et Soties, Oeuvres Lyriques*. Paris: Bibliothèque de la Pléaide, p. 1202.

Manea, Norman. 2012. *The Fifth Impossibility: Essays on Exile and Language*. New Haven: Yale University Press, pp. 92–118.

McQuillan, Martin. 2001. *Paul de Man*. London: Routledge.

CHAPTER SEVENTEEN

Carpenter, Edmund. 2000. *Padlei Diary: An Account of the Padleimiut Eskimo in the Keewatin District West of Hudson Bay during the Early Months of 1950* (with photographs by Richard Harrington). New York: Rock Foundation.

Crapanzano, Vincent. 2004. *Imaginative Horizons: An Essay in Literary-Philosophical Anthropology*. Chicago: University of Chicago Press.

Devereux, George. 1951. *Reality and Dream: Psychotherapy of a Plains Indian*. New York: International University Press.

———. 1967. *From Anxiety to Method in the Behavioral Sciences*. The Hague: Mouton.

———. 1969. *Mohave Ethnopsychiatry: The Psychic Disturbances of an Indian Tribe*. Washington, DC: Smithsonian Institution Press.

Harris, Marvin. 1968. *The Rise of Anthropological Theory*. New York: Thomas Y. Crowell.

———. 1977. *Cannibals and Kings: The Origins of Cultures*. New York: Vintage.

Hart, David Montgomery. 1976. *The Aith Waryaghar of the Moroccan Rif: An Ethnography and History* [Viking Fund Publications in Anthropology 55]. Tucson: University of Arizona Press.

CHAPTER EIGHTEEN

Keats, John. 1899. *The Complete Poetical Works and Letters of John Keats*, Cambridge Edition. Boston Houghton Mifflin, p. 277.

Lawrence, Karen R. 1994. *Penelope Voyages: Women and Travel in British Literary Tradition*. Ithaca: Cornell University Press.

Zweig, Paul. 1974. *The Adventurer: The Fate of Adventure in the Western World*. New York: Basic Books.

CHAPTER NINETEEN

Crapanzano, Vincent. 1992. "Talking about Psychoanalysis" [The Kardiner Lecture]. Pp. 136–154 of *Hermes' Dilemma and Hamlet's Desire: On the Epistemology of Interpretation*. Cambridge: Harvard University Press.

Wilden, Anthony. 1968. *The Language of the Self* (including a translation of Jacques Lacan's *The Function of Language in Psychoanalysis*). Baltimore: Johns Hopkins University Press.

CHAPTER TWENTY

Bourdieu, Pierre. 1984. *Distinction: A Social Critique of the Judgment of Taste.* Cambridge: Harvard University Press.
Crapanzano, Vincent. 1985. *Waiting: The Whites of South Africa.* New York: Random House.
Heidegger, Martin. 1967. *Being and Time.* Oxford: Basil Blackwell, p. 161.

CHAPTER TWENTY-ONE

Baudelaire, Charles. 1954. "Salon, de 1846." Pp. 605–687 of *Oeuvres complètes.* Paris: Editions de la Pléaide, p. 678.
Berreby, David. "Unabsolute Truths: Clifford Geertz," *New York Times Magazine,* April 9, 1995.
Blanchot, Maurice. 1982. "Two Versions of the Imaginary." Pp. 254–263 of *The Space of Literature.* Lincoln: University of Nebraska Press.
Crapanzano, Vincent. 1985. *Waiting: The Whites of South Africa.* New York: Random House.
Geertz, Clifford. 1968. *Islam Observed: Religious Development in Morocco and Indonesia.* New Haven: Yale University Press.
———. 1988. *Works and Lives: The Anthropologist as Author.* Stanford: Stanford University Press.
Kluckhohn, Clyde, and Dorothea Leighton. 1962. *The Navaho.* New York: Doubleday Anchor, pp. 184–187.
Martin, Emily. 2007. *Bipolar Expeditions: Mania and Depression in American Culture.* Princeton: Princeton University Press.

Turner, Victor. 1974. *Dramas, Fields, and Metaphors: Symbolic Action in Human Society*. Ithaca: Cornell University Press.

Wittgenstein, Ludwig. 1981. *Tractatus Logico-Philosophicus*. London: Routledge and Kegan Paul.

CHAPTER TWENTY-TWO

Rovere, Richard H. 1965. *The Goldwater Caper*. New York: Harcourt, Brace and World.

CHAPTER TWENTY-FOUR

De Bary, Theodore, ed. 1964. *Sources of Japanese Tradition*, vol. 1. New York: Columbia University Press.

Odin, Steve. 1995. "Derrida and the Decentered Universe of Ch'an Zen Buddhism." Pp. 1–24 of *Japan in Traditional and Postmodern Perspectives*, edited by Charles Wei-hsun Fu and Steven Heine. Albany: State University of New York Press.

CHAPTER TWENTY-FIVE

Eliot, T. S. 1952. *The Complete Poems and Plays: 1909–1950*. New York: Harcourt Brace.

Nietzsche, Friedrich. 1996. *Human, All Too Human: A Book for Free Spirits*. Cambridge, Cambridge University Press, paragraph 51.

Weber, Nicholas Fox. 1999. *Balthus: A Biography*. New York: Knopf.

CHAPTER TWENTY SIX

Crapanzano, Vincent. 2006. "Eine persönliche Versenkung in Tod, Leiche und Autopsien." Pp. 27–45 of *Verführerische Leichen-verbotener Verfall: "Körperwelten" als gesellschaftliches Schlüsselereignis*, edited by Liselotte Hermes da Fonseca and Thomas Kliche. Berlin: Pabst Science Publishers.

Mann, Thomas. 1995. *Death in Venice*. New York: Dover.

Shapiro-Phim, Toni. 2002. "Dance, Music, and the Nature of Terror in Democratic Kampuchea." Pp. 179–193 of *Annihilating Difference: The Anthropology of Genocide*, edited by Alexander Laban Hinton. Berkeley: University of California Press, p. 189.

Wittgenstein. Ludwig. 1981. *Tractatus Logico-Philosophicus*. London: Routledge and Kegan Paul, section 6.431–2.